VIRGINIA SATIR'S EVOLVING LEGACY: TRANSFORMATIVE THERAPY WITH A BODYMIND CONNECTION

A truly amazing read. What distinguishes this book is its emphasis on the holistic nature of Satir's approach, which recognizes the interconnectedness of body, mind and spirit in the therapeutic process. It was a joy to delve into Virginia Satir's Evolving Legacy: Transformative Therapy with a Bodymind Connection *and rediscover the essence of Satir's teachings within its pages.*

Crafted by esteemed authors deeply immersed in Satir's work and closely connected to her model, clinicians are provided valuable insights and practical techniques. The authors' deep understanding of Satir's teachings, combined with their personal approach to integrating the bodymind connection into therapy is compelling. Through interviews, personal reflections, compelling case studies and experiential exercises, the authors demonstrate how attention to the bodymind connection can lead to profound healing and growth.

This book is a must-read for therapists seeking to deepen their understanding of Satir's model and harness the power of the bodymind connection in their practice."

— Michael Argumaniz-Hardin, PhD
  Director of Training for the Virginia Satir Global Network
  Professor of Marriage & Family Therapy, Fuller Theological Seminary (Houston, Texas)

Virginia Satir's Evolving Legacy *is a fascinating exploration of many ways that the original teachings of Virginia Satir have been adapted, combined and expanded in multiple areas of modern practice. The authors have included case studies and detailed, practical explanations of how they incorporate processes such as the Personal Iceberg Metaphor, sculpting, body work and meditation as well as the philosophical underpinnings of the Satir Model in their work with clients. A most welcome addition to the Satir classics and a must read for all students of the Satir Model of Family Therapy!*

> – Patricia Bragg, BA, BEd
> Counsellor, mediator, trainer, Satir coach
> President and Director of Training of the Satir Institute Society of the Yukon, Canada
> Former longtime Board Member of the Virginia Satir Global Network

The authors brilliantly portray Virgina Satir's understanding of the use of body as an integral part of personal healing. I believe that healing can take place when we connect with our mind, body and spirit. Every word has a spirit, connection is the key.

> – Grace Elliott Neilson. My native names are: *Tiyuqtunaat Wulwisulwut*
> Director and co-founder Tillicum Lelum Friendship Centre
> (Nanaimo, BC Canada)

Virginia Satir's Evolving Legacy *is an amazing achievement and will be a great addition to the literature related to the work of Virginia Satir. For those of you who are trained in the Satir Model, it will add to your understanding of how to help your clients use their body wisdom. For those of you who are new to the Satir Model, it will add to your understanding of the key elements of the Satir Model.*

> – Sharon Loeschen, LCSW
> Author of four books on the work of Satir and the Satir Coaching and Mentoring Program

Bravo to the team of writers! This book provides cutting edge updates on the contributions of Virginia Satir's approach to health and healing in this transformative model of care and healing.

The opening poem of conversation with your body blew me away! How insightful it is to remind us about the power of the body on the soul and the journey called life. This poem sets the energy of what is to come, highlighting that we must look inside to feel, know, and experience the impact of life's transactions on our present and future, as these are forever entwined with the past. The personal sharings of the authors touched me deeply.

The blending of Virginia's teachings, woven like a tapestry, will provide the support needed to shine your light within and without, to achieve peace within, peace between and peace among! Blessings to all readers and those whose lives they touch.

– Dr. Mary Jo Bulbrook, RN, EdD
President of Akamai University, Dean, Integrative Health College
President Energy Medicine Partnerships, Inc.
CEO, Global Healing Alliance

If you assumed family therapy is exploring the family constellations and patterns, you are missing the most important aspects of Virginia Satir's family therapy approach. The essays in this book vividly explore how Virginia Satir, the mother of family therapy, integrated the mind-body-spirit-energy interconnection. Every thought and emotion has a corresponding body response and, in turn, changes and impacts our thoughts, emotions and spirit. It is a must read for any therapist, as it provides a perspective for widening the lens to incorporate soma, spirit and family and thereby provide an holistic healing therapy.

– Erik Peper, PhD
Professor, Institute for Holistic Health Studies, San Francisco State University
Co-author of *TechStress – How Technology is Hijacking our Lives, Strategies for Coping and Pragmatic Ergonomics* by Erik Peper, Richard Harvey and Nancy Faass

VIRGINIA SATIR'S EVOLVING LEGACY:
TRANSFORMATIVE THERAPY
WITH A BODYMIND CONNECTION

VIRGINIA SATIR'S EVOLVING LEGACY: TRANSFORMATIVE THERAPY WITH A BODYMIND CONNECTION

Dr. Nitza Broide-Miller

Leona Flamand Gallant

Julie Gerhardt

Mary Leslie

Anastacia Lundholm

Jennifer Nagel

Dr. Carolyn Nesbitt

Foreword by Dr. John Banmen
Edited by Mary Leslie

Gabriola, BC Canada V0R 1X4

© 2024, Mary Leslie and the other contributors.
All rights reserved.
Without limiting the rights under copyright reserved above, no part of this publication may be reproduced, stored in or introduced into a retrieval system, or transmitted, in any form or by any means (electronic, mechanical, photocopying, recording or otherwise), without the prior written permission of both the copyright owner and the publisher of this book.

*For rights information and bulk orders,
please contact the publishers through*
www.agiopublishing.com

Virginia Satir's Evolving Legacy
ISBN 978-1-990335-22-8 (trade paperback)
ISBN 978-1-990335-23-5 (ebook)

Cataloguing information available from
Library and Archives Canada.
Printed on acid-free paper.
Agio Publishing House is a division of Trelawny Consulting Group Ltd., a socially responsible company, measuring success on a triple-bottom-line basis.
10 9 8 7 6 5 4 3 2 1 0

**DEDICATED
TO VIRGINIA SATIR**

Whose teachings have inspired and enriched each of our lives. And to each of those who have shared and continue to share her wisdom throughout the world. We honour the legacy of Virginia Satir that continues to evolve, with love and gratitude.

FOREWORD

JOHN BANMEN

Virginia Satir (1916–1988), the world-renowned family therapist and world peace advocate, actively included the human body in her therapeutic approach. From conscious breathing to physical touch, to tracking body sensations, to encouraging body movement and body sculpting, Satir did all this in her training sessions and in her work with clients. And she accomplished this in the days when involving the body in any type of therapy was very limited, maybe even discouraged. Fortunately, time has proven her intuitive certainty right. Now the body is often central to the practice of therapeutic change.

The authors of *Virginia Satir's Evolving Legacy: Transformative Therapy with a Bodymind Connection* show us clearly and convincingly how to bring together body and mind within the framework of

Satir's Model. One might say, from practice to theory, each chapter is an outstanding presentation of how a therapist or practitioner can achieve an integrative approach applying bodymind interventions when working with individuals, couples and families.

As you will read in the introduction, the group has worked together for several years broadening their own already-significant understanding of Satir's bodymind approaches. Their discussions and sharing of private practice work and teaching experience has resulted in this timely practical book.

Fortunately, you will not need to be a Satir-trained therapist to apply the valuable teachings in each chapter. As Satir often said, *use what fits*. I encourage you, if you are a therapist, to add to your practice what fits, taking some risks with new ideas, approaches and suggested skills. And I encourage you, reader, to *fully* experience these moments of revelation and discovery. The world will be a better place for it.

    Dr. John Banmen, R.Psych.
    Co-author, *The Satir Model: Family Therapy and Beyond*
    Former Associate Professor, University of British Columbia
    Chairman/President, Banmen Satir China Management Centre

I AM YOUR BODY

Together we have seen and done so much. Inseparable
throughout life. Everything you have felt, I have felt, we have felt.

I have experienced all the emotions, the painful ones,
the beautiful ones and those you were not aware of.

I have absorbed the repercussions of your thoughts, assumptions
and beliefs. You can hear this in my tone, see it in the way I move,

in my shape and how my parts work together – or don't.
I have suffered and thrived as a result of your choices.

So many times you have been unaware of me, punished me
for my limitations or rewarded yourself at my expense.

Many times I have been in the way of what you wanted to do.
I have screamed loudly or held my part in silence, but

that does not mean I didn't feel anything. I hold the memory of
every fall, accident, near-miss, disappointment, fear, worry, hope and
    longing.

I have been the witness and companion to everything that ever happened
    to you.
My tissues are the crystallized matrix record of everything you think

about yourself, about life, relationships, and about the world.
I would like to tell you how this has been for me. I understand you.

I know you so intimately. You have no secrets from me.
Through me you experience yourself and your life.

I hold all the secrets, the things you don't dare tell yourself.
Sometimes I feel you don't understand me.

I would like to serve you in the way you wish,
but without a few changes this will be impossible.

I am afraid we will be doomed forever to work against each other,
even though I am doing my best to serve you. This causes me great pain.

I would like to tell you about life from my perspective
so we might know each other better. Through knowing me,

and my experience, you will better know yourself.
That will be good for both of us. For both of us.

When you feel down, sad or lonely, it is because we crave
to be connected and loved. I know how to pull those strings

so hard it hurts. Because you need love. I always want to motivate you
to do anything it takes to remember you need love and connection,

but sometimes you go the other way, into isolation and self-pity.
It is not my intention that you go there, but it seems to happen a lot.

I wish so much good for you. It is my duty to keep you safe,
warn you of danger and help you cope with life. It is my job

to make sure you survive. Most of all I crave that you feel you are worthy,
that we are worthy, that you feel loved and accept yourself, accept us.

I admit, sometimes my ways of communicating are complicated,
and it seems I am saying the opposite. Making you feel bad is not my
      goal.

I am trying to help you remember. That's my job.
I only want the best for you, for us.

I am you and you are me. We continue to be inseparable.
How do we heal together? How *will* we heal together?

                                            Anastacia Lundholm

CONTENTS

	Introduction to our Collaborative Process and Purpose	1
I	Satir's Enduring And Evolving Legacy *by Mary Leslie*	11
II	Healing At All Levels *by Leona Flamand Gallant*	41
III	My Body, My Self: The Use Of Dance/Movement Therapy And Its Manifestations In Satir's Model *by Dr. Nitza Broide-Miller*	49
IV	Recognition Of Who We Are Through A Body And Energy Lens *by Julie Gerhardt*	79
V	Sculpting: Activating The Body So The Body Can Speak *by Jennifer Nagel*	125
VI	Guided Meditation In Therapy: Surfacing The Unconscious And Connecting To Higher Consciousnesss *by Dr. Carolyn Nesbitt*	159
VII	Bodymind Wisdom In Satir's Model *by Anastacia Lundholm*	209
	Acknowledgements	249

Virginia Satir (1916–1988)

INTRODUCTION TO OUR COLLABORATIVE PROCESS AND PURPOSE

WRITTEN BY MARY LESLIE

Several Satir therapists and practitioners met in 2017 to explore ways to bring into our training programs a greater emphasis on the *centrality of the body* in Virginia Satir's work. We began by reflecting on Satir's use of the body in her writings, sharing personal observations of her work, and watching videos of her training sessions with clients. While sharing how we each integrated the body in our respective therapeutic practices using the Satir teachings – the way such use had transformed our practices and informed our personal growth – it became clear that our original vision in designing training programs was shifting. Collectively, we were tapping into a deeper level of the Satir process as we revisited the gems of Satir's energetic and spiritual way of attending to the body. In February 2020 we decided to write together.

Our goals evolved to highlight:
- Satir's considerable influence on therapeutic practice during the last twenty-five years of her life, particularly through her *prioritizing the body and integrating spirituality into her teaching and therapy practice*. She brought her unique portrayal of the energetic systems within and beyond the physical body into practice before these ideas were mainstream in the West. She anticipated many of the theorists and therapeutic practitioners who focus on the body and energetic systems today.
- Our passion for Satir's ideas and her whole-person approach. Her teaching is still relevant and continues to evolve. Satir's model is taught around the world, including in China, Southeast Asia and Europe. Our respective approaches have evolved in alignment with the values, beliefs and ideas of Satir's teachings.

- Our aim is to demonstrate how each approach might be woven creatively into individual personal growth and into any therapeutic practice.

Satir viewed the body, mind and spirit, not as separate parts, but as one integrated, energetic and indivisible whole. In therapy and in her training programs, her focus was experiential and encompassed a view of human life that incorporated a systemic and deeply optimistic view of humans and their potential for change.

The hallmark of Satir's work was her extraordinary sensitivity to the nonverbal aspects of communication – height differentials, distance, voice, tone, eye contact, posture, touch and movement. Much of the magic of her therapeutic style was the ease with which she used these nonverbal dimensions. She believed that if she could help her clients see, hear and feel more, their personal and interpersonal resources would lead them to their own solutions.[1]

Virginia Satir (1916–1988) is often referred to as the mother of family therapy. She was the first family therapist to begin seeing whole families together, and published her seminal and ground-breaking book, *Conjoint Family Therapy*, in 1964 [3rd edition in 1983], highlighting the importance of working with whole families with the same therapist. This marked a significant shift from the prevailing theories of psychoanalysis of the time. She placed greater emphasis on the therapist-client relationship than on techniques. Her influence was very broad during her lifetime through her many collaborations with other therapists and theorists, including as the first program director in 1963 at Esalen, in California. In many of her collaborations she was the only woman in a field dominated by men.

She had a strong foundation in human sciences and brought creative attention to all aspects of being human. Her colleague, John Banmen, observed that, "She saw herself as more of an innovator and independent thinker instead of a follower of the predominant therapeutic approach

---

1 Simon, "Ten Most Influential Therapists."

of the day."[2] Her overarching mission was to create a more fully human world through working with individuals, with families, and by teaching her approach extensively throughout North America and globally.

The *Psychotherapy Networker* magazine in 2012 quoted Frederick Duhl, a psychiatrist, family therapist, teacher, founder and co-director (1969–2003) of the Boston Family Institute: "Satir was the most gifted therapist in the field. She knew human systems with her fingertips. Virginia probably trained more people than any other family therapist alive."[3]

The Satir Model, a book outlining Satir's approach as it had evolved through her teaching and writing, was begun in 1985 and published in 1991 following her death in 1988. The writing process involved Satir, as well as John Banmen, Jane Gerber and Maria Gomori, senior faculty members of her international process community. Their aim was to formulate the model to that point in time and to highlight core concepts.

Throughout our chapters, we – the contributors to this book – will use the term *Satir's model* (to distinguish it from the book, *The Satir Model*) to encompass all her writing, presentations, video and audio tapes, and articles that evolved over time in harmony with her teaching.

Despite the centrality of the body in Satir's training workshops and practice, we feel that the body aspect was not articulated clearly in her early writing, nor in *The Satir Model* and *SATIR Transformational Systemic Therapy (2009)*.[4] As Satir therapists, practitioners and trainers, we focus on the body; we use it, we talk about it, but we haven't written about the body as clearly as writers from other modalities. This book, therefore, was created to address that need and opportunity. In agreement with Satir's deeply energetic and integrated view of the whole person, we see the body as a way to tap into a person's dynamic energy

---

2   Banmen, *Satir Model in Action*, 14.
3   Wylie, "Changing of the Guard."
4   Banmen, *SATIR Transformational Systemic Therapy*.

system. The body is in constant flow with mind and spirit, always in alignment with the deep energetic "being" of a person.

OUR PERSONAL HISTORIES WITH SATIR'S IDEAS AND TEACHING

In the opening chapter, I will briefly outline aspects of Satir's model that are especially germane to our body/mind/spirit focus to provide a context for the chapters that follow. Rather than being didactic, the contributors chose to lean more towards inspiring readers with Satir's living legacy. We will elaborate on the deep and long-lasting impacts, not only for clients, but also for ourselves, as we seek to bring our whole selves, including a body focus, into our therapy. It is our hope that through the case studies in subsequent chapters, we will be able to convey the energetic and experiential aspects of Satir's ideas and capture the depth and breadth of her way of attending to bodies.

Together we have over 250 years of experience, which includes significant study of Satir's ideas and concepts within both clinical and teaching contexts. We will share our own stories of how we were drawn to the life and wisdom of Satir and Satir's model and how we are carrying her legacy forward. We are therapists, practitioners, coaches, teachers, personal growth facilitators. Each writer's experience of Satir is different. Three of our core group knew her well over many years: John Banmen since 1970 and Nitza Broide-Miller since 1976. Leona Flamand Gallant, an aboriginal elder, met Satir and trained with her starting in the early '80s when Satir held her process groups at The Haven on Gabriola Island on the west coast of Canada. These three, with their rich personal experiences, have greatly enhanced our writing process. I watched Satir working with families on two occasions, several years apart, and the others (Jennifer Nagel, Julie Gerhardt, Anastacia Lundholm and Carolyn Nesbitt) connected with her wisdom through taped sessions, books, and training sessions of Satir's model. Gallant was not part of our initial group process but has long been an enthusiastic supporter of Satir's vision and continues to promote Satir's wisdom, healing and teaching actively in her community in British Columbia.

Gallant and Banmen each had the experience of having Satir lead a family reconstruction around their own families of origin. Gallant has had the opportunity through her training with Satir and Gomori to facilitate family reconstructions on her own, in training programs, and presently for those who seek her out. She is passionate about the relevance and timeliness of this aspect of Satir's legacy, given aboriginal people's need for healing from years of trauma and hardship.

OUR COLLECTIVE OVERALL VIEW AND FOCUS

In the spring of 2020, we began to meet by zoom on a regular basis to attempt to put the non-linear ideas and spirit of Satir into words. This has been a process of feedback and mutual support as we have faced the challenges that Satir named herself when addressing the importance of metaphor. As she said, "There are so many things that have to do with meanings in terms of human beings, and often language is a limiting factor," and as her friend Barbara Jo Brothers stated: "No one has found a way to write a holographic book."[5]

In the spirit of Satir, we have been exploring the body, not just as a key part of therapy, but as a primary focus of therapy; we place it increasingly in the foreground of our work with clients. At the core of Satir's conceptual framework is the unity of the body, mind and spirit. We have chosen to refer to this unitive aspect as body/mind/spirit or bodymind. The two phrases are not far apart in the meaning we give to each of them as authors, but each author's preference is being honoured. The body is not just the "container," but is a clear manifestation of life itself. The body, along with the energy within and beyond the physical bounds of the body, contributes to the vitality of the whole person. Satir

---

5 Brothers, *Well-Being*, 11.

stated, "For every feeling we have, we have a body response."[6] The mind is regarded more as an observer rather than as the leader of change, as we encourage clients to extend their awareness through integration of the messages from their senses, including behaviour, cognition/thoughts and feelings, into all aspects of the therapeutic process. This theme will be expanded upon considerably in subsequent chapters as it is so central to Satir's approach and to each of us in our work with clients.

We will each elaborate on how congruence is expressed in our own particular body/mind/spirit approach; however, as I reflect on the interactions of those of us involved in this writing endeavour, I am aware of the deep level of congruence that has marked our group's interactions and explorations together. Trust and safety permeated our deliberations. This enabled us to be vulnerable together and to enter the sacred space that Satir alludes to so eloquently, resulting in a highly intuitive process, where each offering deepened our collective understanding and the process of exploration. By each sharing what a congruent state feels like and how we experience it in therapy – as a sense of flow between ourselves and our clients, as deep knowing or resonance that invariably is evident and affirmed by and through the responses of our clients – we have achieved, as clients often achieve, a sense of profound connection, and a sense of embodied inner peace and compassion, within ourselves and with one another.

Our discussions and explorations led us to look deeper into what we mean when we speak of the self, both the small "s" self and the large "S" Self. In trying to write from a consistent understanding of what we are each referring to, we agreed that the self (without the capital) refers to that experience of being and relating from an awareness of who we feel we are, the thinking and everyday part of us. When in a congruent state, fully centered and embodied and connected to a sense of universal energy, we experience a state of greater unity with one another; here there is information that we intuit comes from "beyond" our day to day

---

6 Banmen and Loeschen, *Simple but Profound*, 202.

thinking; in this state we may be experiencing the large S Self, even if only briefly, a state that resembles the essence or divine aspect of ourselves. It may also be referred to through out our chapters as life energy, soul, or spirit.

We agreed to primarily address Virginia Satir as Satir throughout our chapters; however, this has its challenges. Some of us, especially those who knew her in person, refer to her as Virginia, a name she preferred. It was commonly known that she was spoken of in many therapeutic venues and circles by her first name only. Our use of her last name, as Satir, does not in any way diminish the deeply personal way in which we and many others hold her and her contributions.

In the ordering of the chapters, we chose to place the contributions of our elders first, as they bring a very personal and deep knowledge and appreciation of her through their many years of training with her. There are a number of ways we could have ordered the remaining chapters. We trust each reader will choose the order in which to read the chapters according to their own interests and curiosities.

SUMMARY

Our group of writers brings an array of unique voices and varied experiences to this book celebrating Virginia Satir. While we each worked on our own chapters, the degree of sharing, support and feedback from the others was deeply enriching and expanding. At times we have each seen our ideas more clearly in the reflections of others. Managing the challenges of living in the real world of work, family and health challenges, while balancing a commitment to write creatively on the side, has been the context of our work together. Our deep passion for Satir's ideas and values, the sustaining support of each other and the many moments of wonderful laughter, have been rich and have enlivened what we have been able to do together.

In the introduction to *Satir Transformational Systemic Therapy* in 2009, William C. Nichols noted that Satir's strong emphasis on growth was one reason she founded the Avanta Network [now called The Virginia Satir Global Network] in 1977, "as a forum for the continued evolution of Satir's theory and practice."[7] He continues: "Whether in the mainstream or not, whether driven by the personal charisma of Virginia or not, the Satir legacy is a different and growing phenomenon throughout much of the world."[8]

Banmen spoke during the 100th birthday celebrations of Satir and her legacy about the inheritance we have been given through her life and contributions. He encouraged us to take that inheritance and share it forward.

It is in this spirit that our group of writers has come together to share creative ways we have used and experienced her teaching; we have seen that growth and transformation can be realized by staying true to Satir's ideas and principles. It is our hope that this writing will reach others, both within the Satir family and beyond – including those less familiar with her work and writing. It is our intent that readers will gain from the depth and expansiveness of her legacy and be inspired to take forward her ideas and passion for this work in creative ways.

---

7   Nichols, "forward", ii.
8   Ibid., vii.

REFERENCES

Banmen, John, ed. *Satir Transformational Systemic Therapy.* Palo Alto: Science and Behavior Books Inc., 2009.

Banmen, John., and Sharon Loeschen, eds. *Simple but Profound: Sayings of Virginia Satir.* Wendell: The Virginia Satir Global Network, 2020.

Banmen, John, ed. *The Satir Model in Action.* Langley: Satir Institute of the Pacific, 1991.

Brothers, Mary Jo. *Well-Being Writ Large: The Essential Work of Virginia Satir.* Hillsboro: Beyond Words, 2019.

Butler, Katy, Gary Cooper, and Mary Sykes Wylie, "The Changing of the Guard 1988, A Brief History of Psychotherapy, A Mosaic of the Psychotherapy Networker, 1982-2012." *The Psychotherapy Networker*, (March/April 2012).

Nichols, William, C. "Forward." In *Satir Transformational Systemic Therapy, edited by John Banmen,* i-vii. Palo Alto: Science and Behavior Books Inc., 2009.

Satir, Virginia, John Banmen, Jane Gerber, and Maria Gomori. *The Satir Model: Family Therapy and Beyond.* Mountain View: Science and Behavior Books, Inc., 1991.

Simon, Richard, "Ten Most Influential Therapists." in "The Most Influential Therapists of the Past Quarter-Century." *The Psychotherapy Networker*, (March/April 2007).

I

SATIR'S ENDURING AND EVOLVING LEGACY

MARY LESLIE

Mary Leslie retired in 2022 following thirty-five years of experience as a registered clinical social worker in healthcare settings and private practice. She taught as a sessional faculty member at the University of British Columbia School of Social Work, presented at conferences, webinars and workshops and has published chapters in journals. Her life and work have been deeply inspired and influenced by Satir's holistic, energetic and spiritual focus.

SATIR'S ENDURING AND EVOLVING LEGACY

PERSONAL STATEMENT

I first saw Virginia Satir work with a family at a gathering at Burnaby Mental Health in 1969 when I was a social work student at the University of British Columbia. I was in awe as I watched her interact with the family members chosen to work with her that day, moving them physically around on stage, and connecting very respectfully with each. Following that first experience, I read and reread Satir's *Conjoint Family Therapy* (1963).[1] In 1988, a few months before Satir died, I had a second opportunity to watch her work with a family in Vancouver and was drawn once again to her attention to the body and to the profound respect she offered each member. She moved with ease in front of several hundred people in the audience. Three years later I began my studies with the Satir Institute of the Pacific and knew I had found my "tribe" as well as support for integrating a spiritual focus into my professional practice.

As a social worker at St. Paul's Hospital, Vancouver, I was introduced to Healing Touch in 2003 and two years later to Therapeutic Touch at the B.C. Cancer Agency where I set up and supervised a Therapeutic Touch Clinic for patients and families. Learning these body-centred energetic approaches significantly amplified my appreciation of Satir and opened up a new depth of understanding of her way of working. Through that energetic body lens, I saw beyond Satir's words into the significance of her use of touch and recognized the value of her spiritual connection with each family member.

Case studies of my practice of Satir's model can be found in the *Satir International Journal* article, "Widening Our Lens, Deepening Our

---

1 Satir, *Conjoint Family Therapy*.

Practice: An Exploration of Energy within the Teachings of Virginia Satir."[2] and in *The Satir in Action,*[3] edited by John Banmen.

Virginia Satir (1916–1988) taught in many countries in her quest to promote peace within, peace between, and peace among. Many of her books have been translated into other languages and her ideas continue to be widely taught. To celebrate Satir's 100th birthday in 2016, 252 people from seventeen different countries came to Surrey, Canada, to share how her work is being used and taught today. There are thirty Satir Affiliates and/or Institutes around the world. Satir's model has been widely taught in China and throughout Asia, Europe and in Africa.

Satir started an organization called Avanta in 1977, a forum for the continued evolution of her work. This organization continues, with a name change to The Virginia Satir Global Network (VSGN) in 2007, to promote and support the teaching of her model and to advance her ideas globally. At the onset of COVID restrictions, VSGN began offering weekly zoom meetings to support therapists and adherents during those challenging times, with participants from Israel, China, Taiwan, Korea, Thailand, Turkey, Serbia, Romania, Bulgaria, Kenya and other countries. These virtual gatherings included a presenter and break-out groups for discussion and sharing of ideas and concerns. Since the fall of 2022, this pattern has shifted to once a month, with weekly hour-long Satir coffee groups providing a less structured sharing opportunity for those interested.

THE EVOLUTION OF SATIR'S MODEL

Satir's model can be placed among the humanistic/transpersonal psychological schools. John Banmen writes: "With the parallel thinking of Abraham Maslow and Carl Rogers, Satir developed a belief system...

---

2   Leslie, "Widening the Lens."
3   Leslie, "An Exploration of Energy."

that advocated a faith in human beings and their ability to manage their lives from a sense of strength, inner motivation, and responsibility."[4]

Banmen outlines four iterations of Satir's model which evolved over time:

1. The Communication Model (1960s) with the advent of her book, *Conjoint Family Therapy*
2. The Human Validation Model of the '70s and early '80s
3. The Growth Model in the mid–'80s (still going strong)
4. The Satir Transformational Systemic Therapy Model (STST) – where spiritual, energetic and transformational aspects, as demonstrated by her in video tapes, evolved with a greater emphasis in the early 2000s.

Banmen writes: "The Satir Model in the 21st century is best described as positively directional goal focused and transformational change based."[5] Our group of contributors to this book has been studying, working with, and teaching versions of the STST model as we and the model have evolved over time. William C. Nichols, a marriage and family therapist, educator and active contributor to the International Family Therapy Association writes:

It appears that Satir's work embodies an invitation to her disciples to "go forth and grow" rather than doing things exactly as she did them. In other words, a broad framework of ideas and values, rather than a narrow and explicit list of prescriptions to be followed without deviation, seems to be the path and pattern expected of Satir-model practitioners.[6]

Banmen refers to Satir's teachings as deceptively simple at first glance, but also states that in many ways we have only scratched the surface of the deeper levels of her wisdom and approach. According to Broide-Miller: "Satir's model really is a journey into a way of living that takes time to grow into and internalize. It does not consist of didactic

---

4   Banmen, *Satir Model in Action*, 15.
5   Banmen, *Satir Transformational Systemic Therapy*, 5.
6   Nichols, "Forward," ii.

information you can learn and copy. It needs to involve internal experiencing as part of the learning." (Chapter 3, Broide-Miller).

SATIR'S TRAINING PROGRAMS

Satir encouraged participants in her training programs, which included family therapists and lay persons, to dig deeper into their own family dynamics and patterns of reactivity to recognize their many resources. Broide-Miller describes meeting and working with Satir in 1976:

> What seemed somewhat different and very welcome to me was Satir's attention to our inner selves and our deepest yearnings, and the importance of doing our own work on ourselves as part of our preparations for working with others. Other therapists also valued this, but it was more consistently and effectively woven into Satir's training and allowed much deeper work with people. (Chapter 3, Broide-Miller).

Satir training sessions included the use of triads where participants in groups of three would rotate through the roles of Star (the client), therapist and observer in an interactive, hands-on process. These roles would rotate, with each person experientially grounding Satir's teaching. Participants explored the influence of their families of origin and early life experiences and supported one another to transform their own patterns in the quest to become more congruent and more "fully human." Satir stated:

> It is urgent that we nourish and develop the buds of sanity and humanness that are emerging. We have going for us a fantastic know-how of technical development and proven intellectual ability. We know how to probe and investigate practically everything. Our challenge now is to develop human beings with values – moral, ethical and humanistic—that can effectively utilize this development. When we achieve that, we will be able to

enjoy this most wonderful planet and the life that inhabits it. WE ARE ON THE WAY.[7]

SATIR, AHEAD OF HER TIME

Satir, best known for her pioneering work in family therapy, was very much ahead of her time. More than sixty years ago she was incorporating the body in therapy with individuals and families.

Barbara Jo Brothers, a friend and colleague of Satir's and a family systems therapist, has stated:

> Virginia was aware, long before body therapies were fashionable, that the human being is a multi-flowing, biocomputing, spiritual, sensate entity. In the late sixties and early seventies when I first made her acquaintance and entered training with her, it was that lack of recognition of the whole, breathing bodied person that was one of the major errors in the world of psychotherapy. The world has caught up with her to some extent in that there is now an intellectual consensus that bodies are more than just structures to carry patients into the consulting room and that they cannot be separated from feelings. *All aspects of this chemistry-and-electricity-of-the-moving-parts-of-a-person is part of [the] flow of communication.*[8]

The Psychotherapy Networker acknowledged Satir's contribution in this way:

> As the *Networker* paid its respects to the trailblazers who'd ignited the clinical imagination of a generation of therapists—people like R.D. Laing, Murray Bowen and Carl Whitaker—there was a palpable sense of the changing of the guard. But it was perhaps the passing of Virginia Satir that stirred the deepest resonance among clinicians who'd been viscerally influenced

---

7   Satir, *New Peoplemaking*, xi.
8   Brothers, *Writ Large*, 55.

by her work, which anticipated so much of the mind body orientation of many approaches today.[9]

In their article, Ten Most Influential Therapists, editors of Psychotherapy Networker noted her attentiveness to neurological aspects:

> It was always difficult for Satir to describe a family in abstract terms. Only when she was engaged with them fully with all her senses would she allow herself to think conclusively about the family system. And she always included herself in the description. So she might say, "I felt a warmth that told me the son was open for some contact." She trusted that her neurology registered the necessary information about the therapeutic system.[10]

Evidence of her ideas and thinking can be found in many writers whose bodymind theories are in use today: for example, Peter Levine, Pat Ogden, Janina Fisher, Stephen Porges, Bessel Van der Kolk, Bruce Lipton, Dan Siegel and Norman Doidge. Of these, only Peter Levine may have collaborated with Satir during her time at Esalen.

SATIR'S ENERGETIC, SPIRITUAL AND BODY ASPECTS

If Satir's earlier writing did not give full expression to the spiritual, energetic and body-based aspects to her approach, that was no doubt influenced by the culture of psychology and family therapy in which she began her work with clients. Her natural and unusual abilities to see energy as it expressed itself in people's lives, bodies and actions (likely deepened by her family's Christian Science background and strengthened by her need to survive in an emotionally challenging early childhood environment) were not widely appreciated by the scientific communities in which she lived and moved. She commented to a few trusted students and friends that she was seeing more deeply into the lives of her clients and students than she was free to share publicly. She expressed an interest

---

9   "A Brief History of Psychotherapy".
10   Simon, "Ten Most Influential Therapists."

in Therapeutic Touch and Touch for Health with Mary Jo Bulbrook.[11] Those with whom she collaborated at Esalen (1962–'69) were also considered on the "fringe" in their appreciation of the body's centrality in healing and therapy. Satir's articulation of energy and spirituality in her teaching evolved at Esalen and continued until her death.

According to Maria Gomori (1920–2021), a co-author, close friend and colleague of Satir:

> Satir's embodied presence and belief in the other person's life force evoked something powerful in those she was with, and her intention was to help people to re-connect with their own life energy, and their own resources and strength to make new choices towards their dreams and growth. The metaphor she often used is that all people have their own lights; she offers a match to light their own lights.[12]

The spiritual nature of Satir's approach is evident in her language and choice of words as she speaks about the high-risk clients she had in the early days of her private practice:

> Many of these people began to blossom as the treatment proceeded. I think now that this happened because I was working to contact their spirits, loving them as I went along. The question for me was never whether they had spirits, but how I could contact them... I consider the first step in any change is to contact the spirit. Then together we can clear the way to release the energy for going toward health. This too is spirituality in action.[13]

Satir's attentiveness to energetic aspects of individuals, families and groups with whom she worked is most evident in the videotapes of her working with clients, and in her month-long training programs beginning in 1969. In an article, "When I Meet a Person," Satir discusses an

---

11   Bulbrook, Mary Jo, personal communication with Satir 1972, shared with author in personal communication, June 2016.

12   Gomori, Maria, personal communication, June 19, 2016.

13   Satir, *New Peoplemaking*, 340-341.

"important element" she refers to as the energy field. She speaks about this in relation to touching:

> Around any well-integrated person there is a circular field that is about three feet in diameter. At the edge of this field, you can feel vibrations – at least I can! These vibrations are like unacknowledged territorial lines around the person... you can physically feel them... I respect these lines. That is why I stay at arm's length. If I go closer to a person, I have already experimented as to whether or not his or her boundary will let me in... There seems to be a relationship between the development of trust and the elasticity of this boundary.[14]

Although few of us would describe the boundaries between ourselves and others in this way, we do experience something. Consider how close to another person you stand in a line-up; sense your discomfort when someone gets too close to you. In an elevator, when a new person enters, others will often shift to maintain equidistance. This happens in response to our intuitive sense of the energy field around ourselves and others, although it remains largely an unconscious process for many people.

Satir knew that the internal state from which the therapist engages in therapy must be fully grounded and centered, with an awareness of self and the field, and focused mentally, physically, emotionally and spiritually on the client. The fullness of this approach can be supported through meditation or other mindfulness processes. This internal state of being is the state of congruence; it applies to the therapist and is also a state a client can access. When connecting with clients from a congruent state, "a therapist's creative life energy shows up in metaphors, humor, self-disclosure, sculpting and many other creative interventions."[15]

Congruence is core to Satir's energetic and deeply spiritual approach, and was a vitally important condition for herself, and foremost in her goals for clients and other therapists.

---

14 Satir, "When I Meet a Person," 193.
15 Banmen, *Satir Transformational Systemic Therapy*, 246.

CORE AND UNIQUE CONCEPTS OF SATIR'S MODEL

MAKING CONTACT AND CREATING SAFETY

For Satir, creating a connection with each individual and member of a family and group she encountered was vitally important for bringing the best out in them, for forming a bond of trust. Safety was essential to this goal: clients needed to feel safe to risk and co-create lasting change. She used a metaphor to describe her relationship to clients:

> When I am completely harmonious with myself, it is like one light reaching out to another. At the outset, it is not a question of "I will help you." It is simply a question of life reaching out to life. All life talks to life when it is in a harmonious state. If my ego is involved or if I need them to get well, then it is a different story. This is one of the secrets of what I do, if there is a secret.[16]

Satir's valuing of the safety and trust in connecting with clients is beautifully stated:

> When people come to see me, I don't ask them if they want to change. I just assume they do. I don't tell them what's wrong with them or what they ought to do. I just offer them my hand, literally and metaphorically. If I can convey to the person that I am trustworthy, then we can move and go to the scary places.[17]

One way she connected with clients was through close attention to the specific words and language they used; she integrated these into ongoing therapy by using a metaphor to shift a client's perspective and meaning making in subtle but powerful ways. She used shared language to establish and maintain a safe and deep connection with each person she encountered, often using metaphors to engage visual and kinesthetic senses energetically, to support shifts in a person's feelings, beliefs, perceptions and assumptions.

Her belief that everyone has resources within, that if made evident

---

16 Satir, "Reaching out to Life," 39.
17 Satir, "Reaching out to Life," 39.

and encouraged, would support healing, along with her deliberate intention to honour strengths and enable clients to actively co-create the change they desire, set her apart from many therapists. In session, she always set the stage by forming a strong connection with clients before engaging them in any change-focused process. She used touch throughout, but always asked permission and carefully monitored the safety and comfort of others. She would shake hands with clients or initiate hand holding if she felt they were comfortable with that:

> One can touch in all kinds of ways. In training therapists, I have told them that to develop "eyes and ears" in their fingers is important. People in families are touching all the time – slapping, pushing, shoving, holding… touch can have different meanings. So it isn't a matter of giving a touch; it is a matter of the message in the touch.[18]

She spoke of assessing a family non-verbally by closely watching their bodies, movement, position, tone of voice and facial expressions before beginning to explore other avenues of assessment:

> We think the most important area of observation for the therapist has to do with body and behavioural clues. There are numerous simultaneous levels of observations around this data… the most important are: the congruency of the body messages of each member of the family with his words, tone, and quality of expression.[19]

She stressed how important it is for the therapist to be fully aware of his/her own body posture and alert to the messages she/he might be conveying.

FIVE ESSENTIAL ELEMENTS

There are five elements considered essential for change in the *Satir*

---

18 Satir, "When I Meet a Person," 184.
19 Satir, "Therapist's Use of Self," 205.

Transformational Systemic Therapy (STST) model. Each of these elements is observable in the taped demonstrations of Satir working with families and participants in her training programs; however, they have been articulated to a greater degree in the *STST* model. The unique components of her approach have been highlighted as: *systemic, experiential, positively directional, change and transformational focused, and the intentional use of self.* These are deeply interwoven with the energetic field of the body. They interact with one another and are not in reality separate or distinct in themselves.

Systemic

Any change in one area can result in or bring about a change in another area. By using the word "systemic," we are referring to Satir's ability to address multiple areas of focus, such as beliefs, fears, yearnings and body sensations simultaneously. Systemic also refers to systems, such as: closed vs open, hierarchical vs egalitarian and differences in power between therapist and client.

Satir focused primarily on two levels of systems: *internal*, the relationships among the constituent parts of a person: emotions, beliefs, perceptions, expectations and yearnings, addressing the different roles or internal (intrapsychic) parts of a person as a system and *interactional*, the relationships among the constituent parts of a family, community or country.[20] Transformational change involves an energetic shift in the intrapsychic system, which then changes the interactive system. Whether Satir was working with an individual, a family or in training groups, she always addressed the vital role that the lived experience of family of origin had in shaping worldview and self-image. The relationship between the client and therapist is also a system that Satir believed requires keen attention.

Satir believed that each human being has what they need in terms of resources, and the goal of therapy therefore is to assist the client to access

---

20 Smith, "Transformations in Therapeutic Practice," 126.

what is already there. From this perspective, she envisioned her clients as co-creators of the outcome of their work together; we each have the capacity to connect with and draw from the universal energy field; it is accessible to each of us, either consciously or unconsciously.

Experiential

Satir consistently articulated the experiential in the energetic focus of her work. For her, experience is located in body sensations, feelings and their interrelatedness, all occurring in the present moment. She demonstrated that emotions, beliefs, expectations and yearnings rooted in our somatic experience must be experienced deeply and processed at a body level before any behavioural changes can be integrated and sustained. She stressed the importance of therapist/practitioner and client moving slowly and incrementally in present time to anchor, reinforce and strengthen the client's resolve and integrate change. This may begin at any level, but eventually will involve the deepest level of the body/self.

Satir held that goals set between client and therapist, including movement towards transformational change, can be supported in many ways, including by an experiential focus on the body as guide, truth teller and monitor, through asking open-ended process questions intended to give the client an opportunity to explore their intrapsychic parts. Process can be entirely experiential or guided with questions oriented toward bringing the client into a deeper inquiry into his or her own being and experience.

Positively directional

The therapist actively engages with the client to help reframe perceptions, generate possibilities, hear the positive message of universal yearnings, and connect the client to his/her positive Life Energy (soul or spirit). By exploring the positive or survival role that our coping patterns provide at times of stress and threat, the therapist shifts clients from self-judgement to more compassionate acceptance of their past responses.

The therapist can link the body sensations of clients to affirmations of their deepest yearnings. This paves the way for the important work of transforming old patterns into new choices and fresh patterns. "The focus is on health and possibilities, appreciating inner resources, and anticipating growth, rather than on pathologizing or problem solving."[21]

This growth-oriented, positively directional component distinguishes Satir's model from others. Satir was committed to supporting clients to move from a negative view of the body associated with trauma to a positive, resourced view of the body. She strived to empower them as participants in the vital change process.

Change and transformation-focused

"The goal of therapy... is transformation in the way the system relates to itself, in essence a change in its way of being."[22]

The focus on intrapsychic change begins with a focus on the body to reveal emotions, beliefs, expectations and yearnings that are stored in the cells and are biologically based in body memory and experience. The body is the storage unit and carries an imprint of one's past, thus attending to the body is a necessary first step for resolving trauma and internalized memory of the past, which the body is still holding. Satir believed that movement towards transformation must first be recognized at this deeply internal body level, and experientially felt and honoured there, before the impacts of past events can be transformed and behaviour can change. When a therapist works interactively with couples or family members, the change will involve connecting people at the level of their emotions, beliefs, expectations and yearnings to help externalize relationship issues or patterns. "Transformational change happens as people embrace the pain of the past in the present and feel the difference in the core of their being."[23] From this place, different choices can be made moving forward.

---

21   Banmen, *Satir Transformational Systemic Therapy,* 246.
22   Smith, "Transformations in Therapeutic Practice," 126.
23   Sayles, "Transformational Change," 114.

Integration of this transformational change by each person is enhanced by "anchoring a change internally," a process that takes place at the level of one's beliefs, assumptions, yearnings and sense of self. This can be supported by the therapist exploring through the body the ways that the client will be, or feel, different given the change that has just been experienced. The importance of the anchoring process will be expanded further, especially in Nagel's and in Broide-Miller's chapters. Timing, in Satir's approach to therapy, is critical to the establishment and sustaining of change. The principles of moving slowly, and integrating change at each level, have been demonstrated with every age group from newborn babies to adults at any stage of their life. This will be expanded further in all chapters that follow, but especially in Gerhardt's Chapter 4, on sessions with infants and mothers who have experienced birth trauma, and Broide-Miller's Chapter 3, on work with movement and dance therapy.

Intentional use of self

The therapist's conscious awareness of herself, of her body, mind and spirit, is a central tenet of Satir's teaching and writings. The actions that follow from the congruent state of the therapist are what we refer to as the intentional use of self. On a surface level this awareness of self helps the therapist to avoid or minimize burn-out and overload; awareness of self can alert us to the need for greater self-care at times of stress. At a deeper level it accomplishes so much more. When therapists are connected, through meditation, grounding and centering, to the deepest core of themselves, they can be fully present to support others' connection to their own lifeforce. In this way clients are supported to embody their own state of congruence and be in touch with their core selves and their inner resources of creativity, imagination and yearning for wholeness, encompassing body/mind/spirit.

CONGRUENCE

Congruence was fundamental to Satir's work and teaching. She saw congruence as a process of aligning one's deep and sustained attention mentally, emotionally and spiritually with and in the service of her clients and students. Satir considered congruence – a state of deep centeredness, at one with self and the other, a deep sense of presence – as the most important aspect of therapeutic interactions. The importance of congruence to client outcome is beautifully expressed in "The Therapist's Story," written by Satir in 1987, a year before her death, and included in the book, *In Her Own Words*:

> I have learned that, when I am fully present with the patient or family, I can move therapeutically with much greater ease. I can simultaneously reach the depths to which I need to go and at the same time honor the fragility, the power, and the sacredness of life in the other. When I am in touch with myself, my feelings, my thoughts, and with what I see and hear, I am growing toward becoming a more integrated self. I am more congruent, I am more whole, and I am able to make greater contact with the other person... The whole therapeutic process must be aimed at opening up the healing potential within the patient or client. Nothing really changes until the healing potential is opened. The way is through the meeting of the deepest self of the therapist with the deepest self of the person, patient, or client. When this occurs, it creates a context of vulnerability, of openness to change. This clearly brings in the spiritual dimension. People already have what they need to grow; and the therapists' task is to enable patients to utilize their own resources.[24]

Congruence will be discussed in each of the following chapters as it is closely linked to a full embodied relationship between therapist and client. When the therapist models this internal state, the client often reaches a deeper level of congruence; the client reflects the patterning of the therapist's state. Broide-Miller and Nagel each explore this in their chapters. Nagel speaks of the flow between Knowing and Unknowing (or

---

24 Satir, "Therapist's Story," 220-221.

not knowing) when she and a client are engaged in a sculpt and in congruent states. For Broide-Miller, congruence is "the metaphorical dance that emerges between the client and myself, when we are each embodying a congruent state."[25]

SATIR IN PRACTICE

PREFERENCE FOR DEMONSTRATION OVER WRITING

Barbara Jo Brothers commented:
> Satir's work was explicitly multidimensional... The awareness of this multidimensional nature, the "roundness" of people, is a major reason Virginia put much more energy into live demonstrations – videotaped and audiotaped – than into writing books. The venue of the book was far too limiting. No one has found a way to write a holographic book. We are limited by the single-file march of the word across the page. Virginia sought to engage the whole person in training and learning events.[26]

MEDITATION

Satir made extensive use of guided meditation, at times with clients, but very frequently in her training sessions. In her words: "I see meditations as a path to the intuitive part of ourselves, which I feel is where everything emanates from."[27] She spoke in her meditations of the importance of centering (in one's heart) and grounding (in one's body) as key ingredients in making contact with and attending to the whole person. "Through meditations, it is as though I'm doing an internal job of bringing together everything that people have, through their senses, through

---

25 Broide-Miller, Personal communication, September 20, 2023.
26 Brothers, *Well-Being*, 11.
27 Banmen, *Meditations of Virginia Satir*, 3.

their feelings about themselves, and through their breathing and relaxation, to enable them to approach tasks."[28]

She also believed that meditations need to come from a state of love. "They have to come from caring and they have to come from a total belief in growth... Before I lead a meditation, I need to prepare myself to be in that state of love and caring... it is not only what you say but what state you are in."[29]

Satir often began training sessions with a meditation. In chapter 6, Nesbitt will elaborate extensively on the multiple ways Satir's meditations supported a state of congruence and set the tone and receptiveness for her therapy and teaching. Nesbitt will also highlight her own use of meditations in therapy with her clients.

CENTERING

For Satir, body awareness and centering, intuition, spirituality and congruence are streams that flow together seamlessly. She was able to work from each level of the stream simultaneously and systemically.

Dora Kunz, in her book *Spiritual Healing*, speaks to the centering process from a Therapeutic Touch perspective, which can add further clarity to our understanding of Satir's process of centering:

> Centering involved, first of all, the intent to be quiet within. It is the focusing of one's energies and attention to a place of stillness within one. One is not reacting to outward circumstances, but one turns to one's own sense of wholeness and oneness for a moment. This leads to a sense of being integrated... Slowly a sense of peace and integration is experienced. Often an intuitional insight can occur... One's intent is enhanced and clarified and so one is more likely to be effective in one's therapeutic encounter.[30]

While Satir did not define specifically what she meant by centering,

---

28   Banmen, *Meditations of Virginia Satir*, 1.
29   Ibid,, 3.
30   Kunz, *Spiritual Healing*, 253.

she frequently shared the following centering exercise with participants "to deepen your experience of spirituality":

> Sit comfortably on a chair with your feet on the floor. Gently close your eyes and simply notice your breathing. Now silently go inside and give yourself a message of appreciation that might sound something like this, "I appreciate me." This is to give your spirit strength from your actions. Next visualize yourself affirming your connection with your creator.

Brothers comments:

> While it might contain some of the elements of self-hypnosis, this centering process was not simply a trick to bypass the conscious into the unconscious. It was a method for affirming the sacredness of the human spirit in each specific person and of bringing that human being into interior and exterior balance and harmony. In Virginia's experience, this movement toward balance and harmony was all part of the congruence process necessary for effective therapy and life.[31]

SPIRITUALITY

Satir's spiritual essence and intuitive gifts were fully present in her interactions with clients and students. Her concept of spirituality is interwoven throughout all areas of her approach and methodology. This is another area of focus that sets her apart from many other therapists:

> I believe (spirituality) is our connection to the universe and is basic to our existence, and therefore is essential to our therapeutic context… We are all unique manifestations of life. We are divine in our origins. We are also the recipients of what has gone before us, which gives us vast resources from which to draw. I believe that we also have a pipeline to universal intelligence and wisdom through our intuition, which can be tapped

---

31 Brothers, *Well-Being*, 49.

through meditation, prayer, relaxation awareness, the development of high self-esteem and a reverence for life. This is how I reach my spirituality.[32]

METAPHOR

Satir often used metaphors in meditations, in training and therapy, to connect people to their own bodies, to help them access their own inner wisdom and to shift beliefs. Satir talks extensively about her use of metaphor and calls metaphors her adjunct (additional) therapist, as they help shape her work with clients in such a profound way:

> There are so many things that have to do with meanings in terms of human beings, and often language is a limiting factor. So when I want to get some special meaning across, I will bring in a metaphor. By using a metaphor, I can make space between whatever is and what I am trying to get across… What I am most interested in is beyond the logical, to engage the intuitive to bring out the pictures, to bring out the sensing which gives juice to the form and possibly allows for deeper change… I believe in and practice the use of sculpting, metaphors, and pictures to activate the whole brain and engage the whole person.[33]

With metaphor, as with sculpting and pictures/visualizations, Satir draws from multiple layers and aspects to engage the client's imagination and help shift their perceptions, and ultimately their beliefs. Physicality is central to so many of her metaphors. She commented that she did not plan ahead what she would use in a session but would allow the images or metaphors to arise organically from her own centered state and life energy. She did not focus on problems needing to be solved but from the outset of a session would address the widest possible context of situations. Metaphor, visualization and pictures were frequently used

---

32   Satir, *New Peoplemaking*, 334.
33   Satir, *Satir Model*, 259-261.

to engage the client so that they would begin to see change possibilities, even in the absence of personal stories.

THE ICEBERG METAPHOR

The Personal Iceberg Metaphor was named by Banmen, but it emerged from Satir's later teaching as a metaphorical structure of how folks experience themselves, "their unexpressed inner life." Wendy Lum addresses how the iceberg can be useful to therapists:

> The personal iceberg metaphor represents the lived experience of a person's intrapsychic world. This metaphor is a specific tool that gives a framework for therapists to reflect, gain awareness, and effectively intervene therapeutically with their clients. Therapist trainees are also encouraged to reflect upon their own internal processes and to gain awareness of their own inner world.[34]

THE PERSONAL ICEBERG METAPHOR

The conceptual components of the iceberg may seem linear in this diagram but, in reality, they are highly interactive. Above the waterline lies visible behaviour. The "waterline" is where one's patterns of coping lie, which are reflected in one's actions (placating, blaming, super reasonable, irrelevant). Below the waterline lie body sensations, the internal aspects of a person, including feelings, feelings about feelings, perceptions (meanings, beliefs, assumptions, understandings and expectations). Still deeper in the layers of the iceberg lie yearnings (yearning to be loved, affirmed, accepted and/or valued). At the deepest level lies the innermost self, what Satir termed "I am," the component which represents the life

---

34 Lum, "Use of Self of the Therapist," 202.

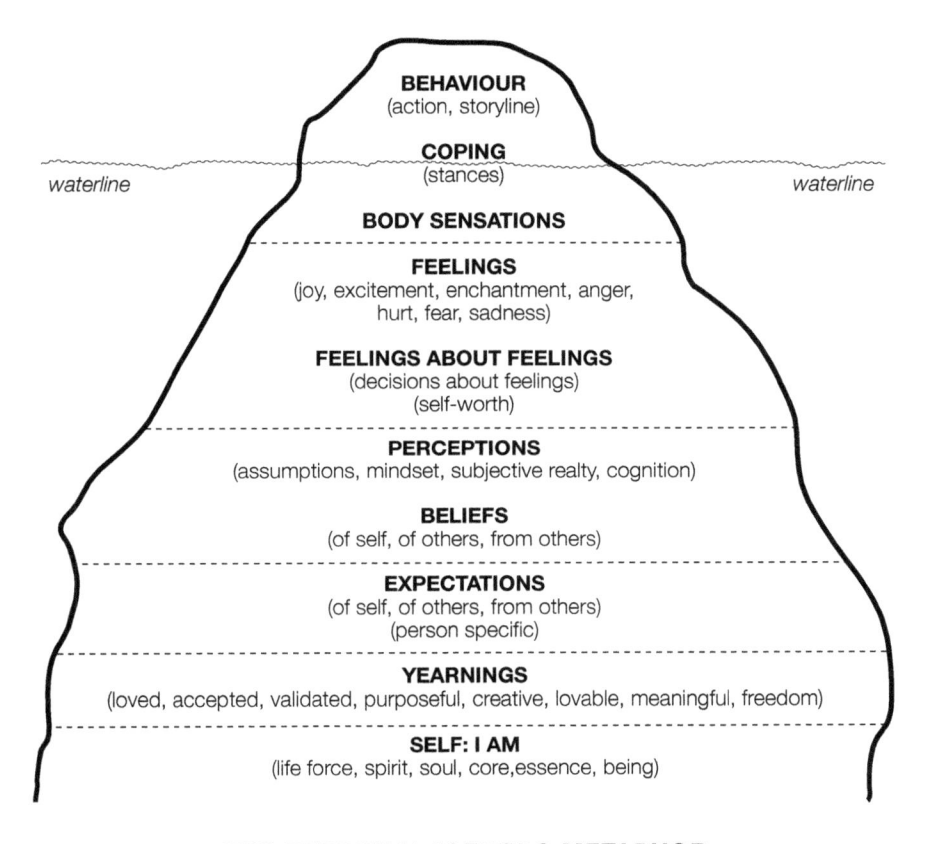

```
                    BEHAVIOUR
                 (action, storyline)
                     COPING
                     (stances)
waterline                                              waterline
                  BODY SENSATIONS
- - - - - - - - - - - - - - - - - - - - - - - - - - - - - - -
                     FEELINGS
            (joy, excitement, enchantment, anger,
                   hurt, fear, sadness)
                FEELINGS ABOUT FEELINGS
                 (decisions about feelings)
                      (self-worth)
- - - - - - - - - - - - - - - - - - - - - - - - - - - - - - -
                    PERCEPTIONS
         (assumptions, mindset, subjective realty, cognition)
                      BELIEFS
             (of self, of others, from others)
- - - - - - - - - - - - - - - - - - - - - - - - - - - - - - -
                   EXPECTATIONS
             (of self, of others, from others)
                   (person specific)
- - - - - - - - - - - - - - - - - - - - - - - - - - - - - - -
                     YEARNINGS
  (loved, accepted, validated, purposeful, creative, lovable, meaningful, freedom)
- - - - - - - - - - - - - - - - - - - - - - - - - - - - - - -
                     SELF: I AM
          (life force, spirit, soul, core, essence, being)
```

THE PERSONAL ICEBERG METAPHOR
© 2022 Revised, John Banmen
Satir, V., et. al, 1991, The Satir Model Family Therapy and Beyond

force, essence, and soul.[35] All parts of the iceberg are continuously experienced by a person, through and with their body.

Lum continues:

> Each layer needs checking out, although Satir's process of transformational therapy can start with an intervention at any level, it invariably involves all levels in the change process towards transformation. This metaphor provides a tool for

---

35 Satir, *Satir Model*, 67.

systematically exploring issues from all angles and a window into how an individual represents and holds their internal world.[36]

This iceberg metaphor portrays the deeply systemic nature of Satir's therapeutic approach, where any change at one level results in change at another level or at multiple levels.

This powerful metaphor, when applied to our day-to-day work with clients and in our personal lives, can highlight areas that need more attention and focus. Combined with a body-centred approach, the iceberg brings awareness to sensations and intuitions deeply embodied in our intrapsychic processing.

SCULPTING AND STANCES

Sculpting is another process Satir used to involve the body, to bring a client to greater awareness of internal states. "Satir developed physical sculpting poses, stances, in order to externalize the internal experience in a non-verbal manner to allow the body memory and wisdom to express itself."[37] Satir saw these physical positions or stances as a shorthand that would allow insight, by therapist and client, into the ways in which people communicate with one another: "I have translated the various kinds of responses into body positions. Within a few moments, I am making mental pictures of the people in front of me and translating them into physical postures that represent their ways of communicating."[38]

Sculpting involves having clients form a physical pose or sculpt (body stance) to externalize the relationship between themselves and another. This intervention is particularly valuable when used in family therapy to support individual shifts in perspective around power sharing and resources within the family. Sculpting can be very helpful in change

---

36 Lum, "Therapists' Experience," 48.
37 Banmen and Maki-Banmen, "What has happened," 119.
38 Satir, "When I Meet a Person," 183.

and transformation processes. To quote Nagel in chapter 5 on sculpting: "Sculpting is one way of 'waking up' cellular memory or familiar energetic patterns of experience..." and "sculpting will shift [clients'] perceptions of themselves more quickly than will verbal therapy." Sculpting can tap into the client's body to bring greater awareness and a wider view to the process and can support their decision to change behaviour.

As with any intervention, timing is a critical factor when using sculpting to tap into the well of body wisdom, especially when the aim is to shift perceptions and beliefs. Satir commented: "I never ask anyone to do anything until they are ready. Timing is very important in how you make trust."[39] Sculpting and stances (placating, blaming, super reasonable, and irrelevant coping patterns) will be addressed in detail in Nagel's chapter 5.

FAMILY RECONSTRUCTION

Banmen refers to family reconstruction as:
> [Satir's] major vehicle for change. This is a three generational, experiential change technique that basically works on various levels of change at the same time. This technique is classically achieved through a dramatic play of re-enacting parts of the three generational family experience with the client (the Star) having the opportunity to see the various connections of experiences from a new perspective and deeper level and make peace with the past in such a way as to be free in the present. It is a major transformational experience.[40]

Sculpting and stances are central to Satir's Family Reconstruction Process where an individual, in the presence of others who offer to "stand in" as members of the Star's family, is supported by a guide to revisit a traumatic situation and gain a fresh perspective of their own

---

39 Satir, "1979 DVD 29."
40 Banmen, *Satir Model in Action*, 17.

actions, those of family members, and of the impactful event they have chosen to explore. The guide supports the Star to see new possibilities, to gain a wider perspective from the feedback of others and by tapping into the body and internal sensing, and to make new choices for moving forward. The ultimate goal is a revision of the meaning-making from that incident and a healthier relationship with family and self. Maria Gomori, a close colleague of Satir's, describes the process this way:

> Family Reconstruction, like all Satir's creative approaches, works experientially with both cognitive and non-cognitive processes. The therapy must be experiential for the Star to experience the impact of a past event in the present with positive life energy. Often body memory is accessed as a way to help experience the impacts of the past. When the Star experiences both the negative energy and the positive energy of their life force, an energetic shift can take place. Satir encouraged this through externalizing the internal processes and coping patterns, making the covert overt, and the abstract concrete, through role-playing, sculpting, metaphor and drama... this context is often seen through the lens of childhood experience and conclusions made at that time. Satir wanted to include an adult perspective and find ways to help a person access new perceptions and choices.[41]

Satir regarded families as our learning laboratories and affirmed the importance of one's family context in the evolution of one's perspective and decisions, relating both to one's past, and one's self-definition. Through the involvement of those playing roles as chosen by the Star, who became contributors in the Star's process of exploration, Satir tried to help the Star gain distance, to see their family and experiences through "fresh eyes"; thus, the Star could gain new awareness experientially for new conclusions and choices. Those playing roles for the Star also expressed how transformational it could be for them as participants.

---

41 Gomori, *Personal Alchemy*, 74-76.

CONCLUSION

This is by no means an exhaustive overview of all Satir's work or teaching. There has been an effort to incorporate and highlight those aspects that most clearly relate to the experiential and body centered aspects on which we are focusing here, and to form a context for those reading, especially those less aware of her work. We were clear that we could not provide a manual, and more information about her model can be found at https://satirglobal.org and https://satirpacific.org. Information for other websites of Satir Institutes and Affiliates can be accessed on the Virginia Satir Global Network site and there you will find information in other languages as well as resources and courses available.

Although the values and ideals modelled by Virginia Satir are held in common across the various Institutes and Affiliates, her model is evolving in unique ways as she intended, and in line with her teachings. The Virginia Satir Global Network continues to provide a venue for sharing between global members and provides resources and education offerings. There is also extensive sharing of teaching staff, and resources among the various Satir Institutes and Affiliates.

We trust our book can be an addition to what is already happening and that others less familiar with Satir's approach will find a path from here to explore and follow their curiosity. Together we will continue to honour Virginia Satir's yearning for "peace within, peace between and peace among, and her passion for healing the world, one family at a time.

REFERENCES

Banmen, John, ed. *Meditations of Virginia Satir*. Burien: Avanta, The Virginia Satir Network. 2003.

Banmen, John, ed. *Satir Transformational Systemic Therapy*. Palo Alto: Science and Behavior Books, Inc., 2008.

Banmen, John, ed. *In Her Own Words: Virginia Satir Selected Papers 1963-1983*. Phoenix: Zeig, Tucker & Theisen, Inc., 2008.

Banmen, John, and Kathlyne Maki-Banmen. "What Has Become of Virginia Satir's Therapy Model Since She Left Us in 1988?" *Journal of Family Psychotherapy* 25, no. 2 (June 2014): 117-113.

Banmen, John, and Sharon Loeschen, eds. *Simple but Profound: Sayings of Virginia Satir.* Wendell: The Virginia Satir Global Network, 2020.

Banmen, John, ed. *Guided Meditations and Inspirations by Virginia Satir.* Langley: Satir Institute of the Pacific, 2020.

Banmen, John, ed. *The Satir Model in Action.* Langley: Satir Institute of the Pacific, 2021.

Brothers, Barbara Jo. *Well-Being Writ Large: The Essential Work of Virginia Satir.* Hillsboro: Beyond Words, 2019.

Kunz, Dora, and Erik Peper. "Fields and their Clinical Applications Part V." In *Spiritual Healing: Doctors Examine Therapeutic Touch and Other Holistic Treatments,* compiled by Dora Kunz, 251-261. Wheaton: Quest Books, 1995.

Leslie, Mary. "Widening Our Lens, Deepening Our Practice: An Exploration of Energy Within the Teachings of Virginia Satir", *Satir International Journal 4,* no.1 (2016): 5-20.

Leslie, Mary. "An Exploration of Energy within the Teachings of Virginia Satir." in *The Satir Model in Action,* edited by John Banmen, 112-133. Langley: Satir Institute of the Pacific, 2021.

Lum, Wendy. "Therapists' Experience Using Satir's Personal Iceberg Metaphor." *Satir Journal: Transformational Systemic Therapy* 2, no. 2 (2008): 45-88.

Lum, Wendy. "The Use of Self of the Therapist." In *Satir Transformational Systemic Therapy,* edited by John Banmen, 188-204. Palo Alto: Science and Behavior Books, Inc., 2008.

Nichols, William C. "Preface", in *Satir Transformation Systemic Therapy.* edited by John Bannen, i-vii. Palo Alto: Science and Behavior Books, Inc., 2008.

Satir, Virginia. *Conjoint Family Therapy, Third Edition.* Palo Alto: Science and Behavior Books, Inc., 1967.

Satir, Virginia. *DVD 29* of a month-long Process Community Workshop Presentation, in Agathe, Quebec, Canada. August 3-30,1979.

Satir, Virginia. *The New Peoplemaking.* Mountain View: Science and Behavior Books, Inc., 1988.

Satir, Virginia, John Banmen, Jane Gerber, and Maria Gomori. *The Satir Model: Family Therapy and Beyond.* Palo Alto: Science and Behavior Books, Inc., 1991.

Satir, Virginia. "When I meet a person." *In Her Own Words: Virginia Satir, Selected Papers, 1963-1983,* edited by John Banmen, 179-196. Phoenix: Zeig, Tucker and Theisen, Inc., 2008.

Satir, Virginia. "Therapist's Use of Self." *In Her Own Words: Virginia Satir, Selected Papers, 1963-1983*, edited by John Banmen, 197-209. Phoenix: Zeig, Tucker and Theisen, Inc., 2008.

Satir, Virginia. "The Therapist Story". *In Her Own Words: Virginia Satir, Selected Papers, 1963-1983,* edited by John Banmen, 211-223. Phoenix: Zeig, Tucker and Theisen, Inc., 2008.

Sayles, Carl. "Transformational Change – Based on the Model of Virginia Satir." In *Satir Transformational Systemic Therapy*, edited by John Banmen, 9-115. Palo Alto: Science and Behavior Books, Inc., 2008.

Simon, Richard. "Reaching Out to Life: The Legacy of Virginia Satir." *The Family Therapy Networker,* 37-43. January/February 1989.

Simon, Richard. "The Ten Most Influential Therapists." In "The Most Influential Therapists of the Past Quarter-Century." *Psychotherapy Networker*, (March/April 2007).

Smith, Stephen. "Transformations in Therapeutic Practice." In *Satir Transformational Systemic Therapy*, edited by John Banmen, 116-133. Palo Alto: Science and Behavior Books, Inc., 2008.

Wylie, Mary Sykes. "The Changing of the Guard – 1988.", "A Mosaic of the Psychotherapy Networker, 1982-2012," *Psychotherapy Networker,* (March/April 2012).

II

HEALING AT ALL LEVELS

LEONA FLAMAND GALLANT

Leona Flamand Gallant is Métis and lives in Nanaimo, on Vancouver Island, B.C., Canada. Flamand Gallant's first experience of Satir followed years of involvement in self-directed and experiential learning. She heard about the presentation of a video of Satir working with a family and had a strong sense this was "meant for me." In 1982, soon after seeing the video, she attended her first month-long training with Satir at The Haven on Gabriola Island. She followed up with two additional month-long training sessions, and other presentations and workshops that Satir presented in Nanaimo through the Northwest

Satir Group out of Seattle. She studied Satir's book, watched and discussed videos with a study group in Nanaimo, and she included Satir's model in her work at Tillicum Lelum Aboriginal Friendship Centre in Nanaimo. She had the privilege of having Satir facilitate her own family reconstruction process, and a parts party. She continued to train with Maria Gomori, including a three-month training group for her workplace, and was certified to train others in Satir's model, which included the facilitation of family reconstructions. She continues to train with science and spirit-based writers and therapists of various disciplines. She is an active member of the Vancouver Island Satir Network Group and continues to have an active role with Tillicum Lelum as a board member. She currently consults and facilitates family reconstructions as requested by those in her community.

HEALING AT ALL LEVELS

Mary Leslie: What memories do you have of first seeing Satir in a taped interview?

Leona Flamand Gallant: As soon as I was offered the chance to see her on the tape, I felt quite drawn to attend. Having seen Satir at work, I knew I wanted to learn as much about her and from her as I could. As she worked with a young man, I witnessed him come alive with a hope that there was a way out of his despair. She provided a light into the darkness of his own despair. He saw that the light was within himself. She created the mirror for him to see his way through despair. I knew without a shadow of a doubt I was going to base my future learning on this woman, Virginia Satir. She spoke the truth clearly, in her choice of language, use of metaphors and humour; it was a universal language.

ML: Can you recall your first encounter in person at the month-long workshop at The Haven on Gabriola?

LFG: That was 1982. I recall that Satir invited each of us to come up to the front at the opening of her workshop, to where she stood, and introduce ourselves. I remember getting halfway up to her and breaking into tears. It was as if her heart had reached out and connected with and opened mine. It was so powerful. I think I had entered her field of love (heart energy) and it was so welcome and needed in that moment.

I appreciated how Satir spoke in pictures and had a deep love of nature. I felt very connected through her appreciation for the natural world. I valued the collaborative way she worked and her collective lens through which she viewed life and the world. She saw that we are all connected to generations before, to nature, to each other and to everything that lives. That spoke to my aboriginal heritage and world view. Satir's appreciation of "context" was important to me. In addressing the Self/Other/Context she used everything to create a wider picture and view of a client's awareness to support change. I recall watching Satir observe bodies closely and make decisions from those observations about how to work further with participants. All parts of us, as well as the world into which we are born, and all the lives from which we came, were considered in her healing and approach. Nothing was left out. I appreciated her emphasis on the reality that we have each come from an egg and sperm because that is inclusive not only of our immediate family, and what they have given or not given us, but of all the generations before our parents as well. It puts our healing and growth into a much wider lens and reality.

In her work that I witnessed, or was a part of, the transformation proceeded like putting a puzzle together. As the pieces were put in place a full picture emerged. All of a sudden, the participant could see an answer that had never been seen before. This raised hope for everyone witnessing this moment.

ML: You have been a strong supporter of our writing efforts since our first conversation about our group's intent. Can you say more about the importance of this information being shared at this time in our history?

LFG: I believe there is a hunger to recognize our own essence, as humans, which includes searching for and valuing meaning in our lives now. That essence was what Satir spoke to, but it is taking us time to move as a culture from seeing ourselves as the centre of the world around us, to seeing ourselves as part of something much greater and more inclusive.

I believe many are living at a higher vibrational level culturally at our time than in Satir's time. She understood everything then that we are learning about now: understanding ourselves and our world energetically, seeing the world from a "we are all One" perspective, and how connected everything is, not only among humans, but with nature and all sentient beings.

Her life messages are like a living cell in each of us who connected with her. Her message keeps expanding and renewing itself. It doesn't stand still. As a culture and collective, we are more able to see her depth, creativity and relevance now. Contemporary writers and scientists have made important connections biologically, spiritually, ancestrally, in line with their regard for all aspects to be included in our understanding of ourselves, and in our view of healing and growth.

As I watched her facilitating family reconstructions in the 1980s, I believed she was doing ancestral healing, going way beyond the family triad of mother/father/child in her work with people. This is more commonly understood in an aboriginal world view, but it is also more present in the scientific world as well, today. That ancestral healing includes the bidimensional aspect of healing generations before and to come.

ML: Can you say more about the family reconstructions you are facilitating, and how you are using stories as part of those sessions?

LFG: I believe Satir's healing and transformative work with people was founded on her belief in the importance of contacting and connecting to people at all levels of her and their being, supported through her open heart and compassion. A sense of belonging is supported through the telling and reframing of stories. The sense of belonging, of being seen and heard, flows from that deep sense of connection.

There are times when a larger group comes together to support the family reconstruction process; however, we often do not have the luxury of involving many people to play the roles of family members. In those situations, I draw on objects of nature, for example, rocks, to "stand in" for their family members. Nature-based objects have an energy of their own and can become a powerful energetic force in the healing process.

I begin my process of family reconstruction with individuals on family healing by meeting over several sessions, a few hours at a time. We do family maps together first, looking at how relationships were formed and developed over time. Over the next week or so, participants write and reflect on the stories of their mother, and their father, one at a time. This involves doing research with other family members or friends as needed. Then they write their own stories. Through this process of telling their story and listening deeply, there is a heart opening that happens. As we share their story, they begin to see their family members and themselves in a wider context. In Satir's view, we don't need to change the child; we need to recognize the holiness of the child and the coping decisions made at that time that carried on into adulthood. Through this process the participant can see more clearly the survival purpose of earlier coping patterns and can make changes now as they choose.

I find the metaphor of the battery helpful, where connecting the negative and positive terminals results in a positive charge. Transformation in our family work is similar. The real and deeper change happens when positive as well as negative aspects are connected, and a wider and more compassionate view is possible.

We heal by integrating each part of the story. Once those parts come together, after several sessions, and shift has begun, we plan a ceremony to celebrate the transformation in how they see their family that has taken place during our time together. The ceremony or ritual as we conclude is a very important part of the healing process and is largely a creation led by the participant.

Satir's experiential way of working, drawing on meditations, visualizing, metaphors, sculpting and parts-party processes can bring a wider view and move participants into a deeper internal place at any time during this family healing process. The sculpt, especially, is what keeps the energy of the process alive, accessible and moving.

ML: Can you comment on how Satir's ideas and overall work relates to reconciliation, as we hear this is needed for our aboriginal communities and for non-aboriginal communities as well.

LFG: Satir's whole approach with people was to work towards healing at all levels, within a person, between people and among communities. This work has been ongoing for many years but is sorely needed currently for healing between aboriginal and non-aboriginal populations, as well as immigrant and non-immigrant peoples. In our country, it is especially needed around residential school impacts and the hardships that evolved from this historical trauma. Satir's model connects individuals, families and ancestors through connecting people and families to their stories. The healing that can come from this connection is vitally needed in our communities at this time.

In my opinion, not only is the content of Satir's teaching important, but her method of integrating all the learning through the body, mind, spirit and emotions needs be an integral part of all learning in our education system.

III

MY BODY, MY SELF: THE USE OF DANCE/MOVEMENT THERAPY AND ITS MANIFESTATIONS IN SATIR'S MODEL

DR. NITZA BROIDE-MILLER

Dr. Nitza Broide-Miller has over fifty-five years of experience as a dance therapist, forty-five of which she has taught Satir's model. She met Virginia Satir in 1976 and worked and studied closely with Satir until Virginia's death in 1988. Her life work has taken her to Israel, USA, Hong Kong, Thailand, China and Taiwan. Broide-Miller's unrelenting curiosity to know more, coupled with keen observation skills, are hallmarks of her work and training style.

She continues to study with body-oriented therapists and scholars, and lives and works in Palo Alto, California. Her exemplary gifts of scholarship and her passion for working with the body have generously enriched our group's exploration of the role of the body in therapy. The following interview took place over several weeks and months beginning in December 2021.

MY BODY, MY SELF: THE USE OF DANCE/ MOVEMENT THERAPY AND ITS MANIFESTATIONS IN SATIR'S MODEL

People need to see themselves as basic miracles and worthy of love.
Virginia Satir

The chapter you are about to read was born out of a work of love… love and acceptance of ourself; love of our body and the spirit that inhabits it. It was also born out of the many conversations between Mary Leslie and myself, allowing curiosity to lead our way; we explored and attentively listened, which clarified our feelings, thoughts, beliefs and yearnings. These talks helped me bring to the foreground the journey of my life in relation to the body. They also highlighted the turning points in my life which re-emphasized what was important for me and what drove me, through opportunities offered and risks taken, to create who I have been and who I have become, and the gifts I discovered in the process.

Recently, my extended family in my native country of Israel helped me celebrate a big birthday. My son, now a mature adult man who was born and raised in the USA, flew there for the occasion. Each person shared their experience of their life with me over the years. When my son's turn came, he said: "I knew Nitza before she knew me." I have dwelt on that statement, and I realize now how relevant his comment is to the chapter you are about to read. My son, while in utero for nine months, learned about his mother and the context of our lives even before I saw him, held him in my arms, before I knew him; he was a viable part of my body, connected to my inner self; he received inner subtle messages through sensations, through the intricate parts of my nervous system in the most congruent way. According to Satir, this receiving was his first birth. By the time he was physically born, he was into the second birth, as Satir called it. He had already internalized subtle nuances that he'd received from my body. Our bodies were the connection transmitter between us; the transmission was nonverbal but steady, congruent and accurate. This transmission is evidence of the power and the gift that our body can share with us as we connect with our true self through our sensations – the primary way we connect with self. The messages we get through our sensations (visual, auditory, taste, smell, and touch) inform us about the inner as well as the outer world and help shape our social and physical connections and relationships.

As I share with you my development as a dancer, choreographer, teacher, psychologist, Satir trainer, and most importantly as a human being, I hope my passion and my learning over the years will inspire you and pave the way to realization of your own discoveries and growth.

Mary Leslie: Dance and movement have been a big part of your life. Can you share more about being drawn to dance in your earlier years?

Nitza Broide-Miller: I started at age eight with ballet, and later that year I choreographed and performed my first solo piece to Tchaikovsky's Flower Waltz, for my grade three class. I was haunted by a desire to dance, but my mother's dream was that I would become a concert pianist. I continued with ballet and modern dance, partly with and partly without my mother's permission. The passion I felt in connecting to my body in that way is difficult to explain. Looking back, I believe the artist in me was born very early and found expression in dance and movement at about two or three years of age. Even at a very young age I was kind of hypnotized by watching people dance.

I performed in theatre from age thirteen until I went to college. I chose teachers' college, as supporting myself as an actor was not an option. I did military service, which was compulsory in Israel, all the while practising modern dance and Israeli folk dancing. I was part of a professional Israeli dance troupe from age nineteen. While performing abroad in 1961, I had an injury which interrupted my professional performing. The doctor told me, "You will never dance again."

ML: Can you comment on your deep yearning to move beyond dance teaching and choreography to pursue dance therapy?

NB-M: After I was injured, I moved back home to Israel. I was quite depressed for six months; however, I didn't give up and continued to dance and to teach dance. But teaching dance, one class after another, did not feel enough for me. I always felt the joy of expressing myself when I danced. The transformation I felt after dancing was very powerful and I intuited that there must be something more to discover. I reflected on the need to learn more about the world of dance; it became clear to me that the dance available in Israel at that time could not satisfy my urge to discover more, so I decided to risk a move to New York City and find a way to learn to use dance differently. In New York City I took classes in a professional dance school while looking for courses using dance and movement for therapeutic purposes. This was the 1960s and Dance Therapy was in its infancy, but after six months of searching, I found a course offered once a year by Marian Chace.

ML: Can you comment on how learning dance therapy inspired a change in the direction of your life?

NB-M: I studied with Marian Chace and Mary Whitehouse. Marian Chace created her dance therapy in the early 1960s after noticing how much her students were getting out of her program, even though a career in dance was not their goal. Mary Whitehouse created her own dance therapy after studying with Carl Jung and incorporating his theories into her movement work. Each of these women had a profound influence on my life's work. From Marian Chace I learned to be a keen observer of minute details and to connect with people where they are. I learned to observe and work with very tiny movements and changes, and to work slowly and deeply.[1] Amber Gray in Porges and Dana's *Clinical Applications of Polyvagel Theory*, comment on Chase's creative interventions for

---

1 Marion Chase papers, 1975 ADTA

working with severely psychotic patients, by mirroring their movements and actions, "which promoted a sense of what is now known as *social engagement*."

Gray continues, "Congruence in movement, affect, and cognition are a sign of well-being and social engagement in safe contexts... From the perspective of Polyvagal Theory and polyvagal-informed Dance and Movement Therapy, social engagement is possible to 'read' through non-verbal markers [facial expressivity, prosody, eye contact, or gaze, mood and affect, state regulation and posture] of engagement."[2]

Mary Whitehouse instilled in me that the body is sacred. Paying attention to boundaries is very important, she believed, and we need to have the permission of clients, at all times, to touch them, and we need to continue to assess how the touch is being experienced by clients as we continue to work with them:

The wonderful thing is that the body is not and never will be a machine, no matter how much we treat it as such and therefore body movement will never be mechanical... it is always and forever expressive, simply because it is human. The body is the physical aspect of the personality, and movement is the personality made visible.[3]

Through my work in dance and movement I realized that we can become more aware and more comfortable with ourselves through our body's responses when we dance. I believe that expressing oneself through the body is a very old and universal form of expression. There is a lot of data by researchers in anthropology who spent time learning about body expression in remote tribes around the globe. They found in many cultures that people express themselves through dance.[4] Movement is our primary language, through which we perceive life, while speech is our secondary language, which is formed later through our left brain.

My practicums and early work experience in New York took me into

---

2 Gray, "Roots, Rhythm, Reciprocity," 210-211.
3 Mary Whitehouse, personal communication, 1964.
4 Hanna, "Anthropological Perspectives".

MY BODY, MY SELF: THE USE OF DANCE/MOVEMENT THERAPY 55

mental health facilities, which, at the time, used few medications, even for very sick patients. With a group of fellow students, I became a charter member and one of the founders of the American Dance Therapy Association (ADTA). Our first conference was in 1966. Marian Chace, my teacher, did not encourage further university training for the work we were doing; as she stated clearly: "all you need to know is in the body."[5]

ML: Can you comment on your desire to learn more in the area of dance therapy?

NB-M: I worked both part and full time in dance therapy, but decided I didn't like being an adjunct therapist. Over time I was not at peace with having to refer clients to other therapists for further work around things that dance and movement were revealing for them. I wanted to be able to take full responsibility for the total emotional and mental needs of people I was working with. I returned to Israel and studied for my BA and MA in Clinical Psychology and Educational Counselling. At the same time, I was always looking for more opportunities to improve my dance movement therapy skills. My academic studies and research in Israel were all focused on nonverbal communication. Since the field was in its infancy, finding courses in dance therapy was a challenge. However, in 1974 I found an intensive summer course at UCLA headed by Alma Hawkins, PhD. I applied and was accepted. This intensive, which included didactic and experiential components, introduced me to more ways of using movement and dance therapeutically. I did not stop training at this point (in 1983), but because I was unable to find a knowledgeable chair to support a dissertation in movement and dance, I pursued my PhD in Clinical Psychology at California School of Professional Psychology in Berkeley, California. I then shifted direction and did my research in family therapy and used art therapy as the tool for my investigations.

---

5   Mary Chase, personal communications, 1963.

ML: How did these studies shift the focus of your work and career?

NB-M: I returned to dance therapy at UCLA with Alma Hawkins. In Los Angeles, I started teaching dance therapy workshops at Esalen Institute, where exploratory workshops beyond formal university studies were offered. These further academic studies enabled me to teach in more varied and larger settings. I taught at several universities. I was working mostly privately with clients and running dance therapy groups, but I was restless to keep learning. I had known about Virginia Satir since the 1960s, when she came to Israel to teach, and was drawn to what I had heard about her from friends who had studied with her, but I did not meet her until 1976, after several failed attempts. When we finally met, I began to study with her. I studied with her for twelve wonderful years, until her unfortunate death in 1988. In 1978 Satir invited me to join Avanta, an organization dedicated to training and advancing Satir's ideas of working with individuals, couples and families. Avanta is now known as the Virginia Satir Global Network. I attended four family camps, and I also did a month-long training with Virginia in 1978 in northern Ontario and in 1981 in Utah.

In 1976 I also had the opportunity to study with Trudi Schoop, who was trained in mime, dance and theatre and had moved to the USA from Switzerland during the Second World War. She worked in a state hospital in Los Angeles with very regressed patients, working slowly and deeply to establish connection with them. Her teaching was complementary to Satir's. They both helped me learn to go deeper internally with my body expression to allow a more congruent external expression of myself. Schoop also helped me to view congruence with clients in a new way. By congruent external expression, I am referring to the inclusion and integration of many body parts in the movement. For example, when people start moving in a session, their body movements are small and repetitive. In her work Schoop encouraged and facilitated bigger body movements. She encouraged opposite movements, differentiating between small and large, high and low, gentle and assertive; she helped participants include

MY BODY, MY SELF: THE USE OF DANCE/MOVEMENT THERAPY 57

more body parts to express themselves. This is similar to Satir's idea of a person "becoming whole" or "more fully human" as more of the person is expressed in movement. Schoop used to encourage participants to make sounds and use words that matched their body movements.

Schoop and Satir both emphasized the importance of congruent expression that reflects the whole person. In session both worked slowly to establish connection and congruence between different parts of a client's body before continuing to explore deeper issues.

ML: How did dance therapy training prepare you for the teaching and work of Satir?

NB-M: Satir paid a lot of attention to body movement and body expression. I had already been trained in dance therapy, so when I met Satir and watched her work, her approach was familiar to me. Familiar too was the stressed importance of starting where the client is and creating connection. By observing small gentle movements in the beginning, I can encourage the expansion of these movements further, making them more visible and meaningful to the observer and, ultimately, the participant. In dance therapy, observation of the non-verbal presentation of the client, and picking up signals from a client's body, lets the therapist know how ready the client is to connect to the therapist. It is also considered important to proceed slowly, to choose small steps, whether non-verbal or verbal, that will allow a positive connection to open up deeper layers in the bodymind with safety and trust. By encouraging participants to increase the volume of the movement and sound, we send a message that we trust the participant to trust their body. This also helps to create and reinforce trust between the guiding therapist and participant. Safety and trust are interrelated. Each step needs to proceed respectfully, with the client's permission. Through ongoing sensitive listening the therapist can identify the client's point of readiness to open up and allow more closeness, whether verbal or physical. These ways of working were already familiar to me, and they are important aspects in Satir's model also. Satir always encouraged participants in an experiential process to increase the volume of their verbal sharing, and thus conveyed the message: "You count, and what you say matters!"

Satir's model incorporates as part of the teaching several embodied positions, also referred to as survival stances, or embodied patterns of relating. The major ones are: placating, blaming, being super reasonable and irrelevant. Encouraging the embodiment of these patterns of relating through highlighting sensations helps to support greater emotional awareness. Satir referred to this process as sculpting. When using the stances as part of a family session, sculpting helps family members embody elements of their relationships by modelling still, embodied "pictures" of a family. I have used movement within these positions or "still pictures" to intensify awareness and meaning for family members and participants.

Movement and moving have always been a part of Satir's work. Satir helped me hone my observational skills and attentiveness to the body to focus more deeply on the inner self. We become more aware of our expression when more body parts are addressed; this awareness helps to create greater overall harmony and brings transformation. Using dance and movement to connect to our unconscious, we discover true and useful information. Movement and dance have proven to be very effective vehicles for the unfolding expression of ourselves.

ML: Can you comment on your first response to meeting Satir and engaging with her approach?

NB-M: Meeting Satir was like "coming home." She was doing so much of what I was already doing that it was very easy to connect to her work. She valued the importance of touch and was very respectful in asking those with whom she was working for permission before she touched them. She was a keen observer and was also very responsive to small changes in a person's body movement. What seemed somewhat new and was very welcome to me was Satir's attention to our inner selves and our deepest yearnings, and the importance of doing work on ourselves as part of our preparation for working with others. Other therapists and teachers also valued this, but it was more consistently and effectively woven into Satir's training and allowed much deeper work with people. The family reconstruction, which is a key aspect of her model, was new to me, but my background in theatre helped me to make the transition to this work almost effortless. Specific similarities between theatre training and Satir's training, from the point of view of the trainer, are as follows:

1. Acute observation of nonverbal behavior and attentive listening to verbal communication.
2. Keeping the balance between focus on an individual and focus on the other group members.
3. Validating minute sensations expressed during the session: by noticing each one, addressing each, highlighting each, and further utilizing each.
4. Addressing the "whole" person and working from wherever the person is, and noticing when the person is ready.
5. Satir believed that each of us is a unique miracle worthy of love, and I believe that each of us has a unique body which stores our history and is an alive partner worthy of love and care. This realization is as essential to training a performer as to training a therapist.
6. While training a performer or guiding a session (individual, couple or group) we need to be fully present and open to our own energy to connect. As Peter Levine said: "To bring our full presence… requires us to go beyond words, to being present in our bodies and feeling our life force in the moment."[6]
7. In the process of growth (for a performer, a therapist or a client) we need to move slowly from where we are. Small meaningful steps bring meaningful sustainable changes.

---

6 Levine, "The Body as Ally".

ML: Can you elaborate on your approach to therapy and training?

NB-M: My own work owes a debt to my early dance and movement therapy training as well as to Satir's training. Here's a glimpse of the synthesis:
1. Satir said: "The words are not enough. It is the experience that counts."[7] It is the experience that brings the transformation; sometimes people can put words to the experience and sometimes they are not able to talk about it.
2. Dance training, Dance Therapy and Satir's approach are all built on a process of discovery and risk-taking and on adding ever more options and new possibilities.
3. I used imagery and metaphors typical in Satir's work frequently in my own Dance/Movement Therapy.
4. Satir advocated and worked to establish "peace within, peace between, and peace among." When I conduct my workshops I start from a place within the individual, then go on to the relationships between people and then connect to the whole group.
5. In Satir's model there is a yearning to become more whole, while attending to the whole body; in my dance therapy the whole body is included.
6. Satir emphasized that people are similar, that we all have universal yearnings; in my dance therapy universality comes with the full expression of the body. This universality is well documented by scholarly research into various cultures.[8]
7. In the practice of both dance and Satir therapy, there is an emphasis on the importance of establishing safety in the process. I take this very seriously.
8. One of the main pillars Satir's model is taking responsibility;

---

7 Brothers, *Well-Being*, 3.
8 Hanna, *To Dance is Human*.

when we use our body in dance therapy, our increased awareness contributes to our sense of responsibility.
9. In Satir therapy, as well as in movement therapy, the focus is always on the experience in the present moment.

ML: Can you elaborate on Satir's impacts on you personally?

NB-M: The importance Satir placed on the congruence of the therapist was very impactful for me. She emphasized that to bring our full presence requires us to go beyond words, to be fully present in our bodies, and in touch with our life force in the moment. Her attention on bringing the internal world of our clients to external expression was very welcome to me, as was her belief that we need to start from our sensations to know more about our deepest yearnings. To receive messages from our sensations we need to attune to them, accept them and use them. All this was hugely important on a personal level.

When I started learning from Satir, I was in a stressful place in my life. With her training I began to be able to rebuild myself from the inside out and to access my own wisdom, strength and resources more deeply to support my healing. Specifically, she helped me to go inside through repetitive centering, and to trust and respect myself. I found that I stopped judging myself so much. "Failing" took on a new meaning for me; it meant I could choose to change and take responsibility for change and accept myself. The more I continued training with her, the more I trusted that I was okay. I am okay The more I integrated the various parts of myself, the more I was able to accept that I was "good enough" and it was okay to love myself. Satir once said to me, "You are a gutsy lady." Before I met her, when I took risks, people used to say, "Nitza is crazy," so her comment was especially poignant and helped me reach a new level of accepting myself.

I found Satir very open to new ideas and ways of doing things. She was a wonderful role model for me in that way. She always encouraged her students to take risks, to try out and integrate new learning. For example, after years of crying into my pillow, knowing no one knew how sad I was, I accepted my sadness and allowed myself to "cry" when I was sad. I found her teaching and wisdom very affirming of what I had learned and gathered to that point in my life's journey and was empowered to learn and grow more. She helped me integrate what I brought to the model from earlier trainings and to continue to integrate subsequent learning.

ML: Can you talk a little about sculpting?

NB-M: The sculpting Virginia did with families seemed very natural to me, given my history in theatre, and I could easily feel how it connected me to my body, to my own energy. Her five freedoms gave me permission to be myself and find who I was in the moment:

1. To see and hear what is here, instead of what should be, was, or will be.
2. To say what one feels and thinks, instead of what one should.
3. To feel what one feels, instead of what one ought.
4. To ask for what one wants, instead of always waiting for permission.
5. To take risks on one's own behalf, instead of choosing not to rock the boat.[9]

In her use of sculpting and stances, Satir demonstrated how the body has the potential to act as an adjunct therapist by giving us information through our sensations. To receive the messages from our sensations we need to attune to them, accept them and then use them.

The body and its senses connect us to the world. Without receiving messages through our senses we would be lost. In her special and *seemingly simplistic way* of describing the way we know about our surroundings, she called the senses "Holes":

…the holes that we have we call the senses, but I would like you to

---

9 Paraphrased from Avanta website.

see or hear "sense" and think, "Hole," and when you think "Hole" you think something moving back and forth, something moving out, something moving in. And without these holes we cannot live. We cannot live… each of those holes is capable of putting something out and taking something in. [they are] the literal channels for taking in and giving out.[10]

Satir's genius was to describe complex sensory systems of our body through the use of images; this helped us "see" and understand and therefore accept the reality and the importance of our body's functions that give us life. Satir then connected the images (the "holes" and the gift of our sensations) to us human beings with our many parts and our yearning to become "whole." The back-and-forth journey of information through our "holes" helps us become "whole." Satir made the following statement often and it has stayed with me: "We are all miracles"; in her words, "The world is a better place because you are in it." This emphasis on valuing ourself left a strong impact on me.

ML: Can you describe some of the features of Satir's model that you found especially helpful?

NB-M: Satir's model is really a journey into a way of living that takes time to grow into and internalize. It does not consist of didactic information you can learn and copy. It needs to involve internal experiencing as part of the learning.

Her model is distinguished by five elements: change focused, positively directional, experiential, systemic, and the use of self of the therapist. I found these elements fit very easily into my movement approach. Regarding change focus: as we move and experience sensations, our mood and energy shifts, whether we intend it or not. Movement is inherently positively directional: as we move the body it begins to open up, energy is freed up, and we become more expressive, our oxygen level increases, which opens up deeper levels of our body, our censorship lowers,

---

10   Satir quoted in Brothers, *Well-Being*, 143-144.

and we can access unconscious material from our inner self. The sensory aspects are activated with movement, cells open up and life force flows along new pathways. Movement is systemic: there is no way to move one part without moving other parts, and all this happens in a very fluid way, without conscious agency. When working with clients I move with them; I need to be one hundred percent present, connected to myself, to be able to relate to everything that is happening in the room, to see and utilize what is emerging, moment by moment; I am using myself.

When Satir worked with people, a lot of movement took place. At times, she stood up during the whole session, especially when she recognized that being at the same eye level with someone was important. At other times, she stood up to create movement within the family, to help to facilitate change. When participants stand up, their energy flows more freely, which introduces more possibilities. Sometimes standing helps them to shift from the emotional or relational positions they are in. Any changes allow the therapist to observe the client's breathing and support the client to access more openness to change and flow. Breath is a symbol of life. It is so important to me to pay attention to the client's breath and use even small changes and any resultant movement to access their readiness and ability to accept more possibilities and move forward. For example, once when working with a family, I noticed one of the participants was not sharing at all; his body was not moving, he was holding his breath. I invited him to "take one breath" which he did, and a flood of tears followed. One breath released his body to express what he was holding back. This small intervention changed everything.

ML: Can you comment further on the role and impacts of the use of touch in therapy?

NB-M: I try to be very sensitive to, and observant of, the impact of participants' past experiences as they show up in their present movement. It is critical to assess participants' comfort level with touch, as everyone's past experience is unique. I feel this area of care needs extra attention. I agree with Pat Ogden, who founded Sensorimotor Therapy, that touch must be adapted moment to moment to a client's boundary needs.[11] One cannot make a general assumption, even on different occasions with the same client, as each can respond differently from one day to the next, to touch and sensations. Some people like to hold hands when they dance, and others do not. Some people are comfortable in close proximity to others, some are not. Preferences need to be continually checked out for comfort in the moment.

Physical touch activates the nerve endings in the skin and touch is an important way to increase awareness of and sensitivity to sensations. Touch can be very important at the beginning of the work to help participants to be more aware of their body parts and sensations. Sometimes, they can be guided to touch their own bodies, such as their heart or stomach area, to bring attention to any sensation and bring awareness to their breathing. Sometimes touch might be from therapist to participant. Touch helps us build somatic resources (greater awareness of the body as a resource) and helps us become more grounded. I always try to encourage participants to make meaning from their sensations, not just from their thinking. When I worked with patients in hospital units, most of the session would take place in a circle. It is important for patients to feel a connection, to have some sense of community. Most patients were comfortable enough to join hands in a circle. Then I encouraged individual movement in the circle formation, so people could move next to each other without joining hands. These variations allow each person the freedom to express certain feelings both individually and collectively.

Stephen Porges first described Polyvagal Theory in his book by the same name (2011). In a later edition (2018) he included a chapter by Moira Theede, who states that our sense of touch is the first to develop in utero, that our skin is our largest sense organ and is in a constant state of readiness to receive messages. Our sense of touch is always "on" and ready to be activated. It is a primary means of experiencing the world

---

11 Ogden, *Trauma and the Body*, 204.

at any age, especially after the loss of other senses. That is why it is so important to continue to touch people, even when they are in a coma.

I feel that we should be very conscious of different cultures' rules and histories around touch. In some cultures the norm is to avoid touch and in others touch is very normal behaviour. We must become aware of our sensations, remember the importance of touch and take care how and when we use it. Touch is like a co-therapist if it is used in a positive way to create safety and security. I often observed Virginia Satir touch people with whom she was working, often on each side of the person; sometimes she'd touch a hand and sometimes their upper body. She would always use her hands on either side of the client's body to provide support, balance and comfort.

There is a sense of touch whereby one can feel another's energy when they are standing nearby, or sometimes even at a distance. For example, another's energy will often determine how close we stand to them in a line, or in an elevator. These sensations are experienced through our skin as well as through other senses. We need to hold in balance other traditions and rules that come from outside the body regarding a person's beliefs about touch, and our own understanding of the important role of skin and body.

ML: What is your understanding of the close connection between the mind and the body and how do you build on this as you work with individuals and groups?

NB-M: I want to start with the teaching I learned from Trudi Schoop, mentioned earlier in this chapter. From her experiences of working in state mental hospitals before the days of medication, she became an acute observer of the body and believed she could tell a lot about a person from this close observation. She believed it was important to get patients to open up, but it had to be congruent with who they are and where they are and how they are. She was very influential for me, in her

MY BODY, MY SELF: THE USE OF DANCE/MOVEMENT THERAPY 67

ideas about congruence. I very much subscribe to her beliefs about the relationship between our mind and body. Her beliefs are:
1. Man manifests himself in his body, and the body is the visual representation of the person.
2. The mind and body are in constant reciprocal interaction. Inner experiences come to full realization in the body and all experience influences the inner self.
3. Whether thoughts and feelings are rational or irrational, positive or negative, split or unified, acknowledged or inhibited, the state of mind becomes embodied in the physical being. It manifests itself in the way the body is aligned, and in its rhythmical patterns, tempo, sounds made, energy and in its relationship to space. One can also assess the potentiality for change through observations of the body (as paraphrased).
4. Man experiences reality of himself through his senses, and these inform his mind and mental processes. They tell him how he is, who he is, and where he is. The senses of sight, smell, sound, taste and touch incite his mental processes.
5. Mind and Body are fused by their reciprocal interaction; their collaboration insures human unity.[12]

Schoop goes beyond Satir; in sessions she would go as deep as possible internally to support the patient's body to express itself externally. She used simple actions, such as getting patients to make sound, quietly at first, then louder until the sound was loud enough to involve deeper breathing and the reactions of internal organs. I found her teaching and wisdom so affirming of what I had learned and gathered to that point in my life's journey and was further empowered to learn and grow more.

Training and working in Dance/Movement Therapy has made it clear to me that mind and body are connected integrally. Once, I had an outstanding experience in a workshop in Canada. A participant said she felt she needed more space – she wanted to widen her space, she was

---

12 Schoop, *Won't You Join the Dance?* 44-45.

feeling too constricted in her body. I guided the whole group to push things sideways, to make more room and space. My suggestions were not specific. People were moving individually. Some were crying as they were dancing, pushing, and moving from side to side. When I came to Canada six months later, one of the participants from the workshop approached me. She seemed shorter than I remembered. "Is it possible that my body has widened as a result of the last session?" she asked. She shared that her body had seemed to widen, and she'd needed a bigger bra, after the "widening your space" session. I understood then why she looked shorter. Her body *had* widened. This is an extreme result of experiential dance, a visible effect of the mind on the body. I learned then that there could be a physical result in the body when the mind does the very deepest work in parallel with the body. Since Dance/Movement Therapy is mostly experiential it affects the mind from inside out. Siegal expresses it as follows: "The mind is an embodied and relational process regulating the flow of energy and information."[13] Peter Levine emphasizes that working through the body can effectively support the mind's capacity to heal. Levine suggested that for the mind to transform, the body needs to be a part of the process.[14] I feel grateful to these researchers who validate what dance/movement therapists were aware of fifty to sixty years ago. All Satir's work and training was experiential. More importantly, her experiential work was derived and based on her own life history. Getting to know ourselves is a prerequisite to being able to relate to others congruently. Satir instinctively understood this. As she says: "I was addicted to the facts about people, so I gave myself permission – in fact, a requirement – that I spoke from experience... I watched the experience first."[15] Brothers adds: "Satir sought to engage the whole person in training and learning events"[16] That teaching deepened our ability as therapists to

---

13 Siegal, *The Developing Mind*, 3.
14 Levine, in "Body as Ally."
15 Brothers, *Well-Being,* 3-4.
16 Ibid., 11.

use ourselves congruently. As Satir therapists, we saw and adopted these clinical phenomena, based on our life experience as well as our clinical experience, even before there was research available to back up such an approach.

ML: Can you tell us about your own unique way of working?

NB-M: Drawing on Schoop's method of starting with very small movements, I encourage the client to make them bigger until the body, moving by itself, opens up, and more innate gestures, guided by the unconscious, join the movement. Clients are then more able to connect to emotions, images and memories as they arise, adding layers of meaning to what, in the beginning, was just a movement exercise. Going further, I suggest clients include as many parts of the body as they can to go deeper. Lost memories may be awakened by the *body memory* through movement. Past triggers buried in the memory can be gifts in the present moment.

When I guide movement, I support individuals to open layers of the body, one after another. The more layers you open, the closer you get to the yearnings and meanings which arise from the deepest self. Let's say a session starts with a client moving from a sense of her external surroundings. When she continues to move following my suggestions, as I suggest visualizations to enhance the scope of the movement, she will enter a sort of trance. Movements that develop in this trance state are guided by the unconscious, and often are accompanied by released memories, images and stories. Once again, it is so important to proceed very slowly, as safety is so crucial; the client must feel safe, or she may shut down when emotions come up too quickly. The externalization of vibrations present inside the body can be very challenging, especially for those who have suffered abuse. I continuously check the client's safety level by watching their bodies closely to determine how fast or slow I need to go to facilitate the process. I have observed many times that people can process information such as unfinished old memories and deep feelings through dance and movement therapy that have not been uncovered in years of verbal therapy. Through movement, they develop their ability to express themselves, they become more aware, and feel more comfortable with accepting themselves.

I encourage students and clients to consider our body as our best friend: our body contains the history of our life, it is the archive of how we felt. Of primary importance to me is to love and listen to the body and accept its wisdom as a partner. Our body, if loved and understood, will enhance deep healing.

ML: Can you elaborate on what you mean by the important elements that can enhance deeper meaning?

NB-M: There are three core elements relating to movement that are always front and centre when I work: RHYTHM, BALANCE and FLOW. These elements stem from biology and from cultural context. Biological rhythms affect our well-being. The main bodily rhythms are heart rate, respiration and vascular functioning. In addition to internal physiological rhythmical systems, we are surrounded by patterns such as: the rhythmical intervals of day and night, ocean ebb and flow, changing seasons, birth and death, etcetera. Our language has rhythmic elements.[17] Certain rhythms keep us safe and calm. They are life-sustaining and we depend on their continuance to give us well-being and meaning, and we depend on the balance among them.

Whether in our physiology or in the rhythms in the world at large, we need to find balance in order to feel well. Satir equated balance with harmony. She saw the sense of imbalance as a sign of change taking place. Satir also paid attention to the need for safety and trust to be present among family members during a session. She maintained balance by giving equal attention to each family member regardless of age, gender, or role in the family. She made sure that each family member is seen and heard. She described the family as a "living mobile" which

---

17 Schoop, *Won't You Join the Dance?*

always moves to seek balance.[18] Balance will always shift because it is a movement concept.

Flow is life force, and the interactions among our internal systems. The flow of our functioning, internally and externally, is necessary to our feeling healthy and whole since flow creates a sense of continuity and well-being.

These core elements make us feel healthy and able to support the energy to face our life, our inner relationships and relationships with others. When we move we feel better. It is a well-known fact that after walking, running or dancing our endorphins are activated; we feel better when we move; the balance of hormones and chemicals in our body is ever changing.

One day, one of the participants in my ongoing dance therapy group (I will call her Jean) whose goal was to work on her relationship with her father, told us that she was going to scream. After letting us know, while other participants continued to dance, she screamed at the top of her lungs. She then continued to dance alongside the others. At the end of the session the participants shared what they had been aware of in the movement process. Jean said that she had never told her father how she felt about him, and she was going to visit him soon. I suggested that she might choose to express herself when she visited him. When she came back, she said that she had expressed what she had suppressed for many years. She felt better. She also shared with the group that she had been on medications for low thyroid function for several years. When she returned for a follow-up with her doctor after the screaming session and speaking with her father, her thyroid was in balance and she did not need medication any longer. It seems that our hormones and body chemistry are impacted when we dance and express ourselves. When they are in balance and flow, they help sustain our life energy and our physical and mental health. After Jean screamed during the session, I pondered deeply what the scream had meant to her. What had it provided for her

---

18   Satir, *Your Many Faces*, 101-109.

at that juncture of her life? First, screaming is the primary sign of life, the way the infant announces their arrival to the world and begins to practise breathing. For Jean, it was perhaps "giving herself a voice" and announcing that she will no longer suppress her feelings. The intensity of her expression seemed a mixture of anger and fear, and possibly anger and fear about her anger. It could be a variety of complex emotions which had been bottled inside her for many years. Satir's metaphor of the Iceberg includes the layer of "feelings about feelings" which allows us to see into and accept the complexity of our inner parts and their systemic way of interacting with and supporting our life energy.

Our intricate nervous system provides connections between various parts of our body and helps us cope with life. These core elements, rhythm, balance and flow, must interact internally to maintain safety and can be brought to awareness through focus on our sensations. When the various branches of our nervous system function properly, we feel safe.[19] Feeling safe allows the harmony of our biological elements to contribute to our sense of aliveness.

ML: How do you integrate these elements into your work with the body?

NB-M: I always start a workshop by asking participants what they hope to learn. It is important to pay attention to each person's pace and not leave anyone behind. I try, in my facilitation with groups, to reflect the rhythm of the participants (go slower with more reticent members). I start with a warm-up exercise to create a delicate rhythmic field. Movement for some participants could be as simple as finger tapping. I may do some "zig zagging," suggesting various different movements until I have the whole group balanced and working from a similar rhythm. I try to enhance what I observe already happening and allow each body the freedom to express itself. My goal is to build trust, for the participants to

---

19 Porges, *Clinical Applications of the Polyvagal Theory*.

become aware of their sensations and allow their body rather than their head to lead them.

In my workshops, I do not make sharing an obligation. I invite "any sharing" at the end of movement sessions *and* wait silently for any response. I do not ask a question or make a comment regarding what has been shared. I feel silence here is validating, an affirmation of what has been shared, and I am careful not to engage participants' left brain. If they have questions of me, I leave those to the end, to help people stay in their experience and accept it for what it is, until the movement and the sharing of the experience has ended. Sometimes I allow time for debriefing someone's experience and this is processed in movement. I believe that an experience can be transformational for the individual without any debriefing. I do not focus on "why" questions about the experience. When I watched Satir work with a family, she never focused on the "why" of someone's request, behaviour exhibited, or on any comments or hopes a client might express. Her acceptance of what people shared was her validation of them and of their sharing.

I sometimes use music, but not always. Choosing the right music to enhance the rhythm and flow of what is happening is very challenging and one of the hardest things to learn and teach. When the movement and music are out of alignment, the whole effect can be impaired. Voice intonation is also very important in leading movement effectively.

Satir always encouraged people to use their lungs, breath and voice more fully. When she invited a participant who had a comment or question to come forward to the stage, next to her, she would encourage them to express their question fully with increased volume to further validate their sharing; she gave active permission to participants to speak out in order to develop their confidence and promote higher self-worth.

ML: Can you comment on what we, as observers, might see in watching you, someone who has integrated dance therapy into Satir's model? How would that look different from the way other Satir Therapy trainers work?

NB-M: It has taken time for me to grow and inhabit my various dance experiences. My journey began with my first course in dance movement therapy in 1963. I started to internalize Satir's model after meeting Satir in 1976 and it took several years to integrate it with my lifelong dance experience. At first the two areas lived in me side by side, with some areas overlapping. As with any internal process, it took time to grow roots and branches, until some of the branches began to intertwine and create new possibilities. Those teaching Satir's model often develop new forms out of their own unique ways of working. When I started to consider teaching her model, I imagined the possibility of teaching the concepts using movement. From sporadic and short workshops I began to offer longer, more frequent workshops internationally, primarily using movement. I believed using the body to express Satir's beliefs and ideas would help both myself and the participants to internalize the learnings at a deeper level. The idea incubated in me for some time until in 2010 it became a reality. The workshops by then were mostly experiential, at times using music, visualization, percussion instruments and more. I trusted that this physiological experience would give participants the opportunity to add an additional pathway to their didactic theoretical knowledge base through their physiological experience.

Satir's work with families involved processing experience on a physical level. Whether it was sculpting or working with internal parts, movement and the possibility of change allowed new connections to open and energy to flow. Energy flows better with movement.

As an observer of my work, you will see intense focus and presence throughout my body. When I work with a group, I do my best to observe even the smallest non-verbal response from everyone and utilize it in guiding the process. I also invite people during the workshop to take risks, to *bring up* their own experiential creation in response to dealing with a particular concept being taught. I usually anchor any experience in the body. For example, I ask the mover, "How do you feel? Where in your body do you feel that feeling? What did your body teach you today? Any discoveries? Did you get any gifts from your body today?"

ML: How do you integrate these elements into your work with the body?

NB-M: I asked one client every weekly session, "Where do you feel it in your body?" He kept answering, "What do you want from my body? I don't feel anything in my body." The body is a living part of us and we need to dialogue with and listen to it. After six months of my persisting, he walked in the door, and even before sitting down for our session, he said, "I finally know what you mean. I finally felt it in my body." My persistence paid off. The take-away? We can all pay attention to our sensations when we can listen to them.

A longtime pioneer of attending to the body, Alexander Lowen, MD, wrote in his article "The Body in Therapy":

> We only feel that which moves. When we know our feelings we know who we are. When we accept our feelings we accept ourselves. We perceive that we are a body – not that we have a body. By identifying with his body, a person realizes he is not a NO-BODY, nor an ANY-BODY. He feels that he is a SOME-BODY. When you know that you are somebody, you move and act with dignity as well as grace.[20]

ML: As we bring our interview to a close, is there anything else that you would like to share?

NB-M: Satir's model was called "deceivingly simple" by John Banmen. I agree with that description. I believe that integrating Satir's approach

---

20 Lowen, "The Body in Therapy", 9.

is a journey. *It is a journey of being and becoming and it gives us an opportunity to discover who we are at a moment in time.* It encouraged me to look inside myself without judgement and find who I have been at various stages of my life. It invited me to see various parts of my personality as positive gifts, to see as positive even the parts that I once judged as "negative." I learned that each part has its own contribution to my "WHOLE SELF" and I can choose how to perceive each part and learn how to use it and further learn from the contribution it makes to the whole. The journey has led me to internalize who I have become and know that who I am is okay and that I always have options. I can choose to change, to adjust to any particular context that fits with the moment. This journey has taught me to be more patient with myself and with others, more accepting and more at peace.

I continue to expand my understanding of the body's experience of trauma and continue to learn from researchers in the field who emphasize the importance of focusing on the body in treatment for healing – such researchers as: Peter Levine, Bessel van der Kolk, Stephen Porges and others. After almost sixty years of practising dance/movement therapy and saying over and over to the participants: "Please listen to your body!" I am delighted to quote Dr. Stephen Porges: "We need to learn more about how to read our bodies' responses... We need to respect our body's reactions rather than continually trying to develop the skill set that rejects whatever the body is telling us."[21] This brings me full circle to Satir's close attention to people's bodies, postures and gestures, and what she could learn from them, and how she used this information. I am grateful for the support of these dedicated researchers. They have provided a bridge for me from my earlier teachers and other pioneers who paid attention to the importance of the body to where I am today. This bridge is the ability of the body to provide us with joy and pleasure.

Schoop, one of my teachers and mentors, said: "The body informs the human (of) the world around him, but the self must be present to

---

21 Porges, *The Pocket Guide to the Polyvagal Theory*, 238.

MY BODY, MY SELF: THE USE OF DANCE/MOVEMENT THERAPY 77

receive that information." She defined her role as a therapist: "I use every available means to give the body back to its owner."[22] Schoop concluded her book by laying out her "theory" about the human body and its potential for healing:

Those are my facts. They compose the "theory." Somehow, there is one very important something missing – the very spirit of dance itself. But there are just no words to impart the measureless sense of joy, the love of life, the enchantment with existence that envelops the dancing human. Have you danced lately?[23]

Satir said that each of us is a unique miracle. She certainly was a unique miracle. When she emerged and started evolving and developing her observations and ideas in the 1960s and '70s, the world of psychotherapy was focused on analysis and on verbal therapy. She relied on embodied experience; this is highlighted in her family reconstructions, which included the body in every element of the process. She demonstrated the "bodies are more than just structures to carry patients around."[24]

Satir said, "For every feeling we have, we will have a body response."[25] Satir said, "We cannot talk about wholeness without taking into account our physical being."[26] She also said that "what I have found, is that every experience has a dance to it… there is no such thing as being able to stand still… movement is always going on."[27] She preceded and maybe anticipated researchers like Stephen Porges, when she said: "Our bodies continually give us messages. Take a moment to listen, for this has survival value."[28]

Thank you for listening.

---

22 Schoop, *Won't You Join the Dance?* 100.
23 Ibid, 158.
24 Brothers, *Well-Being*, 55.
25 Banmen and Loeschen, *Simple but Profound*, 202.
26 Brothers, *Well-Being*, 103.
27 Paraphrased in Brothers, *Well-Being,* 82-83.
28 Satir (1989), "Thoughts and Feelings" (pamphlet).

REFERENCES

Banmen, John and Sharon Loeschen, eds. *Simple but Profound: Sayings of Virginia Satir*. Wendell: The Virginia Satir Global Network, 2020.

Brothers, Barbara Jo. *Well-Being Writ Large*. Hillsboro: Beyond Words, 2019.

Gray, Amber. "Roots, Rhythm, Reciprocity: Polyvagal-Informed Dance Movement Therapy for Survivors of Trauma." In *Clinical Applications of The Polyvagal Theory*, edited by Porges, Stephen W., and Deb Dana, 207-226. New York: W.W. Norton & Company. 2018.

Hanna, Judith Lynne. *To Dance is Human: A Theory of Nonverbal Communication*. Austin: University of Texas Press, 1979.

Hanna, Judith Lynne. "Anthropological Perspectives for Dance Movement Therapy." *American Journal of Dance Therapy* 12, no. 2 (1990): 115-126.

Levine, Peter. *In an Unspoken Voice: How the Body Releases Trauma and Restores Goodness*. Berkeley: North Atlantic Books, 2010.

Levine, Peter. "The Body as Ally". *Psychotherapy Networker*. (May/June 2020).

Lowen, Alexander. "The Body in Therapy." ADTA 5th Annual Conference, October 23-25, 1970.

Ogden, Pat., Kekuni Minton, and Claire Pain. "Trauma and the Body: A Sensorimotor." *Approach to Psychotherapy*. New York: W. W. Norton & Company, 2006.

Porges, Stephen W. *The Polyvagal Theory; Neurophysiological Foundation of Emotions, Attachment, Communication, Self-Regulation*. New York: W.W. Norton & Company, 2011.

Porges, Stephen W. *The Pocket Guide to the Polyvagal Theory - The Transformative Power of Feeling Safe*. New York: Norton & Company, 2017.

Porges, Stephen W. and Deb Dana, eds. *Clinical Applications of the Polyvagal Theory*. NY: Norton & Company, 2018.

Satir, Virginia. *Your Many Faces*. Berkeley: Celestial Arts, 1978.

Satir, Virginia. *The New Peoplemaking*. Palo Alto: Science & Behavior Books, Inc., 1988.

Satir, Virginia. "Thoughts and Feelings," brochure from Avanta Network, 1989.

Schoop, Trudi. *Won't You Join the Dance?* Palo Alto: National Press Books, 1974.

Siegal, Daniel, J. *The Developing Mind*. New York: Guilford Press, 2012.

IV

RECOGNITION OF WHO WE ARE THROUGH A BODY AND ENERGY LENS

JULIE GERHARDT

Julie Gerhardt has been a Physical Therapist for over thirty years. The primary focus of her holistic practice is women's health and supporting babies and young children. Julie's manual therapy weaves together advanced osteopathic training, energy work and psychosocial approaches, including Satir's model, somatic experiencing, infant body psychotherapy and recently with Hakomi Education Network. She has developed and teaches Cranial Sacral Therapy and pelvic pain/pelvic floor workshops. Julie was director of the Healing Pathway at the Naramata

Centre for several years and continues to run body/mind/spirit retreats. She is completing her Training for Trainers with Satir Institute of the Pacific and, as part of that program, is facilitating retreats and workshops that integrate Satir's model. Julie lives in Naramata, B.C., Canada.

RECOGNITION OF WHO WE ARE THROUGH A BODY AND ENERGY LENS

At a family gathering years ago my dad's blessing to us was "Remember who you are and where you come from." His words had a deep impact on me. I knew he was speaking about the soul essence of who I am, honouring the lineage of our clan and the spirit of the land we grew up on. These heartfelt words came back to me during my training in Satir's model and have become a foundation for my own healing and life's work.

The core of who we are is not the identity we attach to, what we do for a living or what roles we connect to, it is our soul essence, which I will refer to throughout this chapter as Self. Other words for Self are life force energy, I am, soul, essence. When we are in touch with Self, we can be lovingly connected to our inner world and the shared creative energy of the universe simultaneously. Intuition and trust arise from this bridge of connection. I believe Self can be palpable in our body and experienced at all levels of our being, right from our early formation in the womb, through infancy, childhood and throughout the rest of our lives.

When I discovered that Satir honoured spirituality and body wisdom in herself and others, it felt like coming home. This sacred, deep river continues to be central to Satir's approach. "We are all unique manifestations of life. We are divine in our origins. We are the recipients of what has gone before us which gives us vast resources to draw."[1] This connection to the larger spiritual context and our ancestry attracted me to her model. I continue to celebrate the model's focus on awareness of body and energy, and the accessibility of the teachings for personal growth and becoming "more fully human."

The overall intent of this chapter is to show how I have integrated Satir training into my practice and into my life. The case studies emphasize key concepts and processes of the model, and are based on the timeline of conception, pregnancy, birth, infancy and the early years.

---

1 Satir, *New Peoplemaking*, 338.

I will invite you, as you read, to reflect on your own conception, in-utero development, birth and early years. There will be pauses for you to be present to your own embodied response.

Several interconnected themes will be explored:
1. Our unique life force energy is present in each of us, whether we aware of it or not. When we become conscious of Self within ourselves and others, connections deepen; we have greater access to healing within, between and amongst.
2. Awareness of our body and energy within us and around us is integral to transformational change. The abundant resources of our body and energy system give us a treasure box to create new possibilities.
3. Through embodiment, we get to a state of congruence; through presence and connection to our body, Self, the Earth, and Universal Energy, we come home to ourselves. Being congruent and embodied enhances any relationship and is especially important in therapeutic relationships.
4. Intuition arises when we are lovingly present and connected to the flow of Universal Life Force Energy. We each have unique gifts of knowing and can choose to develop different ways to access our intuition. Intuition is a vital part of creativity and change.

PERSONAL BACKGROUND AND DISCOVERING SATIR'S MODEL

Before I integrated Satir's approach clients were coming to me to "fix" their physical problems. As a new physical therapy graduate, I grappled with the client's expectations and assumption that I was the expert and should know more about their body than they did. Anatomy, physiology, neurology and functional movement always intrigued me, but my excitement was in the individual gaining greater access to their body's potential for health. I sensed that a collaborative process through both hands-on work and goal setting was essential for lasting change. This relational style of therapy was reinforced early in my career through training in cranial sacral therapy and energy work. I developed a deep trust in my body and in the client's body; each body and each whole being has an innate capacity for balance, release and transformation.

I was fortunate to have exceptional mentors in Somatic Emotional Release, Somatic Experiencing, Healing Pathway and infant body psychotherapy, each of whom taught the importance of grounding, boundaries, titration, pacing and containment. My own deep yearnings were met to find mentors and training where mutual respect, intuition and safety were paramount. Prior to the Satir trainings, I experienced subtle and profound shifts in offering or receiving sessions, but when I returned to daily life the change was not always tangible, it had not been integrated or anchored.

When I started training in Satir's model early 2000, I was hoping to gain more capacity and confidence in dialoguing with clients and keeping a focus on change while they were exploring their inner worlds. I was familiar with supporting clients and students to access their feelings and yearnings through their body's expression and spiritual guidance. I was looking for more ways to help them anchor their experience. In Satir's approach I discovered new ways to explore clients' perceptions, beliefs and expectations. I knew this work would help me to create shifts and healing in body/mind/spirit. Landing in her model was a fit.

INTEGRATING SATIR'S MODEL

I immersed myself in Satir Level 1 and 2 trainings in 2000 and 2001. During those same years, I took a course in infant body psychotherapy training. Both in-depth trainings helped me understand more about my family of origin and our unique ways of coping under stress. This time was particularly important for clearing some unfinished business of my own in utero time, birth and early childhood. I began to transform emotions, expectations and limiting beliefs I had been holding in my body for years. I gained insight into my early intuitive, empathic and kinaesthetic gifts and I now appreciate this way of being as a resource. To sense subtle shifts in the energy field and in bodies – my own and others – without taking on energy or pain is an ongoing practice. Over the years, I have supported my personal growth through commitment to spiritual retreats, trainings in Satir's model, working with counsellors and body/energy therapists of diverse backgrounds. I believe it is essential to do personal growth work in order to hold a compassionate, therapeutic space for clients.

Satir's teachings have become the container for holding myself and my clients in this kind of awareness. In the words of my university professor Joyce Manton – "This work is as much art as science, and you need to remember you are working with a whole person" – echoes the message of Satir.

The first case study I want to present is an example of the therapist connecting to the whole person by consciously considering the Personal Iceberg Metaphor throughout the bodywork session. For a discussion of the Personal Iceberg Metaphor, see Leslie's Chapter 1.

Briefly, the iceberg represents our history/behaviour, our postures, coping stances, body sensations, feelings, feelings about feelings, beliefs, perceptions, expectations, yearnings and Self. All these aspects of our being have corresponding sensations in the body and qualities in our energy field. Most of us spend a lot of our time in a state of duality, accessing different parts at any given moment rather than experiencing being whole. Our unique life energy is present in each of us whether we are aware of it or not. In the moments we become aware of our essence we may sense our light radiating through all aspects of our being, the whole iceberg. As a therapist my capacity to be open, embodied and accepting of all aspects of myself throughout the session, invites the client to stay curious and deepen to their own self-discovery and potential for wholeness. In Satir's approach, we hold the image of two unique "icebergs": therapist and client in genuine exchange with each other. The relational field that emerges between us is full of possibilities and creative sparks for change.

Case Study: *Cheryl*

Cheryl is a regular client. She is a teacher and has two young children. I have supported her through both pregnancies and have had sessions with her children since they were infants. She is feeling very overwhelmed by all the reading she is doing about Black Lives Matter and Every Child Matters (relating to the history of Indigenous children in residential schools in Canada). Plus, she is navigating getting herself and her kids back to school from COVID restrictions. Today Cheryl shares she is having frequent dizzy spells and headaches. "I am literally off balance on so many levels."

I start with the intention of grounding by holding her feet and guiding her with an embodied meditation. After a time of following her breathing pattern, I feel energy rising and vibrating. I ground even more in my own body and in my connection to the Earth. "What's happening now?" I ask.

"I feel a tightness in my chest and it is almost like my skin is shaking."

"Are there any areas open to touch? Can you let your hands move there? Perhaps the touch feels best slightly off the body?"

She moves her hands and arms out to the sides of her body. "Yes, it feels like my energy is poofing out and I can't get inside my body."

I move to her knees and increase the pressure of my touch and ground more. "Can you let your arms move and sense the energy with your hands?"

She pulses the motion almost like wings, and then her hands come to land gently on her breasts.

I feel the energy shift and there is less vibration. My sense is that her energy field is full – like she is holding so much collective trauma and energy of others. I check it out verbally. "I sense you are carrying a lot of others' energy… does that fit for you?"

"Yes. I am feeling the suffering of so many people and children who are marginalized. It breaks my heart."

"Can you send a message of acceptance inside to any pain or emotion you're feeling? Is that possible?"

She takes a long deep sigh.

I ask, "Is there any other way for you to deeply care rather than carrying the pain? What might that look like or feel like?"

"Not sure yet."

"Can you let the question float through your body and energy field?"

After a long pause… "I can make room for the sadness, but I don't want it to close off my heart energy."

I shift my touch so one hand is on her sternum and the other on her back between her shoulder blades. I lead her through a breathing sequence with long pauses between breaths. "What are you sensing between my hands?"

"A pink hue with a small dark green ball."

As this area starts to soften, something shifts in her whole body. "What's changing?"

Her face is getting red and her hands shift to her lower rib cage. "As my heart tries to open, I feel super-hot, and there is a gripping in my throat."

"Is there an emotional tone?"

"I'm really angry."

"Are there any other parts of your body expressing the anger?"

"In my jaw and in my fists."

"Is it related to any expectations you have of others, yourself or what you think others expect of you?"

"I'm mad at myself… I can't believe I didn't know so much of the history – of our First Nations especially. And I've been teaching for years. I should have known more." She lets out a guttural sound and I invite her to pull some of the feeling into her hands. She holds her fists tightly for a few minutes and spontaneously throws the energy out towards the ground.

"Are there other feelings? How is your body responding?"

"Guilt… it feels sticky and thick under my ribs."

I change my touch to release around the lower lungs and ribcage – she shifts her own hands to her belly. "What would have been different if you had known more?"

"I would have had so much more compassion for the kids and families I have worked with in the past."

"Can you connect back to your heart…" Long pause. "What would you like to be different going forward?"

"I want to support… and create ways to share the truth in a way that children of all cultures can take it in."

"Can you send a message of appreciation for your capacity to be part of the change?"

"Yes." As her breath deepens, her jaw releases.

I hold silence while I release and align her neck and shoulders. I can sense Cheryl is actively tracking sensations and needs space to integrate.

Clarity – when to dialogue, remain in silence or change physical touch or pace – comes from the therapist being congruent and staying in tune with Self and with the client. Being grounded and centered in my body and deeper essence allows me to track nuances and shifts in the client's body. I must be very discerning about what to share regarding what I see or sense in a session. What is most important is the client's experience. If something keeps nudging, I will check in with my intuition to find what words, touch or presence is most needed.

Cheryl's breath starts to get fuller and even, and her weight is sinking into her back.

"I sense more of your being is present in your body."

"Very much so. I feel like I am hugging myself back inside."

"Can you open to your soul essence as you are hugging back inside? What unique qualities describe or represent your Self? This might come in an image or perhaps a time in your life that you connected to who you really are?"

I shift my hands to her womb area and wait. Her eyes flutter lightly and an expression of ease comes across her face. I feel more life force flowing in her lower body. "What is coming into your awareness?"

"I see myself when I was backpacking in Thailand and sense my free spirit – hair blowing in the wind, sun on my face." Tears start to flow.

"What are you yearning for?"

"Freedom." Big sigh. "As I feel that part of me it makes me so sad because as a child, I was able to travel with my family and it formed who I am. I am so scared my children will not get to travel with all the COVID restrictions and they won't ever know that freedom."

"Is that true?"

"Logically, I know the restrictions might not last forever, but, oh, how I long to take my whole family on a two-month trip overseas."

"Are there other ways to invite freedom in present time as a way to practise?"

Cheryl is quick to say she has already talked to the kids about all the local camping trips they can do next summer. She also acknowledges there was a strange sense of freedom when they had to stay home and do things more simply together as a family.

After inquiring about what a client is experiencing in their body, I will name what I am noticing, which can open a wider lens of awareness. *I may not know where the session is going but I always trust in the process and deeper knowing*. Guidance and intuition flow within the relational field, which includes Universal Energy and divine support that is always available. Verbal and non-verbal dialogue are a bridge to what can be remembered and what changes are possible when the client leaves the session.

Coming to the end of Cheryl's session, I want to integrate and anchor any changes within her and connect to how things might now be different in her family and community. "What is different in your body?"

"I feel a balance between the right side and left side of my body. I can find my centre."

"How would you like to see yourself in the days and weeks to come? Or perhaps what might friends or others in your family see or sense that is different about you – in your body, posture, affect, your communication?"

"I would like to connect to my core and see my free spirit in my eyes in the mirror in the morning. I will let more things roll off my back and not be so impatient with my husband and kids. Believe me they will notice!"

"What steps are needed to sustain this change?"

"Getting back to my morning yoga, even if it is only ten minutes. And making sure I get more fresh air."

"Who will you connect with about your goals and wishes?"

"My friend Barb is going through a similar kind of experience. I'm going to ask if we can set up a hike once a week."

Inquiring of the client what experiences from the session may be possible to commit to and connect with when they return home, highlights two of Satir's model's essential elements – being change-focused and systemic. The essential elements are explained further in Leslie's Chapter 1. Whether the commitment is to self-care approaches or to transform a difficult emotion, the process of change will be unique to each person, based on their resources available.

There are numerous ways within Satir's approach to help anchor the awareness of something that comes to the surface from the past, to bring it into the present moment and explore possibilities for change in the future, while including the body. Movement and bodywork have always seemed inherently experiential to me. By integrating and working with Satir's model, I have a deeper understanding of what it means for therapy to be experiential. The key is for the therapist and the client to be present *and* aware of their inner worlds. Slowing things down, each naming what they see and sense and accept in the present moment, makes the experience more tangible and more retrievable for the client when they leave the session. I continue to learn from Satir mentors about the experiential and how to bring use of self into therapy and group trainings in more conscious ways. By being positively directional, change focused and systemic, I have built a navigation system that orients towards wholeness and transformation while working with clients and in my personal journey.

On days when I have high *self-esteem* and *self-compassion*, I can explore the sensations in my body and being, even the painful ones, with acceptance and love. I can choose to honour and *be responsible* for my feelings, feelings about feelings, perceptions, expectations and yearnings. My yearnings lead me back to my resources and essence. When I am grounded to the Earth, aware of my body, accepting all parts of me, aligned to my essence and spiritual support team, *I am congruent*. When I am congruent, I can listen to the "still small voice" inside and *make choices* that are right for me in the moment and for my future. "[…] congruence is being in harmony with our Self and our life energy, spirituality or God."[2]

Being congruent is tangible when I am preparing to be with clients after years of practice and being aware of what it feels like in my body and energy. I create a sacred space around me. Simple things like having a rock from my favourite beach, a plant, or feeling the natural light through a window, connect me to the Earth's elements and support me to stay aligned and centred. Once grounded, connected to Self and Universal Life Energy, I can make contact with each unique being coming to me for support; I can meet them where they are.

 I consider the first step in any change is to contact the spirit…
 then together we can clear the way to release the energy towards

---

[2] Satir, *Satir Model*, 171.

health. The question for me was never whether they (clients) had spirits, but how I could contact them.[3]

This quotation from Satir is for me a golden key; whether we offer body-focused or psychosocial therapy, it is so empowering to trust in the spirit and resources of each person we support. When I'm connected to my heart, body and energy, I can sense, in our first meeting, what contact is best for the client. Do they need me to be physically close or do I position my chair farther back? Should I adjust my energetic presence? My energy field may need to be open and spacious, or more grounded and drawn closer to my physical body.

The way I show up as a therapist is influenced by my personal journey and the unique resources that have been with me from the beginning. I feel a kindred spirit in Virginia Satir. I too grew up in a family with a rich spiritual foundation and on a farm, tending animals and growing food. As a child, I had so much freedom to explore and developed a deep reverence for nature and spirit. So many magical moments: lying in a wheat field at sunset, waiting for the moon to rise over the hills – I felt spirit and my own life force coursing through my body and a sense of oneness. It wasn't just seeing the beauty of the Earth, but feeling the beauty reflected in my soul. These precious moments continue through my life. They are not just memories, they are the fabric of who I am, and can be accessed in a heartbeat, as though there is no time.

> Knowing that you love the Earth changes you, activates you to defend and protect and celebrate. But when you feel the Earth loves you in return that feeling transforms the relationship from a one-way street to a sacred bond.[4]

I feel most embodied when I am communing with nature, immersed in Earth traditions and my spiritual practice, both in community, and on my own. The Satir trainings have supported my lifelong quest to experience and understand embodiment. Though the word embodiment may

---

3   Satir, *New Peoplemaking*, 340.
4   Kimmerer, *Braiding Sweetgrass*, 124.

not be explicitly defined in the Satir books and written documentation, the experience of it is very present in the training.

EMBODIMENT

We might say that embodiment is a state in which your entire "intelligence" is experienced as a coherent unity attuned to the world.[5]

Embodiment is beyond being grounded or simply aware of touch and physical sensations. It is soul energy inhabiting our body and being aware of the inner and outer world moment by moment. We are present to spirit, intuition, creativity; we experience through our senses, including our subtle senses. This level of embodiment, modelled so beautifully by Satir, is necessary to get to a state of congruence.

Satir's sculpting is a way to explore embodiment within ourselves, clients, families and in group trainings. In her work around the globe, she noticed that individuals took on similar postures, facial expressions and energetic presentations when in a particular pattern of coping. Sculpting grew from these observations. Arranging clients into different postures to represent different patterns of coping while being congruent is a powerful way to explore a wide range of embodied experiences. Watching videos of Satir using sculpting in family therapy, one can witness her congruence and embodied presence. This is expanded on in Nagel's Chapter 5 on sculpting.

Each person has a unique experience of embodiment. The access for some may be visual (the beauty of great art), for others auditory (inspiring music), for others an overall sense of expanded consciousness. Nature was my first teacher, but I also discovered embodiment through dance, authentic movement, Qi Gong, yoga, Feldenkrais, breathwork and various traditions of meditation and prayer. The key in these practices is being present to Self and the Divine at the same time as being

---

5 Shepherd, *Radical Wholeness*, 53.

mindful of the sensations and movements of my body. I bring presence and awareness to moving in and through my world, to gardening, to being with clients or loved ones, hiking in nature or being creative. Yet, there are days I notice how disconnected I am – from myself, others, the environment. The beauty is, with awareness, I can make a different choice. By simply taking a breath, grounding and inviting myself inside for a moment, I can return to the world with a message of acceptance and get back to my centre:

> We can more easily reach this wise part of ourselves when we are calm inside, when we feel good about ourselves and when we know how to take positive approaches. I refer to this as being centered.[6]

In a guided meditation Satir said, "Our body works best from a state of rest." This is also true for our mind and heart. Today scientific research is validating her intuition. Studies have found that yoga, meditation, prayer, conscious movement, cranial sacral therapy and energy work activate our parasympathetic nervous system. These practices slow our systems down. And slowed down, we are in touch with our body and Earth energy, open to inspiration, creativity and peak experiences. Satir tells us:

> Also remember that being in the universe, we have access to the energy from the center of the Earth, which brings us our groundedness; and from the heavens, which bring us our intuition. These are there for us to use at any time. We are already part of it. Our job is to know it and access it.[7]

We are supported from above and below; our body and energy field are a conduit for energy to move in us, through us and around us. Paying attention to all sensations and our energetic space informs us: What are we feeling emotionally? How are our thoughts or beliefs affecting us?

---

6 Satir, *New Peoplemaking*, 338.
7 Satir, *Satir Model*, 81.

What expectations are we holding or projecting? What are we yearning for? How are we impacting others? The full range of life's experiences, from feeling euphoric to deep grief, feeling puzzled to an aha moment, being exhausted to highly energized, all happen in our body. When we embody our sensations, movement and stillness, we honour all that comes from above and below; we are in a more intimate trusting relationship with our body and our whole self.

I am in awe of the complexity and creativity of our body and energy system, and how the psychological and spiritual aspects of ourselves interrelate with experiences in our body and energy. I am curious about embodiment and continue to discover new conditions that allow us to experience it more fully… right from our arrival in this world.

CONCEPTION

In *Meditations of Virginia Satir*, Satir often reminds us that we each begin from an egg and a sperm; we are unique manifestations of that union. Satir considered the uniting moment of our parents' sperm and egg as our first birth.[8] Satir invites participants to send appreciation and gratitude to all our resources within, to our beautiful bodies and to our ancestors and to take time to truly celebrate the miracle of who we are.

I invite you to pause as you read and reflect on your conception. What was happening in your family, environment, the world at that time? We each begin from an egg and a sperm, and we are unique manifestations. Read Satir's words again and appreciate and celebrate who you are. Honour the unique manifestation of who you are. What body sensations, images, words, subtle senses arise as you check in? Is there a gesture you want to make? Maybe there is a place on your body you want to place your hands?

The relationship between who we are and where we come from is being studied in epigenetics, neuroscience and perinatal psychology.[9] Is

---

8   Satir, "Life's Beginning Brings Joy," 34.
9   Shore, *Affect Regulation*, 13.

research catching up with what we intuitively know – that resources and challenges are passed down our lineage? The potential for who we are and will be is available right from the beginning. From the moment of conception, life force ignites in you; your intelligent body is designed to grow and develop:

> I feel overpowered when I try to comprehend how this very tiny human embryo can produce something as big and multifaceted as a person...The life force not only oversees the growth in each seed, but channels the energy so each part gets what it needs. Is this not a miracle?[10]

When conditions are right, cells multiply exponentially in fetal development in a relatively predictable way, but the ability to survive and thrive in utero is dependent on many diverse factors: genetics, mother's health and wellbeing, environment, etc. After conception a significant percentage of embryos do not continue to become new human beings. Beyond physiological conditions, what other states of being or invitations allow a spirit to land in a physical body? Some couples have shared with me their experience of conscious conception, where they sensed a soul communicating and felt a deep knowing that it was the right time to conceive, even though on practical levels it was not. Some women have reported they just "knew" the moment they became pregnant. It remains a great mystery.

Some women may be very clear about the timing of when they choose to become pregnant and for others it happens unexpectedly. I had years of yearning to be a mother and was not able to sustain a pregnancy. I hold compassion for those who are having difficulty with fertility. Working with Satir's processes and continued therapy ensures that my own unfinished business is not interfering as I hold space for clients. A percentage of my practice is women seeking support as they prepare to conceive or are pregnant. They may have a goal of preparing their body to enhance fertility and pregnancy; some might be having pain with

---

10   Satir, *New Peoplemaking*, 336-337.

intercourse and need pelvic floor rehabilitation and need a safe place to share issues of sensuality and sexuality. Others desire to explore more globally the body/mind/spirit connection in preparing for conception, birth and motherhood.

Case Study: **Holly**

Holly has come to see me because she is starting to see a fertility specialist. She is particularly interested in releasing any restrictions around her reproductive organs. As Holly shares some of her history I'm aware of how stiffly she is holding her posture, and her hands are interlaced so tightly her knuckles are white. Her voice is quite sharp and she is very succinct in the initial dialogue. She works as an emergency nurse and one of her passions is photography.

I start with a guided meditation and cranial sacral therapy, then go to the abdomen and pelvic area. Since her goal is to increase circulation and motion around her organs, I invite her to be grounded and present in the lower half of her body. I meet her at the intellectual level by discussing some of the principles behind the parasympathetic nervous system (rest to digest) in neuroscience literature and this contributes to her feeling more settled.

Holly is quite articulate about the variety of sensations she is experiencing and the visuals arising. Her resources of visualization and knowledge of anatomy help her move easily into experiential processing. She says she is feeling the subtle rhythms and sensations in her body. "I am surprised that I'm able to relax so deeply. I don't ever relax. I really can't stand lazy people."

"Is that a family belief?"

"Absolutely not," she scoffs. Then she adds, "No one in my family was reliable when I was growing up. And at work I'm way more capable than everyone. I just get things done."

As she is sharing, I assess her abdomen with gentle touch and there is a lot of restriction under her ribcage and throughout the whole abdomen. I ask, "What is the feeling-quality where I'm working?"

"Guarding and protection... feels like hard rubber. And it's hard to get a deep breath."

"Is it my touch or presence?"

"No. The sensation is very familiar." We explore her beliefs and resources through this part of her body and she says, "Maybe it is connected to being able to handle the toughest emergencies without letting my guard down. I don't even let down my guard with my husband or with friends."

"Do you think that can change?"

"I can practise softening my body when I'm with my husband. He is my 'safe person.'"

Her belly softens as she speaks about him and the deep love they have for each other. I shift to release around her uterus and ovaries. I invite her to bring a blessing to her womb space and be open to any messages or images from this area of her body. I wait for a long time. Then I ask what she is noticing.

"I have the image of slow-burning embers and the feeling is gentle and powerful at the same time."

At the end of the treatment, Holly shares how much energy flow she can already feel in her belly, and she feels excited to start a meditation ritual, which for years she has resisted. Holly herself comes up with a plan to use a photo of a gentle fire as a focal point to connect to her womb space. I share my appreciation of her resource of creative visualization and her capacity to create a plan!

We work together over the next couple of months before she goes to the fertility clinic. Holly comes in afterward and reports the in-vitro procedure was not successful, but she is still determined to try again. I sense her body is very relaxed, her energy centred, and her eyes are bright. I bring this to her attention and ask, "What has changed?"

"Well, I feel more connected to myself and to creativity than I've felt in a long time. I've begun to reach out to more friends, and my husband and I have ignited our sexual intimacy outside of the regimented fertility process! I am not willing to give up my deep desire to be a mother, but

I'll accept it if it doesn't happen. I have many other loves and resources to fill my heart. When I'm in my heart, my mind and body are not so far apart."

It humbles me to be with women who clear and prepare all levels of their being as they step into the journey of becoming a mother. A question I often ask women of all ages and stages is, "What is your relationship to your womb space?" If there has been emotional and/or physical pain many women cope by closing off this part of their body. From an energetic perspective our womb space is our second chakra and very much about our relationship to emotions, intimate relationships and feminine nature – it is the element of water. When our energy and emotions are allowed to flow, we are receptive, sensual and creative. It is always rich to offer body/energy work to women and to share the ceremony of embracing their womb clearing. Taking responsibility and courage to transform our fear and pain, we can open to our natural feminine capacity to create. For me, this birthing energy has led to inspiration for me to hold women's circles, retreats and writing projects. For many women the tangible form of creating involves giving birth to a new human being. What a miracle!

BIRTH

"Your birth, my birth, everyone's birth is a spiritual event and cause for celebration."[11]

I have been blessed with a glimpse into the raw, primal and sacred space of birth in my work as a doula. A woman's capacity for surrender, to soften, open *and* stay connected to her body and Self amidst the pain and intensity of birthing, is a true example of embodiment. Women's bodies have innate wisdom to create and birth a baby. Through pregnancy and giving birth, hormones influence women's capacity to receive and offer love; often troubles roll off women's backs, though

---

11   Satir, *New Peoplemaking*, 337.

others may feel more vulnerable to chaos and negative influences. Some women I have worked with processing their labour remember in great detail things perceived as harsh or judgemental that were said by someone in the room. When a woman perceives she is being supported in her labour and is given choice every step of the way, there is far less postpartum emotional trauma, even when the birth is intense or ends in an emergency C-section. Even with the best of health, positive intentions and great support, birth can be full of complications. No matter how the experience unfolds, birth is powerful.

I have specialized in pelvic-floor rehabilitation and women's health for over twenty-five years, and heard hundreds of birth stories from women. Some have shared that giving birth was the first time they had a tangible experience of their deeper essence or Self. Through their bodies, intuition and connection to the universe, they found their power. This can carry them into early days of motherhood with their life force bolstered and guide their natural instincts of caring for their babies, opening them up to love in ways they may not yet have experienced. More often, I hear birth stories from women who did not feel empowered by the experience. They come to me because they had a birth that resulted in pelvic pain, organ displacement, pelvic floor/abdominal restriction and weakness, sexual dysfunction or bladder issues. In our first meeting and assessment it can be quite clear that there are many layers of complexity to their inner landscape that have been exposed by the birth experience and early post-partum time. Satir's model is especially useful in helping women shift into being positively directional and goal orientated, especially if the birth was difficult or resulted in physical and/or emotional trauma.

Satir's process of change (Status Quo, Introduction of a foreign element, Chaos, Integration, Practice, New Status Quo)[12] has been invaluable for me as a practitioner supporting women preparing to give birth and processing all the changes through pregnancy and after giving birth.

---

12 Satir, *Satir Model*, 98.

There can be so many periods of chaos without much time between to settle into a new status quo before the next roller coaster of impacts arise. Offering a woman a grounded, loving presence can help invite acceptance that chaos is part of change. Trusting and holding space for the body's innate healing capacity can help her access her whole being and her own creative ways to practise and integrate new steps towards change. A therapist holding the process of change with compassionate grounded presence is also a lifeline for women who have experienced pregnancy loss. My passionate hope is to help resolve some of the impacts of pregnancy to help women access their body wisdom and intuition going forward.

Case Study: **Maxine**

Maxine comes in early in her pregnancy wanting support for settling anxiety. I inquire if this anxiety is familiar.

"I've had anxiety in the past, especially when travelling. It's often about feeling something could happen to me medically. What if I couldn't get to a hospital? So in every town or country I always had to find the nearest hospital or first aid station. Generally, that settled me down. But this present anxiety is much more intense physically."

"Tell me how."

"Sometimes I can't breathe, and I get heart palpitations. They don't stop even with yoga and meditation."

We spend a couple of sessions focused on grounding and centring with breathwork and bodywork.

"Maxine, can you explore what is within and amongst the strong sensations of anxiety? What do you see or hear?"

"I see myself pulled in like a snail, yet there is a large white shell of protection all around me."

"How do you want to see yourself in the next days and months?"

"I see myself uplifted in my posture and want to feel the strength of a Ponderosa tree."

By connecting her to perceptions, visualizations and her deeper yearnings while engaged in the sensations arising from bodywork, she has more capacity to lift out of the intense feelings.

The next appointment Maxine shares that last week she started bleeding and felt the life force leave her body. The miscarriage was confirmed by blood work and ultrasound. But the pregnancy hormones were increasing so there was concern about an ectopic pregnancy. Medication was given to stop the growth.

"I am intensely anxious. The surgeon encouraged me to go up the mountain and exercise, but I feel I have to stay close to the hospital. I have a foreboding feeling that something is really wrong. I have gone to emergency twice with this pain in my side, but they say everything is fine."

We spend the session with energy work and cranial sacral therapy to support centring and to calm her nervous system. Two weeks later, Maxine calls to say that she is recovering in hospital. She barely made it in time to emergency with a burst fallopian tube from the ectopic pregnancy.

During her recovery from surgery, our sessions focus on resolving the trauma of her loss and supporting her body to heal. In one session, she shares the intensity of what she experienced.

"I knew something was *really* wrong." Her tears flow and I observe a lightness and calm around her. I bring her awareness to what I am experiencing in her energy field. She says again, "I knew something was wrong, my body and anxiety were telling me loud and clear and now I *know* I can trust my intuition."

Over several sessions, we continue to anchor her experience of that deep intuitive knowing in her body and energy field while working around the scar tissue. Her own touching of her scar connects her to her intuition. One session, as we are releasing fascia around the scar and uterus, Maxine drops into a deep, still point and I feel the whole room lighten. It feels similar to my experience of being in deep prayer.

"I sense spiritual support coming in for you. Is that a fit for you?"

Maxine nods. "It feels like an angelic presence."

"What are you experiencing?"

"I'm getting a replay of my near-death experience… it's like I'm watching it on a big TV screen. I was lifted out of my body up to the ceiling towards an amazing white light and there were two bright lights off to the right. I can see these two lights now, but there's a third light."

"Is this familiar?"

"Yes… they are the same two lights I saw in the emergency room. I felt like I was leaving this world. I knew it was my grandpa and my brother and thought they were there for me, but now I know they were there to welcome the baby soul that was leaving. I now know I chose to stay here."

Long deep breaths for several minutes and we hold space for her tears. Then, while we work around her organs and low pelvis, her facial expression shifts to show curiosity and I feel her energy expanding out to the right.

"What is happening?"

"I see the third light… it is the soul that was trying to come in. I need to name him…" Long pause… "Michael. My archangel, Michael." As soon as she says this out loud the whole pelvic area softens. When I bring her attention to this, she notices the changes in sensation and feels warmth through her entire spine.

"What quality or message is in the sensations?"

"Power and peace."

"Is there anything you could see yourself doing to help connect to this experience when you go home?"

She smiles. "Yes. I have an image of me and my husband doing a ritual with candles and prayers to honour Michael."

About a year after her surgery Maxine comes into her session with the news that she is pregnant again. She says she has done a lot of processing with her counsellor and EMDR about her young years and the pregnancy loss. She feels strong and centred. Her sense is that her premonition about something going terribly wrong has already happened and now she trusts her deeper knowing and her body's wisdom. Now we work together balancing her body and drawing her into the deep well of her resources in preparation for her giving birth. Anxiety does start to surface when she begins to think about going to the hospital. She has not been there since her near-death experience. "They didn't listen to me before when I knew something was wrong." With tapping and grounding techniques, she is able to shift her perspective, and says, "The hospital is not a scary place but a place that saved me."

Maxine gave birth to a baby girl with her husband and doula by her side. She was able to stay deep inside, completely quiet and centered amidst the intense pain. She felt her body and her baby working together. She told me it was the most beautiful and powerful experience she had ever had.

INTUITION

I can't light your light. I can only light mine so that I can illuminate for you to see your own light.[13]

If we as therapists can trust our own energetic sensing and intuition, it will help open that access for our clients. When two fields of energy interact, there is greater light and spaciousness available for the client to allow parts that have been out of awareness to be held in compassionate presence. Centeredness and acceptance is portrayed nonverbally to the client, so they can access their own insights and body wisdom. It is inspiring to watch Satir in videos, from many years ago, and see her energetically tracking the slightest shifts, using touch in creative ways to access the body. She had a brilliant access to her intuition.

Sometimes in a session I am unsure if my words or what I sense will be a fit for the client, so I simply say, "This might not be a fit for you but what I am sensing is..." In our writing group's discussion about intuition, Broide-Miller commented: "As therapists, we need to learn to take risks and check things out; often when we follow our instincts, we are right

---

13 Banmen and Loeschen, *Simple but Profound*, 16.

on track. The key is like so many things: following our intuition takes practice." We may have one way of sensing that is stronger than others, but we can open up and practise other ways of perceiving as well.

Facilitating workshops and retreats offers me the greatest growth in tracking energy. Such workshops and retreats remind me of the power of coming together with a shared intention of allowing healing grace to flow through us and around us in a group space. As I grow, I open to more ways of perceiving intuitively. Being with groups who are discovering more of who they are allows access for all to a deep well of grace and healing. Such workshops and retreats support my belief in the power of where two or more gather.

There have been times in sessions with a female client that I was aware of a new soul before the client knew she was pregnant. This has been a great teaching to trust what I sense. Often when working with pregnant women I have strongly connected to the qualities and energy that I sense of the baby in their mother's womb. So delightful. Recently, a mom I worked with through her pregnancy brought her three-week-old baby to improve their success with breastfeeding. When I saw the baby, there was such recognition at a soul level that I spontaneously exclaimed, "So good to see you again!" The mom looked at me a little funny. "You haven't met her yet." I just smiled and winked.

Babies have been my greatest teachers. They have taught me to trust my intuition. In their presence I naturally attune to energy and gain greater understanding of the vocabulary of our body's exquisite language. Being with women during pregnancy, birth and the early days of bonding, I have witnessed our innate human design supporting embodiment and loving connection. I have also experienced stress, intense emotion, physical trauma and injury during pregnancy and at birth. It can interrupt the capacity to stay connected to the body and Self. This holds true for both baby and mother – they are impacted by each other's internal and external experiences.

OUR ARRIVAL

From our very first breath, we are in relationship. With that indrawn draft of air, we become joined to everything that was, is and ever will be.[14]

Being born is not only about surviving; it is about coming into relationship with the air, our family and the universe in a whole new way. Satir refers to the moment we come out of the womb as our second birth. Anyone who is alive has made it through two births.

What do you, reader, know about your own arrival? Even if you don't have details, take a moment to sense what your body and being remember about your birth and early days. Connect to your deepest essence, it has been with you from the beginning, and send a message of gratitude – to you, from you. Send gratitude to anyone who supported you. Take a deep breath. Remember the first time you felt air come into your lungs. The breath of life is available right now. Invite your life force energy to express itself in your body, your heart and in your mind. Are there images, metaphors or colours? Breathe deeply or softly and, as you do, send a blessing of gratitude. You arrived here on this planet. Celebrate your birth day and honour the treasure that you are.

When we are ready to be born, we are actively part of the process and our body is designed with hormones, neurological wiring, primitive reflexes to help us survive. When our birth experience is uninterrupted by excess stress or trauma and we are welcomed into loving arms, we land in our body, orient to our surroundings and experience embodiment outside of the womb. For some, the experience of trauma and distress in infancy creates patterns of coping that last a lifetime. Some of the infants that come to me for therapy are in distress. Though the events around their arrival cannot be changed, it is my greatest hope that the impact can be reduced or resolved. It is amazing to witness the huge range of infant responses to impacts suffered while arriving in this world. It is a

---

14   Wagamese, *Embers*, 44.

privilege to work with their unique resources and see into their families of origin.

Early in my career I was part of a rehabilitation team that supported children with traumatic brain injury and neurological disabilities. Parents and families were included in therapy, but the primary focus was the child. My women's health private practice is generally one-on-one. Satir's model and infant body psychotherapy training gave me the confidence to hold space and dialogue with mother, father or partner and their infant or young toddler all together: the primary triad. Sometimes it becomes clear that the goal must shift to support the mother or the partnership (while always including the infant or child).

Satir is known as a pioneer in family therapy and was one of the first in her profession to offer sessions with all family members present. "It is now clear to me that the family is a microcosm of the world… to change the world is to change the family."[15]

Case Study: **Baby Cora**

Emma and Jerry bring their infant Cora to me because she has been diagnosed by her doctor as having "colic"; they were told she would grow out of it in time. They share that Cora cries inconsolably without any clear reason. She might be just fed, diaper changed, and go from peaceful cooing to alarmingly intense crying, sometimes continuing for over an hour. Nothing they do will settle her. None of them are getting enough sleep and they are not sure if she is in pain. Cora is asleep in her car seat on the floor next to Mom. I let them know we will be talking for a time so invite them to take her out and hold her. Both are very quick to say an adamant "no." That it is better to leave her, as she has just fallen asleep. Mom is sitting at the edge of her chair and Dad says he prefers to stand. As we chat, I observe their body language, posture, breathing rate, voice quality and general energy. Sometimes the first session is about making contact with the parents, exploring inner states and anchoring resources.

---

15   Satir, *New Peoplemaking*, 2.

We discuss Emma's pregnancy, Jerry's involvement, and the birth.

"Can you sense or imagine what it might have been like for baby Cora?" I ask.

Emma says, "The pregnancy itself was a breeze. The only thing that was of emotional upset was Jerry losing his job. We had to move in with my parents." Space opens up for each of them to check in with what life was like then and now. "I was feeling frustrated. I was caught between my parents' expectations and Jerry's… and then I got anxious about not having space to prepare for the birth."

"I saw myself as 'a loser'," Jerry says. "If we were starting a family, we should have our own home."

I invite them to connect with their deeper yearnings.

"I want to feel more connected," Emma shares, and Jerry says, "I hope I don't second-guess everything."

I encourage them to trust their instincts. "Can we reflect on how your experiences may influence Cora's ability to feel safe and secure?"

There is silence and I ask them if they are willing to do a short meditation to anchor into their bodies before continuing with the birth reflection. My hope is to invite awareness of how their internal world may have had an impact on Cora in the womb, at her birth, and now.

Emma begins to replay Cora's birth story. I notice her voice rising in pitch and she is talking faster.

"Take a moment, Emma. Take a few breaths and notice what is happening in your body."

Baby Cora startles several times to Dad's voice and to the sound of the chairs moving. When she wakes she goes into a high-pitched scream and her body goes into a rigid arching position, her eyes tightly closed, fists tight. Emma picks her up and starts bouncing her quite vigorously and making a loud "shushing" sound in her ear. I know that these techniques are recommended by some experts, so I continue to quietly connect to the three of them and ground. Emma is able to settle Cora enough to breastfeed and Cora's body starts to soften but is still in a very erect posture. This posture is quite common if the birth reflex is heightened and is sometimes an indicator of trauma or that something interfered in the baby's being able to complete the reflex of pushing out of the womb.

I prompt Emma to continue telling me about the birth. There are several key times I notice her body change to being more pulled in at her core and she taps her foot excessively. "The labour was very long, twenty-eight hours, and the specialist wanted to give me an epidural which I did not want. But when the baby's heart rate dropped, I felt I had no choice. Things went quickly after that but then Cora got stuck. I was too weak to push and lost any focus."

Jerry confirms. "That was very hard to watch. I couldn't stay in the room with her."

Emma goes on. "A decision was made to use the vacuum to get Cora out because her heart rate was still dropping with every contraction."

I ask, "What is happening now, in this moment, as you tell me about the birth?"

"I'm cold and feel shaky inside my belly."

"Is it alright to support you with touch? Jerry, are you willing to participate?"

Both agree. Jerry instinctively holds a hand on her back, behind her chest, and I place my hands on her knees. I invite us all to breathe deep and allow the shaking to discharge down and out her legs and feet into the ground.

This is Satir's concept of use of self. The therapist, by connecting to their own body and being congruent through the use of touch, voice and intuitive guidance, can invite clients to ground and center amidst the chaos of emotion or intense body sensation. I chose to move into a posture of strength, used deep pressure in my touch and breathed deeply along with Emma to affirm a sense of safety and connectedness. Holding space and simple potent inquiry while Emma was in the experience helped her anchor into the present moment and access her resources.

All the while baby Cora nurses vigorously, with one eye peeking out at me. I am orienting to her the whole time, letting her contact me and responding by shifting my energy to give grounded containment and yet staying soft and spacious. Emma takes a deep sigh and reports feeling more solid and this is confirmed in her body by her sitting back and leaning into Jerry's hand. Her breathing slows and drops into her belly.

We all acknowledge how much emotion and charge is still being held in Emma's body from the intensity of the birth. I ask, "Can you appreciate the courage and resources you have in this moment to allow this release?"

"Yes."

"Do you want to continue the session for your own healing or is it okay to return our focus to Cora?"

The decision is for us to continue with Cora and book a separate session for Emma. She is open to getting in touch with a counsellor as well.

When there are interruptions in the birth, both the mother and the infant may need to complete the part of the process that has not had a chance to move organically through their bodies and whole beings. When I am holding the whole family capable and connecting to their resources a myriad of new options becomes possible. I follow instincts to move things in a positive direction and trust what creatively evolves in the group connection.

Focus now goes to baby Cora, still in Emma's arms. Moving into gentle touch, assessing baby Cora's body, my instinct is to tap into places where I find flow and ease versus restriction. I invite Jerry to stay close and feel free to touch Emma or Cora as he feels drawn.

Being curious about what resources are there to anchor into and what is possible are themes I have absorbed from the Satir approach. It is so important to work within the family unit as opposed to working with an infant separate from their caregivers. Acknowledging what is happening in the whole family system in an open and loving way can build self-confidence and empowerment for all present.

I cue both parents to take deep breaths and ground again so we can all create a therapeutic container for Cora. I talk openly to baby Cora about her birth and ask what it was like for her, communicating at the same time through touch and presence. She begins to make more direct eye contact with me. I focus first on her diaphragm, holding her in what I call a sandwich hold, connecting 3-D through her centre. Her body is excessively tight. In particular, she pulls up in her upper chest and throat – possibly due to all the excessive crying and the drive of the reflexes putting her nervous system into "flight, fright, freeze" mode. Her energy is very high in her body, but the grounding touch starts to invite her back into her center.

Satir was known for using touch and having a hand on the front abdomen and also on the back as she invited a client to go inside and notice what was happening.

I ask Emma and Jerry to notice Cora's energy and focus on that part of their own bodies as well. Baby Cora relaxes more and we shift her to be more open on Emma's lap so I can cradle her head and the base of her spine. Cora and I negotiate the right touch that helps her settle into a natural rocking rhythm. I feel her nervous system calming. After ten minutes of following this rhythm a gradual shift to calm is experienced by everyone in the room. I ask Emma and Jerry if there is an image or word that might help them access and return to this sensate experience at home over the coming days/nights.

Jerry says, "Water, flowing water."

Emma has the image of a star.

I let Emma and Jerry know they can continue to do this at home, and we discuss their own ways to relax and centre Cora.

This is the start of a series of weekly family sessions for baby Cora. Emma comes alone for a couple of additional sessions to continue to process her birthing experience and early post-partum time. In one family session the parents explain how hard it is to hear Cora cry so intensely.

"What do you know about your own births and early years?" I ask. "What was going on in your families when you were in utero and when you were infants?"

What emerges for both of them is a family belief that big boys and big girls don't cry. Emotions were suppressed and not talked about, ever.

I check in with their present beliefs. "Are you willing to practise sharing emotions authentically with each other?"

They look at each other. Jerry cocks his eyebrow and smiles. Emma nods.

"What would it look like if you shifted your expectations? Right now you want Cora to stop crying. Would it be possible some of the time to simply listen and hold her in her cries?"

My intention here is to focus on the whole family system, rather than Cora as the problem; to hold a container and awareness for the parents to interact differently with each other. One shift in Emma or Jerry may allow a new experience for Cora, and then Cora's response may in turn affect the parents.

Sessions with the whole family concluded when Emma and Jerry shared that they felt confident in listening to Cora's language and her cues. They were excited to share some of their newfound creative ways to settle themselves and her, even when big emotions were triggered.

Each life is truly a miracle. The way each of us grows and develops is unique, based on our resources and early experiences within our family and communities. If in our early development our universal yearnings – safety, belonging, love, respect, appreciation, acceptance, freedom, validation, being seen, being heard – are met, a foundation of self-esteem forms and we can express the essence of who we are.

WHAT'S IN THE ATMOSPHERE?

Every child that is born into this world comes into a different context and a different atmosphere from every other child, even when born to the same parents.[16]

What is happening in our environment and the dynamics of our family when we are in utero and during the first eighteen months after we are born has an absolute impact on our early attachment and our

---

16   Satir, *New Peoplemaking*, 241.

sensate experience. Major transitions, such as moving home, loss of a loved one, or the undercurrent of unfinished psychic business in the parents' families of origin, leave deep impressions. An infant's sleep patterns, feeding patterns, the way they move or don't move may indicate physical limitations, but often these are manifestations of a combination of factors: their birth experience, the state of their nervous system, and how their mother or family system is surviving or thriving. There are tangible signs of an embodied life force in infants and toddlers; they will move and explore their world with groundedness and ease. Or they may seem stuck, bracing or collapsing through these early developmental stages.

If there have been significant impacts on the baby, mother or in the family during pregnancy, birth and/or the first months afterwards, babies may carry the message that it is not safe to "be" here and the nervous system can dysregulate early on. The emotional charge of these experiences can be stored in the tissues, bones, nervous system, organs, hormones and fluids. There is a single field of energy shared by mother and baby, some say, for up to eighteen months. What is felt and experienced by the mother is experienced by the infant and vice versa. This field, created in our physiology and energetic container, enhances bonding and safety. This design ensures that the infant/toddler is safe and gets their needs met at all levels of their being. However, if they experience stress and chaos in the shared field, perhaps due to the energy between their parents or in the community/world, the first patterns of coping develop. Coping patterns develop well before executive functions and show up in our nervous system, body, energy and movement.

I believe infants and young children have much to teach us about being whole, especially when they are getting their needs met. The body/mind/spirit is unified in this preverbal explorative time. Few conscious memories can be recalled before three years of age, as that is when the hippocampus and amygdala develop and we begin to retain memory. But we are not blank slates before the age of three. We have body memory and consciousness tracking all our life events and experiences. "Neonates and infants are conscious, sentient beings who make decisions about their experiences and take shape accordingly."[17]

Gentle and attuned body and energy work with infants can restore their ease and flow and connect them to resources obscured by entrained patterns in the nervous system. The infant before three does not have a differentiated self, so attention by the therapist to gentle, respectful boundaries is of utmost importance. I engage nonverbally and work with the relational field of the family. My experience is that babies and young children are very clear about when a caregiver or therapist is congruent or not. They will inform you through body language and vocalizations that your approach is too quick, or you are too close, or what you are doing does not match what they need. Their bodies and nervous systems want to be settled. First, I establish connection through eye contact, I mirror them, I use grounded sensitive touch, affirming words and tone of voice; in short, I send them a message that they are being seen and welcomed. "One can touch in all kinds of ways. In training therapists, I have told them to develop 'eyes and ears' in their fingers."[18]

We don't need our parents to be perfect for us to thrive in our development; in fact that would do us a disservice. Satir said "Who wants to be perfect anyway?" Ultimately, we learn from the fluctuation of life's experiences, as long as they are within a range that allows for growth. It is natural to have times of stress and emotional upset, but the repeated return to loving connection and touch creates the building blocks for resiliency in the baby's nervous system and whole being. Holding space for parents to share what is happening within them and in the atmosphere of their home can connect them to parts that have been held out of awareness. Satir is most recognized for her gifts in working with families. Instead of diagnosing the problem child or parent, she created a space

---

17   Sills, *Craniosacral Biodynamics*, 252.
18   Satir, "When I Meet a Person." 184.

of love, acceptance and curiosity for all. "I like the feeling of loving. I consider it the highest form of expressing my humanness."[19]

AND ON WE GROW...

"We learn a great deal before the age of two. Our parents may communicate with us in words but we interpret their messages from their touch and tone, their hands and their voices. Parents are not necessarily aware of or intending these nonverbal messages."[20]

The developmental stage – from three months to approximately eighteen months old – is all about getting our physical and emotional needs met. This time is all about nurturance. We develop our full sensate palate through exploration of our world and through locomotion. We feel the full range of our emotions, and if they are received with loving connection and touch, we experience intimacy with others and begin to develop healthy boundaries. Given our strong drive towards growth we will usually reach all the developmental milestones, but our bodies may compensate for stress and trauma in ways that create discomfort or expend a lot of energy. Parents and family may try to respond to our needs based on their own family-of-origin experience, but that may not match our desires. Beliefs can form like "life is too hard" or "I never get what I need" and these beliefs set up patterns in our subconscious and personality early on. Personality and body language are to some extent based on these patterns.

Whether infants are learning to roll, exploring their feet, crawling, and eventually standing, walking, climbing, I want to give them space to be curious and to fill out the full range of movement and possibilities. In a world full of baby classes, new gadgets, and a culture that praises doing and intellectual learning, I am drawn to support stillness and the parasympathetic nervous system in young children. Sometimes I remind

---

19   Satir, *New Peoplemaking*, 229.
20   Satir, *Satir Model*, 56-57.

the baby and their parents that it's okay to slow things down and settle. Why not linger longer in each stage of development? There is no need to rush. Attuning to babies and toddlers in subtle ways can demonstrate slowing down, and being on baby time creates a magical experience for all family members. We can all afford to be more embodied and aware of the nuances of nonverbal communication.

Case Study: *Max*

Max is nine months old when his parents bring him in, concerned he has no interest in locomoting. He came into the world via a planned C-section. "Max loves to just 'be'," his mother says. And, for sure, he does not seem to have a lot of interest in movement at all. He is relatively calm in his demeanour but not happy if he is pushed into different positions by one of his brothers or anyone else. He sits fairly steady, but if anything takes him a few degrees off centre he either falls to the ground in distress or braces back to his upright position. Max has a soft round appearance in his torso and it's striking how little he moves his legs. His dad says, "Overall he is very calm, but we wonder why he doesn't even roll or move out of sitting – he just doesn't seem interested."

I am curious about the imprint of the planned C-section. And I wonder about his two siblings. Do they swoop in to give him his toys or lift him into a new location? Perhaps a belief has formed: "I don't need to initiate; everything is done for me."

With Max I work very slowly and positively directional to celebrate even the smallest shifts towards reaching or rotating away from his center. We have several sessions with just Max and his mom where he is able to rest into her support and release around his spine. We then invite his brothers in. We play and move on the floor, navigating to find just the right boundaries for him to feel safe to move on his own within the big bolstering energy of his family.

Intimacy, boundaries, beliefs about life, orientation and emotional patterns are often set up in the body and psyche right from birth and our early development. Our caregivers' capacity to meet our needs for safety, love and belonging with healthy boundaries builds a foundation for self-esteem and self-love that we in turn can offer others as we grow and mature. "I want to love you without clutching, appreciate you without judging, join you without invading, invite you without demanding, love you without guilt, criticize you without insulting. If I can have the same from you, then we can truly meet and enrich each other."[21]

Case Study: *Audrey*

Diana books an appointment for her three-and-a-half-year-old daughter Audrey. I am familiar with the family as I worked with Diana during her pregnancy with Audrey and with her youngest son Greg, who is now eighteen months. Mom wants to check Audrey's physical alignment as she has had a few significant falls – on her head and tailbone. She is also concerned about Audrey's big emotional outbursts and her defiance, especially around issues of safety. For the first visit, Mom and the kids come. Dad works out of town, sometimes up to six weeks at a time, and is away right now. Diana says, "He's only home for a week or two at a time. It's pretty difficult to be mostly a single mom. And on top of that, we recently had to move house."

As they settle into my office space, I invite Audrey to explore the toy box while I chat with Mom, who has Greg on her lap. Diana launches into all the things Audrey has done wrong of late, her voice strained by irritation and her facial expression very stern.

"Can we talk about Audrey's resources?" I ask. "What is going well?"

"Audrey just creates so much chaos in the house. I get so mad. I can't believe how many times she's put herself and her little brother at risk!"

Audrey is watching Mom closely. The little girl quietly chooses a book and positions herself away from us but still watching us. Her body starts to pull in, almost like she wants to get small. She has a pout on her face.

"I'm going to connect through play," I tell Mom, "before we do any

---

21 Satir, *Making Contact*, 3.

body work. Let's continue this conversation over the phone after the appointment."

Diana nods.

I get down on the floor and invite Audrey to read the book to me. She beams a big smile and sits close, her back against my torso. I open my heart space and ground even more, with the intention of creating a field of love and safety for everyone in the room. "I am going to massage your belly while we read the book, is that okay?"

"Yeah."

"Where would you like Mom and Greg to sit?"

She points to the office chair which is close but facing away towards the desk. Clearly, she wants to have some of her own space but still have Mom close.

Satir used to work with families by positioning them, sensing the right distance and location for individuals to be comfortable within the group energy. She emphasized getting on the same level when communicating, especially with children and even used adjustable stools to achieve this.

As Audrey leans back, I place one hand on her belly and the other on her back; engaged in the pictures and story, she naturally follows my touch by sinking into her spine more, all the while holding the book. Her body seems to be asking for more pressure. It feels like she is pulling herself back inside and her energy is rooting down. I deepen my breathing and ask her to take a big breath. "Like you are gonna blow out a birthday candle." She does and I can feel she's more centered and more relaxed in her body. "Maybe Mom and Greg can come join us and Mom could read the story while you lie on your belly so I can massage your back. Is that okay?"

"Sure," she chirps.

I hold her hand and when she turns to face me, I gaze into her eyes for a while. "I really appreciate you listening. I can see your special sparkle."

"Where?"

I lightly touch her eyes and her heart. Then I bring Mom over... "Can you see Audrey's special sparkle, Mom?"

Diana gives a sigh. She can see where I'm going.

"Could you give Audrey a touch or hug that shows her?"

She nuzzles Audrey's head into her side and tousles her hair.

I check Greg to see if he's alright, not wanting to bring him into the connection yet. He seems content to observe, and I want Audrey to feel like the star for a moment. I assess her spine and back. Her muscles are surprisingly tight, especially around her neck. It truly feels like she is carrying a heavy backpack with emotions and expectations all bundled in. I mention this to Diana and we dialogue a bit about expectations.

Diana says, "I need her to be the good big sister, but often Greg is the one being 'good.' He's always sharing his toys and looking for hugs even when Audrey is being mean to him."

"What would it be like if Audrey was good?"

"Well, I would be calm and peaceful."

"Is there any way you could feel calm when Audrey is emoting or not listening?"

Diana shakes her head. She looks really exasperated... she really doesn't know how.

"Are you willing to take that question away and think about it and we could arrange a follow-up phone call?"

She agrees. Audrey starts whining and getting restless at the end of the session and her mom matches the energy of frustration and impatience. It gives me a window into how quickly the emotions escalate for both of them.

The phone consult focuses on Diana finding ways to have some time to herself to regroup. She realizes she needs to find more emotional regulation so she can hold space for Audrey. She reflects on how she was parented at that age. Both her parents worked for the Air Force. There was no way for her to be defiant. Family rule was: "you just follow the rules, no questions asked." Diana still wishes that Audrey would just listen to her but says she can imagine gently laughing at herself about how strict she has been. She is willing to look at creative ways to give Audrey more choices and to pick her battles as a parent unless there's a safety concern.

The next two sessions are Audrey with Mom. Dad is at home with Greg. Along with body work, we play games and colour a big sheet of paper, *You're Awesome*. Mom and Audrey draw pictures and write words of things they love about each other. At three-and-a-half, Audrey sure has some amazing things to say about herself and her mom! Their homework is to make a poster for the whole family.

FIRST STEPS IN BECOMING A CHOICE MAKER

As we develop autonomy, when we first begin to sense we are the centre of our universe, things may not always go well. If we choose an unsafe or destructive path, we may get shut down. Hopefully, with the support of our parents providing a healthy structure, loving feedback and creative options, we can learn to make different choices. But if the reaction to our choices is shaming, criticism and control, we can develop coping patterns that stay with us into adulthood. Our bodies can hold big feelings, opinions and creative impulses that did not have a safe space to be expressed. We learn what is expected of us and we follow the family rules, spoken and unspoken. Deeply held perceptions and beliefs, once set up, will play out in life. Blind spots based on early trauma make setting healthy boundaries challenging. We need to experience nurturing relationships to grow. We need to shift from surviving and coping to new ways of thriving in order to meet our full potential. There is alchemy in holding space for what may seem like polar opposites.

I invite you to sit back in your seat and feel your feet on the floor and the Earth beneath you. Take a big breath and allow the out breath to be long and slow. As you ride inside on your breath, take inventory of your body and energy and connect to where there is ease and spaciousness. Notice what's happening as you move from thinking about what you are reading to being grounded and centered. Be present, invite your sky connection or spirit support team – whatever language works – and breathe in the energy from above and below and within your body and around you... your sacred space.

Now time-travel back to your early steps as a decision maker. Notice any visuals, sensations, posture etc. Let your body remember the resources. This young part of you may have insights to share. Are there puzzles, feelings, or did you hope something could be different? Send appreciation inside to all parts of you and bring acceptance to whatever is arising.

Let's reflect on your capacity to be a choicemaker now – feel into your body and energy field. How do you feel when you get a "yes" or a "no"? What comes forth to guide you? Honour all. Take another breath or a stretch as you return to reading.

Every life experience happens in the body, nervous system and energy field. Our postures, habits and tensions can give us insight into what may underlie a pattern of coping. Awareness of our bodies, energy and Self can remind us of joyful moments and freedoms and give us a doorway to unlimited resources. If all parts of us have resources to guide us to new ways of being, we can hold loving presence for all that surfaces. Sometimes what has been stuck or is a status quo from early childhood can shift and transform organically. But often we must make the choice to check in and be willing to be surprised. Ultimately, it is up to each of us to take responsibility for our own lives. Satir's belief is that "change is always possible."

> Each of us emerges as a bud on a universal spiritual tree. That tree links all human beings through its roots. Each of us can become a wise leader who will love, take care of and nurture the precious life we have been given.[22]

We are not alone. We can tap into the roots that connect all of humanity, this beautiful planet, Universal Life Energy, Spirit or Source energy. This "spiritual tree" can bolster us through times of challenge

---

22   Satir, *New Peoplemaking*, 336.

and times of joy. Yet, it is up to each of us to be responsible for our own life by making life-enhancing choices, practising self-love and being congruent. These are intrinsic qualities of a wise leader. Imagine if each of us on this planet could be this kind of leader and take responsibility for the one precious life we have been given.

CLOSING

> Creating caretaking approaches and crystalizing the inner recognition (what I call bone knowledge) is the realization that we are spiritual beings in human form.[23]

Our life force energy is expressed in our bodies, literally in our bones. We may thrive for a period of time and then drop back to coping or surviving when life becomes challenging. The deep essence of who we are is always available to us, no matter the circumstances. Whether coping, thriving or co-creating we can connect to Self; throughout our life we may get glimpses of oneness, love, connection to the cosmos; we yearn to return.

We can access states of creativity and spirituality at any age. Babies and children have shown me their capacity for bliss and joy. Their life force energy is so palpable. The environment they are in may be chaotic, and yet there they are beaming. This speaks to the unique resources that are with us right from the beginning.

As a growing human being, I continue to find repeating patterns from my early years and family of origin that still take me off track. My frustration, grief and unworthiness send me back into the same old potholes and I lose sight of my inner light. Through it all, I am deeply grateful. Grateful for my parents and some of my extended family who met my yearning to be seen and validated at a soul level. My mother was always open and curious when I came home from the woods and shared my experiences of seeing angels in the trees and hearing whispers

---

23 Ibid, 336.

from the animals. This acceptance and love gave me a foundation to seek spiritual experiences from a young age and throughout my life. These moments are tangible in my body and help me remember who I am.

Spirituality and consciousness have always infused Satir's therapy and trainings, but she became more engaged in putting her ideas on this topic into more tangible discussions and writings near the end of her life. John Banmen and others share and write about this stage of her life and career. Some of Banmen's questions are embodied in me. In our practices we see people move from surviving and coping to thriving; if we as therapists and leaders become co-creators in life, will that organically encourage clients and others in community to co-create? How do we invite clients to connect to Self, the Divine and creative energy of the cosmos? Can we reach and sustain a state of I am or oneness?

I believe we come into this world with our divine spark and leave with it. Some say we are walking stars in this amazing galaxy. The ongoing inquiry is, how do we tend our own unique spark and that of others? I have deep gratitude for Virginia Satir. She saw each person as nothing less than a spark of the Divine. She forged the way for so many people, in so many cultures, to honour the wisdom, resources and language of our bodies and energy. I have felt the powerful transmission of her energy and her passionate message: to love and hold hope for change and peace for all of humanity and for our beautiful planet. Though I did not have a chance to meet her in person, she inspires and teaches me still.

REFERENCES

Banmen, John, ed., *Meditations of Virginia Satir*. Burien: Avanta, The Virginia Satir Network. 2003.

Banmen, John. *In Her Own Words*. Phoenix: Zeig, Tucker & Theisen, Inc., 2008.

Banmen, John, and Sharon Loeschen, eds. *Simple and Profound: Sayings of Virginia Satir*. Wendell: The Virginia Satir Global Network, 2020.

Kimmerer, Rose. *Braiding Sweetgrass*. Minneapolis: Milkweed Edition, 2015.

Satir, Virginia. *The New Peoplemaking*. Mountain View: Science and Behavior Books, Inc., 1988.

Satir, Virginia, John Banmen, Jane Gerber, and Maria Gomori. *The Satir Model*. Palo Alto: Science and Behavior Books, Inc., 1991.

Satir, Virginia. "Life's Beginning Brings Joy into Your Life," In *Meditations of Virginia Satir*, edited by John Banmen, 35-36. Burien: Avanta The Virginia Satir Network, 2003.

Satir, Virginia. "When I Meet a Person." In *In Her Own Words: Virginia Satir, Selected Papers, 1963-1983*, edited by John Banmen, 179-196. Phoenix: Zeig, Tucker and Theisen, Inc., 2008.

Satir, Virginia. *Making Contact*. Wendell: The Virginia Satir Global Network, 2020.

Shepherd, Philip. *Radical Wholeness*. Berkeley: North Atlantic Books, 2017.

Schore, Allan. *Affect Regulation and the Origin of Self*. Hillside: Routledge, 1991.

Sills, Franklyn. *Craniosacral Biodynamics, Vol.2*. Berkeley: North Atlantic Books, 2004.

Wagamese, Richard. *Embers*. Madeira: Douglas and McIntyre, Ltd., 2016.

V

SCULPTING: ACTIVATING THE BODY SO THE BODY CAN SPEAK

JENNIFER NAGEL

Jennifer Nagel, MA, RCC has extensive training in Satir's model and has been leading trainings for therapists, educators, school programs, community groups, at-risk adolescents, therapeutic programs, non-profit organizations and corporate groups. She has presented many workshops and training programs internationally, working in Canada, China, Kenya and Thailand. Jennifer is a member of the British Columbia Association for Clinical Counsellors, the International Family Therapy Association, the Virginia Satir Global Network and a clinical member of the Satir Institute of the Pacific (SIP). She is the Director of Trainer Development for SIP, and on faculty as a senior trainer for the Banmen Satir China Management Centre. Jennifer also works with individuals, couples, families and youth in private practice, and provides clinical supervision to other therapists. She is the author of *Magic in the Muck: Finding Grace in Chaos* and the collaborative book *Therapists are Human Too: The Healing Journey of Reciprocity*. Jennifer is passionate about teaching Satir Transformational Systemic Therapy programs around the world.

SCULPTING: ACTIVATING THE BODY SO THE BODY CAN SPEAK

How do we wake up the experiences and memories that are stored in every cell of our bodies? How do we shift blocks in our flow of energy and vitality? How do we access those stuck places? When I pause to reflect on my journey so far in this lifetime, I am struck by the way each memory holds its own response in my body – from the exhilaration, racing heartbeat and butterflies in my stomach when falling in love, to the tightness in my chest, trembling of all the cells around my pericardium, and tears in my eyes after a tragedy. We have a visceral experience in the present moment when we remember our various triumphs, tribulations and ecstasies, and it is essential to include our bodies in any therapy or intervention for transformational, lasting change to occur. One of Virginia Satir's therapeutic interventions to bring about deep change is sculpting – she invited people to take on movements and postures that reflected the internal and external dynamics she was observing in the session. This chapter explores how the therapeutic process of sculpting allows access to the body's stored messages and brings these to the surface of awareness. When we bring greater awareness into each moment, new decisions can be made about how we would like to live; we will tend to be more healthy and whole in relation to ourselves, others, and to the world.

FINDING VIRGINIA SATIR

Since I'm not sure I can articulate exactly what I was looking for at the time I discovered Virginia Satir, it feels more accurate to say that Satir found me. I had the sense that something was missing from my graduate school courses, but I did not know what that something was. I felt the lack of a solid theoretical orientation. I had learned bits here and there from a whole variety of theories, and had accumulated a collection of ideas, techniques and interventions that seemed to fit with how I wanted to work with people. As I searched for a theoretical orientation that I could call "home," I simply considered myself "eclectic" in my approach. I was drawn to experiential approaches that went beyond dialogue, sensing there was an important element to the therapeutic relationship necessary for any approach to be effective that I hadn't quite discovered yet. Only when I learned about Satir's model did I find the language and framework that truly resonated with my own views and beliefs about humanity.

My first introduction to her model was in 1998 during my clinical counselling practicum for my Master's degree at the University of British Columbia. Dr. John Banmen (who had worked closely with Satir) was my clinical supervisor. What attracted me to this model was the way it prioritized the articulation of internal experience by encouraging clients to reflect, to go inward to gain a new depth of awareness to their whole experience, outer and inner. This moving beyond mere cognitive awareness and understanding, to a deeper transformation of old patterns and ways of being in the world affected me tremendously. The model spoke of transformational change, along with the belief that we all have the internal resources to support healing and growth. This fueled my own energy and gave me renewed hope for each of my clients. Finally, everything I had learned, everything I believed about people and the possibility of change, had a place to land. For me, this model was much more than a theoretical orientation; it aligned with the person I wanted to be in this world and in relation to others. I was curious to know more about Satir, the person, and how she worked with people. I wanted to see and experience in action her ideas of "becoming more fully human" and more "whole."

I dove right into learning, practising, and eventually, in 2003, began supervising and teaching Satir's model and Satir Transformational Systemic Therapy for the Satir Institute of the Pacific (SIP). In 2008, SIP acquired the entire collection of recorded videotapes from a month-long intensive Satir had led in Quebec in 1979, which were then transferred onto 122 DVDs. I had the privilege of watching and documenting countless videos of her teaching and working with people. I suppose I can now say that I once attended a month-long intensive with Virginia Satir! It became clear just how intuitive and ahead of her time she was, that this way of working with people went way beyond talk therapy. I noticed how attentive she was and how clients responded to her presence, her use of touch, to the questions she asked of their inner experience. Satir would gather information from the wisdom of the whole body when asking clients to move into various postures and positions rather than ask questions about the details of the story or context. Witnessing the shifts and transformations made in sessions showed me that there was (and is) a depth to this work that had and still has not been clearly articulated. Perhaps this lack of articulation can be attributed to language being somewhat limited; it isn't possible to find words to encapsulate something so experiential and, some might say, magical.

In this chapter, I will focus on sculpting and its use within therapy as a vehicle for experiential, transformational change. Sculpting is the externalization of what is going on internally – within oneself and in relation to others. Sculpting is an experiential, action-oriented process that utilizes body postures and spacing to represent the internal and interpersonal dynamics of what is going on within an individual, couple, family or group, especially when under stress. I remember the first family-of-origin sculpt I experienced as a participant in a Level 1 Satir Transformational Systemic Therapy training program. Chosen to represent one of the star's[1] family members, I experienced a surprising jolt of body sensations and emotions the moment I entered the sculpting process; I was initially directed by the facilitator (according to the information on the family map) to enter the sculpt in a body posture that represented sacrificing my own needs for the sake of pleasing everyone else in the family. Even though I knew nothing about the actual person I was representing, the words that I spoke when asked questions had a profound meaning for the star. Not only did the star experience profound shifts in this session,

---

1 "Star" refers to the client, as Satir said, "we are all the stars of our own lives." In this chapter, the words "client" and "star" or "Star" may be used interchangeably.

I also gained new insights and a greater awareness of my own patterns in relationships. I was even more determined to learn more about this fine art of experiential processing work to facilitate positive change within clients and groups.

In Satir's approach we are working on resolving and healing impacts from past events and experiences. Bringing these impacts into conscious awareness through experiencing them in present time is necessary for them to shift and change. Sculpting a physical position is one way to access impacts from our past in present time. As soon as we invite a client to shift their physical position or posture, they will feel a shift in their body and in their energy. Asking a client questions about body sensations, feelings, thoughts, beliefs, expectations and yearnings as they are experiencing the old impacts in the here-and-now brings awareness about what might be changed, let go, or added in, to transform the effect or residue of the impact. I would like to emphasize that therapists using the model work to change the impact's effect on a client, not to retraumatize the client.

In my experience of teaching and clinical supervision, I have met many helping professionals who have expressed initial trepidation and even anxiety about using sculpting in their work. When starting out as a therapist, I was also nervous about using this process with clients and groups; however, I have discovered by taking the risk and just trusting the process, sculpting goes places that talk therapy alone cannot; it really can speed up the process of change. In a sculpting process, clients have the opportunity to experience their internal dynamics in a visceral way. Sculpting can be used in a variety of contexts, including with groups, families, couples, individuals, to work with present lifetime impacts as well as to explore family-of-origin reconstructions.

BUILDING SAFETY AND CONNECTION WITHIN THE (SACRED) SPACE

With any experiential process we are inviting people to be vulnerable in their connection to themselves and to others, including the therapist.

The process of building connection and trust among all those who are present is necessary so that clients can experience emotional, physical and spiritual safety, which will allow their vulnerability to come through. Sculpting is one way of accessing information the body is sharing; it does this by magnifying the present energy/experience. When emotions are activated, we might see tears, physical discomfort or pain. Trust and safety are important; there needs to be an unspoken contract of support and strength that connects to the wisdom and information the body is holding.

The intention of the sacred space is to foster interpersonal connections that go beneath the surface of roles and expectations. Whether meeting an individual client or a couple, a family, or a group of people who don't know one another, the therapist begins by finding out who they are and what they appreciate about themselves. The objective of asking what qualities they are bringing with them to the therapy process, and/or what brings them joy in their lives, is to activate life energy and get it flowing in the room to begin setting the space for deeper connection. In a group situation this could be inviting each person to share some of the inner resources they are bringing with them to the session.

WAKING UP FAMILIAR ENERGY PATTERNS

With sculpting we are constantly working with the intra-psychic experience (internal feelings, thoughts, beliefs, expectations, yearnings) of each individual in the sculpt, as well as the process of what is happening interactively among all participants. Sculpting can allow faster access to the body's memory and experience. This is a very fluid process with endless potential variations. Within the sculpt many possibilities emerge based on the uniqueness of each family or group, each person, and the uniqueness of the therapist or guide who is leading the process. These possibilities indicate movement and hope. Sculpting truly is a therapeutic art with techniques to learn and follow, yet within the form there is room for the creativity of the guide as well as the creativity of the star and the other participants. *The drawing depicts Satir working with a star in a sculpting process.*

© Jennifer Nagel. Illustration by Aleksandra Gammer based on a workshop photograph courtesy of Virginia Satir Archives.

How does this internal experiencing of outer dynamics unfold? We know that emotional and energetic memory of our experiences is held physically and carried within the body. Much evidence supports this[2] Our bodies can manifest these memories in a multitude of ways, such as through muscle tension, aches, pains, changes in breathing, and changes in heart rate. These physiological manifestations can be viewed as our body's language for communicating that something is happening now that might need our attention and care. Rather than medicating or using other ways to armor ourselves, we want to find ways to access these messages and listen to what needs to change. For example, in the photo we see Satir checking in with the star as she experiences the tall person pointing his finger and looking directly down at the person on one knee,

---

2 Levine, *Waking the Tiger* and Pert, *Molecules of Emotion*.

who is reaching out and looking up towards him. We can imagine into this. Might the kneeling figure be feeling something in present time in her body? Satir is engaging with the star as she processes what is happening. Allowing the body to have a voice can bring new insights into what is still being lived out. What in one's present life might need to change?

Sculpting is one way of "waking up" cellular memory or familiar energetic patterns of experience. What follows is the case study of a couple I worked with, "Laurie" and "Doug,"[3] and shows how a familiar energy pattern was accessed.

Case Study: *Laurie and Doug*

Laurie has been complaining that her husband focuses too much of his attention on her and has no goals for himself other than to "make her happy." Doug cannot understand how this is a problem for her. Laurie is visibly uncomfortable with this dynamic and I have a picture forming of Doug having Laurie up on a pedestal. I share with them that I have a picture I am curious about exploring and wonder if they would be willing to see how it fits for them. Inviting them to stand, I guide Laurie to step up onto the chair and Doug to kneel on the ground looking up at her while extending his hand toward her. They both express immediate discomfort with this physical position, yet Laurie says this is exactly what her experience feels like. She says she feels lonely all by herself up on the chair and that she yearns for her husband to be eye to eye with her.

"What would be different if you were both eye to eye, Laurie?"

"We would be able to connect more."

"What about you, Doug?"

"It is so exhausting looking up at her all the time. My neck aches."

"Anything else?"

"Yes. It's true I've not put any energy into my own dreams. But I really want to please others. I want to feel accepted and loved."

"Is this a new experience for you?"

---

[3] Pseudonyms will be used throughout this chapter to protect the identity of any clients mentioned.

"No. It's very familiar."

"How old is this familiar experience, Doug?"

"It's quite old.... I remember feeling this when I was quite young."

This sculpting process allows for new awareness to surface for both clients; and based on this new perspective, new decisions can be made about what each wants to work on, both for themselves and in relation to each other. We process their hopes for change in the immediate present while recalling the pain they have been experiencing in the relationship.

Therapeutic elements considered essential in Satir's model for transformational change to occur include: experiential, systemic, change focused, positively directional, and the therapist's use of self see the Introduction chapter.[4] The sculpting intervention was experiential; we were processing what was happening in the present moment and working with the energy and dynamics in the room. I worked systemically to explore what was happening internally for each person, interactively in the relationship, as well as bringing into focus impacts from families of origin. Change was uppermost in our minds, and positively directional as we explored Laurie and Doug's hopes and wishes. Meanwhile I listened to my own body's responses, acknowledging its wisdom, following my intuition and fully present with unconditional positive regard for both clients – as we co-created a safe space for us to engage in the sculpting process.

EXPERIENTIAL PROCESS

Sculpting is an experiential process – we access and bring to the surface internal dynamics associated with a pattern of interaction usually outside the client's awareness. When the therapist intentionally invites the client to position and move their body in a sculpt, the client becomes more consciously aware of body sensations, feelings, thoughts, expectations, and yearnings; these can then be associated with a pattern

---

4   Banmen and Maki-Banmen, "Introduction", v and vi.

of interaction with others or with various inner parts[5] We are surfacing the memory of an event or interaction that happened in the past that is impacting current relationships. By bringing this internal experience into awareness, the client can make new decisions, which can open up the possibility of transformation. For example, as a client within the sculpt connects with sadness and a sense of disconnection from others, they might notice physical sensations, such as trembling or a lump in the throat, and maybe, beneath that, a longing for more connection. Working with the client's new awareness can support them as they investigate what lies under the sadness – perhaps anger, confusion, loss, unexplored expectations and yearnings. It has been well documented that our bodies store profound emotional experiences at a cellular level[6]. By focusing on the parts of the body that are "speaking up," we are able to "listen" to their "messages" and facilitate a greater depth of lasting change.

Different postures and body positions result in different manifestations of our energy. To experience this, I invite you, the reader, to slouch over with your head hanging low. Notice what you experience in your body and what happens with your energy. What are you noticing? Do any emotions and thoughts come up for you in this position? Do you have any expectations of yourself? Of others? What it is that you need in this moment? Is your energy somewhat down or heavy? Do you notice any areas of tension or physical discomfort?

Now I would like to invite you to shift from slouching and slowly allow yourself to sit up tall and straight, expanding your chest and rolling your shoulders back. What shifts and changes in your body do you experience now? Any changes in your breathing? Do you notice any emotions? How do you perceive yourself? Has anything shifted in your expectations of yourself or of others? What do you need now?

---

5   Satir often worked with parts within her stars and these parts would be represented by others in the group in order to bring the internal dynamics of these parts into the star's awareness. The intention is to transform the relationships among these parts, to integrate them into a more harmonious whole, and access deep resources within the star.

6   Siegel, *Pocket Guide,* and Porges and Dana, *Clinical Applications.*

Some positions can seem familiar or bring up memories of the past. Bringing this positional body awareness to the surface gives us information about our deepest selves; we can then explore and process, with the aim of making more conscious decisions: what could be different for us, and what would we like to change?

When our clients connect with what they would like to change, they are in touch with their wisdom. Sculpting can help them to access yearnings, and yearnings are the universal deep needs that all human beings have – the need for love, to belong, to be accepted, to feel safe, peaceful, and free. As our clients gain more awareness of that deep place within themselves, they will be able to choose healthy ways of meeting and expressing these yearnings.

Case Study: **Kristy and Dave**

Kristy and Dave both say they are experiencing tension in their relationship. I ask them each to tell me how they deal with stress. Kristy admits she has a tendency to blame Dave for not meeting her expectations. Dave agrees and says when things become too stressful he simply withdraws and distracts himself with the internet. I invite Kristy and Dave to stand and ask Kristy to, "Blame Dave. Put one hand on your hip and raise the other one and point at him." I then arrange Dave to turn slightly away from Kristy. "Let's put a bit more physical distance between you and Kristy by taking another step away."

We process and explore the internal experience of each and what is happening. I encourage them to move in response to their energy. "Feel where it wants to take you."

Kristy moves to face him directly and stands tall, radiating energy. This results in Dave walking to the far side of the office and completely turning his back.

When asked what she is feeling, Kristy says she is in touch with her anger.

"Are you criticizing him?"

"Oh, yeah."

"Anything else?"

"He won't let me in!"

I ask her what needs she is really trying to get met.

"I just want connection and to be understood." As she voices these yearnings, her shoulders noticeably soften and her pointing arm starts to lower.

I turn to Dave. "What's happening for you now, Dave?"

"Phew. I'm feeling some relief at the moment, something's changed!" Clearly, he resonates with the desire for connection, understanding, to be heard and loved.

For the remainder of the session, both are more open and willing to explore new understandings of what can be possible for them. In subsequent sessions it becomes clear that they are both trying to meet the same yearnings (to be seen, heard, more connected) but just in different ways. We then explore new body positions to find alternate ways to be in touch, with the ultimate aim of finding how they want to be together. Anchoring these shifts through movement and stances, Kristy and Dave become more aware of changes in their personal energy. They are able to articulate new decisions. The intentional step of making a new decision is integral to sustaining the changes made within a session.

Sculpting dynamics in a relationship is a very effective way of letting clients experience different ways of coping while also connecting with the deep longing that each person has for change. By exploring internal experience, a client may discover that what they are really yearning for is love, connection, safety, and to be heard. When clients begin to hear each other at the level of yearnings, there is a shift in the energy. They will often move to a new physical position and find a new place of connection and understanding.

THERAPIST'S USE OF SELF

Satir stated that one of the most important tools the therapist has in their toolkit is the use of self. What does this mean? Let's imagine a session in progress. The therapist is as much a part of the process and the dynamic flow of energy in the room as the client(s). The therapist is not separate from what is transpiring, not some automaton observing the process from a distance, making calculated decisions about what should happen. The conscious therapist brings their whole presence – body, mind, energy and spirit – to support the safe container needed for clients to process and transform overwhelming emotions and impacts.

Sculpting, or any process that invites the client to access the wisdom of their full internal experience of themselves, requires preparing each person present. For authentic work to unfold, safety and trust within the space is required. I believe this begins with the therapist or facilitator preparing their own inner state. It is necessary to cultivate a belief and trust in the overall process, knowing that the outcome or the way the process will unfold is not known. This "grounding" or "centering" puts me in touch with a power and wisdom greater than myself. Meditation and mindfulness on the part of the therapist contributes to the physical, emotional, and spiritual safety of the container that supports the therapeutic work. Prior to meeting with clients or a group, I have my own personal ritual of meditation and prayer. Guiding a meditation for clients and groups also helps me to be fully present and connected with my Self, the client or group; and listening to my intuition connects me with universal wisdom, which sets the space for the work to unfold. Satir would often use guided meditations and mindfulness with groups she was working with:

> I now know that the ability we have to go into the unknown is due to the resources we have. It is not because we know what is there or that there are guarantees. I can go anywhere because I take with me my resources. If I can center people and allow them to become aware of their resources and secure in the knowledge that it is their resources that will take them somewhere, then I can reduce their fears.[7]

---

7   Satir, "Purpose of my Meditations," 1.

I really see this work as sacred. Guided meditation allows space for going within and connecting with Self, bringing awareness to the breath, to body sensations, emotions, thoughts, beliefs, expectations, yearnings; we connect with life energy and our internal resources. Meditation and centering in a group prepares all present in the room to contribute to the safe and compassionate space for therapeutic processes to unfold.

I begin each session with an underlying trust that what can happen is bigger than the mind's conscious understanding. In other words, I might not have a clear sense of what will happen during an experiential process, yet I trust that whatever happens will serve a bigger picture for all involved. There is a large "Knowing" that umbrellas or encircles the "unknowing." By trusting the bigger picture – even when the picture is unclear – the magic within the process begins to unfold. The "magic" is the dance of life energy that flows, moves, blends and interacts among all involved in the process. For me, it is about knowing that all that is unfolding is much bigger than myself. It is alright to "not know," to trust the bigger picture and hold space for the process to unfold. Satir said: "I believe [spirituality] is our connection to the universe and is basic to our existence, and therefore is essential to our therapeutic context."[8] Satir's words resonate with this idea of intuitive knowing when in connection with universal life energy one does not need to be clear about how the process might unfold.

Case Study: *Jenny*

I am teaching a Social Trauma program for social workers, counsellors, and other helping professionals in Hong Kong. The city is in the midst of upheaval. Protests are happening literally all around the area we are in. One participant, Jenny, talks about the fear she is experiencing. I invite her to bring awareness to where she feels this fear in her body.

"My heart is pounding, and my stomach is clenched tight."

The energy I feel from her in this exchange prompts me to ask if she

---

8   Satir, *Peoplemaking*, 334.

would be willing to choose people from the group to represent her heart and her stomach. "Trust your intuition and go with what fits." (This is the first time I have ever sculpted an individual's organs.) I experience my intuition as an inner voice and a gut feeling and this leads me to follow the direction we are going. Jenny chooses two people to represent her heart and one to represent her stomach (following the energy of her own intuition) and they go to the centre of the room. Without prompting or instruction or even talking with each other, the two heart representatives link arms and begin alternately jumping, to represent the jumping and pounding of the heart. The person chosen to represent the stomach comes to stand near the heart and I invite her to hold her body in a way that represents the clenching. She crouches down, holding her body tight and clenched. We continue adding various parts to the sculpt – including the part of Jenny's body that is experiencing peace in the midst of this fear, and resources such as caring, and courage. Meanwhile, I keep an eye on the star. Having a visual representation of all the movement and flow of each part with their respective influence on one another is clearly profoundly moving for her. I walk with the star to each of the parts and we check in with their experience in the moment. Each part shares words about their experience, and each says what their loving intentions are for the star. As the star listens to these positive intentions, she begins to weep. As the parts hear one another, they find new ways to move and communicate. A general energy of support for the star fills the room.

There were many profound and moving moments during this sculpting process. There was a general shift away from fear, anger and despair toward reconnecting with life energy through hope, compassion and love. The huge gift of this experience for me – and this is true of countless other sculpting experiences – was to witness and hold space for the intuition, wisdom and creativity of each participant chosen to represent various parts of the star. The wisdom of their responses, the trust in their own energy to move them, not only contributed to the star's process of transformation, but also promoted learning and new shifts within others in the sculpt and all those observing the demonstration.

By tuning into our own energy and the energy of our clients, in the belief that we all have innate resources and wisdom that can be accessed, we support the clients' connection with life energy in a very interactional way. The roles of "giver" and "receiver" can blur. Therapists and clients are engaged in an intuitive inner dance. All involved in this dance can better discern internal resources available to each of them for healing and growth. Internal resources include wisdom, creativity, intuition, love, compassion, caring, assertiveness and tenacity. When the therapist believes that every person has within themselves all the resources necessary for survival, healing and growth – even if they don't know or believe it – the therapist can connect with the resources. The therapist can accept the client in their pain, while not colluding with their suffering. In other words, the therapist is congruent.

Congruence is a state of being in which one is aware of what is happening within, is loving and accepting of self and others, and is fulfilling one's own yearnings. One can connect with others at their essence rather than via their behaviours. The congruent person also accepts as given the environment, context or culture. When the therapist is congruent and connected to the essence and dignity of the other person(s), and is providing a safe container, any chaos that comes up in session can be experienced as unfulfilled yearnings. In turn, clients experience themselves as being loved, accepted, heard, acknowledged and safe, and can do the work necessary to transform and heal painful impacts from the past. Satir modelled this way of using one's self in the therapeutic process and in her training programs:

> When I am completely harmonious with myself, it is like one light reaching out to another. At the outset, it is not a question of "I will help you." It is simply a question of life reaching out to life. All life talks to life when it is in a harmonious state. If my ego is involved or I need them to get well, then it is a different story. This is one of the secrets…[9]

---

9   Simon, "Reaching out to Life," 39.

FOCUSING ON CHANGE

When using sculpting, it is important to establish a picture of what clients want to change or have different for themselves. If we do not have a clear goal or picture, then sculpting becomes merely a means for exploration and processing what is happening in the moment. Knowing what our clients are hoping for provides us with a collaborative structure for movement and change. Clients get in touch with what is really going on deep inside their experience and can connect with a felt sense of what could be possible.

When we move into sculpting a picture of the change that is hoped for or imagined, our bodies have the same visceral, experiential response as if the change were already happening in the present. This might bring up a range of emotions. Clients may experience the tension between the pain of how it has been and the hope of what could be possible. Experiencing both at the same time leads to the need for a decision: Where do I want to focus my energy?

When working on transforming old patterns into new ways of experiencing oneself, it is important to remember the change-focused goals. We need to move beyond pure awareness and begin to facilitate new choices and decisions, find what could be different and then anchor the change: What WILL be different?

Case Study: **Laurie and Doug revisited**

Let's go back for a moment to Laurie towering on the chair above Doug, who is kneeling on the ground looking up at her. What happens next? At this point I invite them to move their bodies to positions they want to experience each other in. Without speaking a word, they immediately shift. Doug stands up and extends a hand to Laurie. She steps down from the chair and takes his hand. They stand facing each other, holding hands. Laurie lets out a sigh of relief and her shoulders relax. Doug looks directly into Laurie's eyes and his tears flow.

When I ask him later what he felt, he says he finally understands what was getting in the way of their connecting more intimately. In short, experiencing this "hoped for" change in the immediate present, in contrast to the pain of the old relationship pattern, has led them to a mutual decision to continue working on new ways of connecting to each other.

POSITIVELY DIRECTIONAL PROCESS

During sculpting, the therapist keeps the process moving in a positive direction towards healing by holding the knowledge that within each person lie the internal resources needed for healing and growth. This *knowing* is what strengthens the container that allows for the alchemy whereby each person connects with their own wisdom and hones their ability to make new and different choices that support them in relation to themselves, to others and to the world. Connecting with the "gems" beneath painful experiences and with coping mechanisms allows new energy to enter the system; all sorts of new possibilities arise, and these new possibilities are such a joy to "play" with in sculpting!

Case Study: **Ben**

Ben is very aware of the fear that is interfering with his life and his work. As we explore the fear, Ben names reluctance and worry as further obstacles to his stated goals of happiness, ease and feeling free. I am curious about what helps him get through these challenges, given that they seem scary for him. He says he connects with his courage, caring and determination. As we are processing this in the context of a group setting, I invite Ben to choose participants to represent Fear, Reluctance, Worry, Caring, Courage and Determination. Ben chooses six people to come up to the front to be enroled[10]. When the sculpting process begins, the parts dialogue and shift their postures and positions in response to what Ben is

---

10 *Enroling* (sometimes spelled as *enrolling*) involves guiding each participant to embody the role they have been assigned. For example, the person in the role of "Determination" is guided to go inside and say, "I am Determination," to see what that feels like, and then hold their body in a way that shows what they are feeling.

saying. As each part is addressed and explored through process questions and corresponding answers, we hear a uniform desire to support Ben and keep him safe; each part expresses its positive intention for his life. Further, the parts discover new ways of connecting to and supporting one another. These verbal and physical exchanges resonate for Ben. New awareness is born as he witnesses their interactions and new positions in relation to him and he is able to internalize and anchor within himself compassionate self-support. Suddenly he is in a new relationship with the fear and all of his resources.

Anchoring involves having Ben dialogue with each resource, reiterating what he has learned from each, stating how his relationship with each has shifted, then saying how he plans to integrate them moving forward. De-roling[11] each participant is the final part of the process. Ben has in a single sculpt recognized and internalized his resources (and reminded the participants that they, too, have a multitude of resources within themselves).

It would be a mistake to interpret "positively directional" as "stay away from the negative." To truly shift and let go of past painful experiences, it is necessary to encounter the pain. This does not mean retraumatizing our clients, but it does mean allowing painful emotions, old beliefs, expectations, and unmet yearnings to surface in order to process them and foster change. By sitting with our clients through their discomfort and keeping them grounded in the present (in the here-and-now) we help them to move in a positive direction. One participant from a program I taught summarized this beautifully: "When we strip away what's underneath the coping, we find the wisdom – the gift – and the gift is wrapped in pain sometimes."

---

11   *De-roling* (or *de-rolling*) is essential at the conclusion of a sculpt so each participant can shed the role ascribed to them but hold on to any learning and new awareness, and to remind them of who they are, with their own multitude of resources.

SYSTEMIC PROCESS

The use of sculpting is systemic, whether we are working with just one client or a whole family or group. The process is non-linear as every aspect of one's experience and every interaction is affected by everything else going on in that moment in time. If one person is down on one knee with one hand over their heart and the other hand reaching out towards another person (either in the room or imagined), we can explore the whole intra-psychic system (what is going on in their experience) and we can also explore what is happening to others or other parts of people either physically or imagined in the sculpt. For example, the person down on one knee reaching toward another might have feelings of sadness, hurt, resentment, frustration, and feel shame or anger about having these feelings, might have a small or weak self-image and see the other as strong or powerful and believe the world is unfair. They may expect to stand up or stay down, expecting the other person to see and understand them or think the other person expects them to serve them. Perhaps there are deep yearnings for connection, love and belonging. All of this can be accessed and experienced in the present moment when the person is connected to the energy aspect of the sculpt. We can ask questions such as, "How is this for you right now?" "What are you feeling?" "What are you hoping for at this moment?" Our internal experience is dynamic and ever-shifting; once one part starts to move there is a domino effect as other parts come into awareness and begin to shift. Only a systemic approach can address such an array of moving parts. The following case study illustrates how becoming more conscious of internal dynamics can start to shift relationship patterns.

Case Study: **Betty and Jill**

Betty says she has been exhausted for weeks, trying so hard to do whatever she can to ensure her partner is happy and getting everything she needs. She feels blamed by Jill when anything does not go according to plan and works extra hard to keep the peace in the relationship. In a sculpt, Betty is on her knee with one hand over her heart and the other hand reaching toward Jill. Jill is standing with one hand on her hip and the other pointing in an accusing way at Betty.

"Jill what's happening for you right now as you see Betty?"

"I'm irritated that she is down on the floor looking up at me instead of taking a more active role in making plans together."

Betty speaks up: "But I feel that's exactly what I HAVE been doing and nothing ever seems good enough for you."

"Jill, what are you doing with what you're hearing from Betty?"

Jill then shares her own disappointments and expectations. After some time processing what is underneath disappointment and expectation, each expresses a deep yearning for a more intimate connection with the other.

I invite Jill to notice any shifts in her energy and move her body in a way that fits for her.

"My arm wants to relax and I want to connect more with Betty."

"And Betty, what is happening for you right now?"

"I want to stand together with Jill, facing her, or maybe joining hands and facing our journey ahead together."

We play with various movements and postures, allowing for deeper realizations about themselves and each other.

The process questions are determined by what is happening internally for the therapist and the client(s) at a particular moment in time; the sequence will follow the energy, intuition and wisdom of what is arising from within the exchange between therapist and client(s).

While we are working with the intra-psychic system we are also working with what is going on with others in the sculpt. For example, after processing one person's experience we can check in with others; "Did you know that?" "How is that for you to hear?" "And what are you experiencing inside as you stand here?" We explore what is happening in external relationships while bringing into conscious awareness what is going on inside each participant. With greater awareness comes a greater range of choice. "What do you want to change within yourself?" "What do you want to change in the way you relate to others?"

Sculpting is not a static process. Initially, it might arise as just a picture, but as we process the experience of each person in the sculpt there is an interactive flow and exchange that shifts and changes. When looking at the flowing dynamics over time, we can identify many opportunities to pause and process. We need to explore the nuances of each person's internal process as we explore the interactive system. How does the dance unfold?

The next section of this chapter will elaborate on common patterns of survival coping. We will take a closer look at some of the dynamics that become visible and can be heightened and processed in therapy.

PATTERNS OF COPING AND THE STRESS RESPONSE

Life is not what it's supposed to be. It's what it is.
The way you cope with it is what makes the difference.

Virginia Satir

We have wonderful evolutionarily developed resources – physical, emotional and relational – that we utilize for survival. Satir observed four main patterns of coping that people adopt when experiencing stress. The stress response may or may not be related to an external situation, but is at essence a deep internal response to what is going on, whether imagined or real. To survive we need to protect ourselves when we are threatened, but some of the ways we have learned to do so are psychologically costly. Coping patterns arise from our early childhood experiences with our caregivers. Family-of-origin impacts influence how we learn to navigate stress in relationship. The way a parent (or caregiver) learned to cope with stress will impact the coping patterns learned by the child.

Satir sculpted postures to illustrate these patterns so that people could experience the familiar energy, discomfort and dynamics. It's important to note that there are many coping patterns, and many nuances within these patterns. I have found, over time, that Satir's four main patterns are wonderful starting places. Physical postures open the way for the therapist to ask questions of the client that directly access their internal experience of a specific pattern of coping: what has it been like for them and how has it protected them? Once the element of protection is brought into the light, we may explore the costs as well as the benefits of this method of protection. What follows is a brief description of the most common patterns of survival.

SURVIVAL COPING STANCES

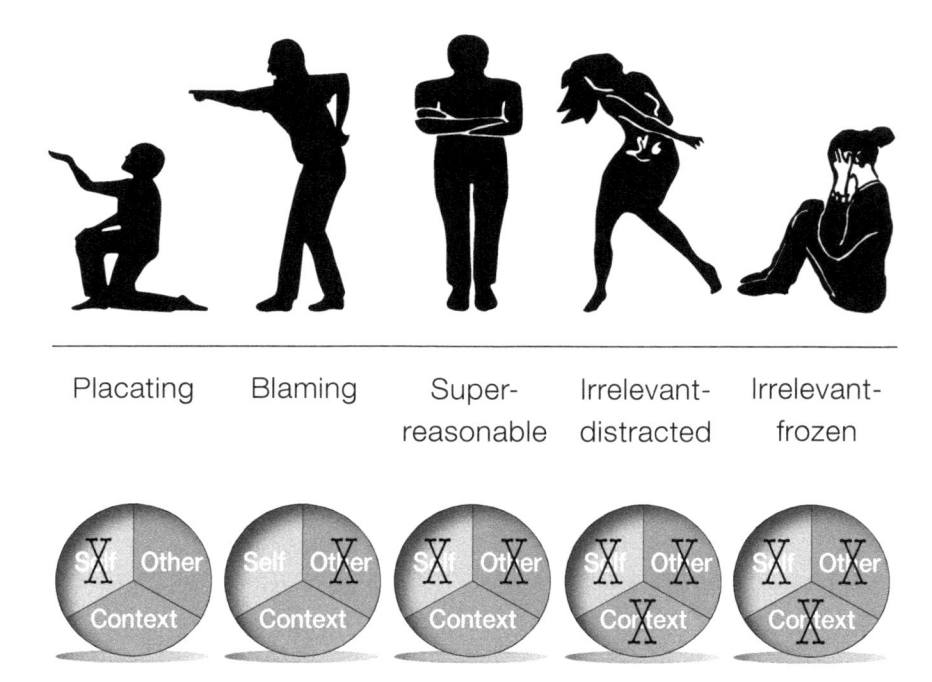

| Placating | Blaming | Super-reasonable | Irrelevant-distracted | Irrelevant-frozen |

© *Jennifer Nagel. Artwork created referencing images provided by the Hong Kong Satir Center for Human Development.*

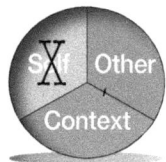

PLACATING

By placating, one puts others' needs and expectations ahead of one's own. Using this pattern of coping, we discount our needs and stifle our voice for the sake of pleasing others.

Lisa

Lisa complains of feeling exhausted and burned out. She is taking care of everyone at the office, looking after her children, driving them to their after-school activities and helping them with homework, while also being the friend that everyone calls when they have problems. She is so busy taking care of everyone else that she has no time to take care of herself.

The posture that Satir used to illustrate placating involves being down on one knee with one hand outstretched and reaching up towards another (real or visualized) person. The other hand protects the heart or is tucked in under the arm.

This posture will heighten the experience of feeling needy: that one needs others in order to survive. Staying in this position will create physical discomfort. One's knee might become sore and stiff, balance may be thrown off when leaning towards the other person, and the neck might get tense if one looks up for too long. Physical discomfort will open awareness into other feelings and perceptions, perhaps of hurt, anxiety, frustration, fear; feeling "less than," believing that others are more important, and that the world is unfair. We might hear from the person placating: "It's my fault," "I'll do anything for the sake of our relationship," "I'm sorry," and, "You're right."

BLAMING

In blaming, one is self-involved and aware of the context, but the other is discounted, along with their voice and needs.

Bill

Bill expresses his frustration with others in the family. They are not meeting his expectations. They don't behave the way he thinks they should behave. He literally points his finger at all the things they are doing wrong. His children do not listen to him. They do not do what he asks of them. His partner won't agree with his opinions. He feels anger, resentment and hurt. Bill knows that his way is the best way and others should respect him. He might see the world as unpredictable and out of order.

The blaming posture involves standing with one foot slightly in front of the other, one hand on hip, and the other arm stretched out, pointing a blaming finger towards the other. Staying in this position also creates physical discomfort. One's pointing arm will start to feel heavy and tired, and one's balance may be thrown off from leaning forward.

This posture demonstrates an experience of needing to show power to the other. While the stance might initially seem to express anger and control, holding it can lead to the client getting in touch with what is going on under the surface. Someone who is blaming might say, "It's all your fault," "I'm right," and, "You're wrong." Underneath all this is a yearning for connection, to be heard and understood, a need for emotional safety and validation. There is often a desire to be validated, as well as feelings of hurt, fear and loneliness.

SCULPTING: ACTIVATING THE BODY SO THE BODY CAN SPEAK ✸ 151

Asking questions of someone standing in a blaming posture allows them the opportunity to speak from a place of deeper awareness. They may be able to say how this stance impacts them personally and in relationship with others. Once the yearnings are recognized, the process can shift to exploring new ways of expressing these yearnings – to one's self and in relationship with others.

SUPER-REASONABLE

The super-reasonable pattern of coping is context-focused: while ignoring the relationship with self and others, one rationalizes problems by connecting facts and using logic. Feelings and experiences are discounted, only the "facts" count. Here is an example of the super-reasonable pattern of coping.

Claire

When asked how things are going, Claire states the facts of what is going on. She tells others in the room that she likes to view the situation in a somewhat detached manner. Focused on the details of time and place, she seems not connected with her own experience of what is happening. And, she says, she doesn't trust the experience of others.

The super-reasonable stance involves standing rigidly erect, feet close together, with arms crossed tightly over the chest, chin tucked in, and looking slightly up and over the head of the other. Holding this stance for any length of time will likely result in feeling off balance (feet so close together and standing so rigidly), and feeling physical tension through the whole body, together with a sense of being completely cut off from emotions.

This stance represents intellectual superiority, and an attitude of knowing better. Those who demonstrate this way of protecting themselves often come across as rigid in their beliefs; they are "right." Yet there is underlying insecurity and loneliness. When questioned, a person in this stance might answer with long, impersonal explanations such as, "Statistics show that..." and, "Let's be objective and analyze the problem."

Inviting them to notice what they are experiencing in their body will bring their attention to the tension and discomfort. From there we can explore what else is going on in their emotions, perceptions, beliefs, expectations and yearnings in relation to themselves and to others. It's important to stress that there is always an underlying need for safety and predictability within every sculpt.

IRRELEVANT

The irrelevant pattern of coping disconnects us from self, others and the context we are in. This way of coping under stress shows up in two very distinct ways, yet each reflects the same internal experience of disconnection.

IRRELEVANT-DISTRACTED

This version of the pattern shows up as constant movement; the person is utterly absent from any connection, with no focus on anything or anyone.

Matt

Matt has difficulty staying focused on anything and changes the subject or makes a joke when he is uncomfortable and stressed. He is in constant motion. Rather than stay on task, he keeps shifting to other tasks. He seems unrelated to what is going on in the moment. He says it is a huge challenge and scary for him to slow down. It's impossible in those moments to be present with his internal experience. He has to distract himself so he's not flooded with overwhelming emotions.

The Satir sculpt for this pattern involves constant movement. The distracted person is never still and remains disconnected from others in the room. They divert attention away from other dynamics among relationships in the sculpt by making large, exaggerated movements or quick shifts in direction.

IRRELEVANT-FROZEN

Someone involved in the frozen version of the irrelevant pattern of coping can present as almost catatonic.

Ann

Ann, triggered by a conflict going on around her, suddenly loses focus. Her eyes glaze over and she stares off into space. She says that when anything really stressful happens she either physically leaves the room and hides or remains frozen in place.

In the irrelevant-frozen stance one either stays still in a sculpt, not focusing on anyone or anything, or one hides under a chair; in either case the star separates entirely from the others in the process. The person in this posture is then asked to become aware of tuning out everything and everyone. "What is it like to be out of touch with what is going on in the room?" "What might lead you to this protective way of survival?" "How has escaping helped you to feel safe?"

When a client is using the irrelevant survival pattern, in either its active or passive form, the therapist needs to focus first on presence, grounding and safety. Before any exploration and processing can happen, the therapist needs to be present with the client, with their breathing and with their physical body here in the room. Once grounded in the present moment, we can look into past trauma without triggering the survival pattern.

SUMMARY OF SURVIVAL COPING PATTERNS

Coping patterns can come into play for a few seconds, a few minutes, or for longer lengths of time. Whether the pattern shows up as placating, blaming, super-reasonable, irrelevant, or some other combination, they are all behaviours refined by continuous use over a lifetime – or sometimes over lifetimes; they come into play each time the person is under stress. If not resolved through some kind of examination, through awareness and transformational shift, these patterns will be ongoing, and it may seem to ourselves or others that we live habitually at a level of coping. A person is not limited to a single coping strategy. Different coping patterns might be activated in different contexts and with different relationships. How one manages one's patterns of coping will depend on one's awareness as well as one's ability to self-regulate. Being conscious, aware and grounded are excellent ways of responding to stress – much better than reacting.

I want to make a distinction between experiencing these patterns as they arise when under stress and allowing them to play out in a safe container. When we are more accepting and open, our relationship with self and other can flourish in any context. When coping patterns surface under stress, it is important to remember that they are the tip of the iceberg, representing the visible manifestation of deeper forces, positive intentions for our survival. We must learn to use the resources and abilities within.

Coping exists on a continuum that ranges from automatic subconscious reactions (out of our awareness) to real or perceived stress, to a set of physical symptoms – real impacts on our physical and mental health. For example, placating can range from slightly giving in to others' needs while discounting one's own, to symptoms of depression or anxiety. Blaming can be an internal unspoken energy of frustration, anger and fault-finding, or, at the other end of the continuum, can present as violence, paranoia or antisocial traits. The super-reasonable pattern can make one an excellent physics teacher, but, at the far end of the spectrum, can lead to obsessiveness, compulsiveness and depression. The irrelevant pattern can make one the life of the party or a creative artist, while at the other end of the spectrum can lead to poor impulse control, depression, anxiety and lack of focus. Coping patterns do not indicate a personality "type," nor do they define a person. Coping is an entrenched pattern of behaviour for survival that tends to be used when there is real or perceived stress. By allowing coping patterns to automatically arise, one or more relationships is sacrificed: relationship with self, with other, or with context will be discounted – at some painful personal and interpersonal cost.

Whenever a person is somewhere along the continuum of whatever coping pattern, the hope of the Satir model of therapy is to move them towards more congruence, toward making more conscious choices (responding rather than reacting) while honouring self, other and context. When aware of being triggered into familiar patterns of coping, we can choose an alternative way of responding. For example, I can use caring creativity and problem-solving resources when feeling stress at a committee meeting, thereby remaining connected to self and others while staying grounded in the context. I can choose compassion when I want to support another person by remaining present to my own needs and checking in with myself. In other words, let us find and use all of the gems and deeper yearnings underlying our coping patterns; here are resources that can be accessed, and if used congruently can contribute to a world of deeper connections to Self, Other and Context.

What is so hopeful and positive about Satir's model is that these patterns point to what needs to be unearthed in order to experience wholeness. Helping our clients honour their internalized relationships is a key part of our work, the ultimate aim of which is greater congruence.

Helping clients sculpt these coping patterns brings the trapped dynamic energy right into the room and allows all involved the opportunity to work through old patterns of relating by processing the impacts and reclaiming the discounted parts of self, other, and/or context.

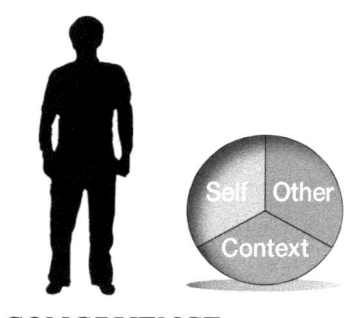

CONGRUENCE

Congruence actually is not another stance, but another choice of becoming more fully human, as well as a state of wholeness... a sense of being and becoming.[12]

While congruence is not a pattern of coping, it is possible to view it as the only alternative to subconscious, automatic, reactive patterns. Congruence is a more conscious meta-state of being. Satir said that we are all congruent at our essence. When congruent, we fully experience our life energy and are in harmony with all our parts. We are open, accepting, and connected in our relationships with others, and the world around us.

The sculpting posture for congruence involves standing comfortably,

---

12 Satir, *Satir Model*, 65.

feet slightly apart, in a balanced way, head centred, eyes gently open, neck soft, body relaxed, arms loose at the sides with palms open.

This posture conveys openness. The person is grounded in Self while relational and loving towards others. Validation comes from within. There is no looking to others for a sense of worth. When asked to report from this stance, the congruent person will say: "I feel accepted. I feel love and understanding. I accept and love myself in this moment, and I accept and love you just as you are in this moment."

Once again, I want to emphasize the importance of the therapist's congruent use of self. The therapist must be honest with their feelings, thoughts, expectations, and hopes as well as listen closely to clients in a respectful way. My aim is always to be fluid, creative, grounded, connected and intuitive in order to guide and facilitate transformational change.

CONCLUSION

In this chapter we have considered some forms of sculpting and seen how sculpts can activate the body to heighten awareness of stored energy patterns. We have delved into the essence of sculpting and found healing and transformation processes. We explored survival coping patterns human beings unconsciously access under stress and observed how sculpting these patterns can be useful to shift old ways of relating to one's self and to others. We have seen clients discover new possibilities.

The artistry and magic in sculpting emerges when the therapist supports each person in the room, whether they are part of the sculpt or holding space as witnesses. The therapist's intention is to support and facilitate, through techniques and sequencing, each person's movement towards congruence. That said, I believe the essential components for the process to be transformational are the congruent therapist and trust in the biggest possible picture of the overall process; allowing wisdom, creativity and intuition to weave and flow within, between and among all present in the room; allowing the dance to unfold in surprising and unexpected ways as people connect with these interweaving resources.

Finally, it is wisdom and intuition that magnifies the trust in the process and ultimately gives birth to the possibility of transformation.

I hope this chapter has conveyed my wonder and excitement; I am awed by sculpting. By tapping into the wisdom of the body and allowing the body to have a voice through deep exploration of postures and movements in a sculpt, I have found vibrant energy patterns and relationship dynamics in clients and participants. I have witnessed expanded awareness making way for new choices. I have experienced movement toward greater Wholeness on this human journey. Certainly, Virginia Satir's brilliance in pioneering this therapeutic process is a major contribution to the field of therapy.

REFERENCES

Banmen, John, ed. *Guided Meditations and Inspirations by Virginia Satir*. Langley: Satir Institute of the Pacific, (2020).

Banmen, John and Kathlyne Maki-Banmen. "Introduction." In *Applications of the Satir Growth Model*, edited by John Banmen, v-vi. US: Avanta, The Virginia Satir Network, 2006.

Levine, Peter. *Waking the Tiger: Healing Trauma*. Berkeley: North Atlantic Books, 1997.

Pert, Candace. *Molecules of Emotion: The Science behind Mind-Body Medicine*. New York: Simon & Schuster, 1999.

Porges, Stephen, and Deb Dana. *Clinical Applications of The Polyvagel Theory*, New York: W.W. Norton & Co, 2018.

Satir, Virginia., John Banmen, Jane Gerber, and Maria Gomori. *The Satir Model: Family Therapy and Beyond*. Palo Alto: Science and Behavior Books, Inc., 1991.

Satir, Virginia. *The New Peoplemaking*. Mountain View: Science and Behavior Books, Inc., 1988.

Satir, Virginia. "The Purpose of my Meditations." *In Guided Meditations and Inspirations by Virginia Satir*, edited by John Banmen, 1-3. Langley: Satir Institute of the Pacific, 2020.

Siegel, Daniel. *Pocket Guide to Interpersonal Neurobiology*. New York: W.W. Norton & Co., 2012.

Simon, Richard. "Reaching out to Life: The Legacy of Virginia Satir," *The Family Therapy Networker,* January/February, 1989.

VI

GUIDED MEDITATION IN THERAPY: SURFACING THE UNCONSCIOUS AND CONNECTING TO HIGHER CONSCIOUSNESSS

DR. CAROLYN NESBITT

Dr. Carolyn Nesbitt has been playing with, working with and exploring states of consciousness for over 45 years. She found Satir's model as she was completing her PhD in Psychology and felt an important synchronicity as she moved forward, working with trauma in various hospitals and private practice.

Carolyn is currently Co-Director of the Satir Center For Becoming More Fully Human at Akamai University (AU) and associate professor with the

AU College of Integrative Health. She is a senior faculty member for the Banmen Satir China Management Center and has taught in several countries around the globe. She has a continuing private practice with individuals and group retreats. Teaching and facilitating group retreats are her passions.

GUIDED MEDITATION IN THERAPY: SURFACING THE UNCONSCIOUS AND CONNECTING TO HIGHER CONSCIOUSNESS

MEDITATION INVITATION

Wherever you are reading this chapter, I invite you to put your feet flat on the floor, sit up a little straighter, lower your shoulders, connect into your belly… and breathe. Be aware of your breath.

I invite you to allow to come to mind your own experience of giving a meditation… receiving a meditation… experiencing a meditation. Allow yourself to pause from time to time in your reading while you bring awareness to the moment, then move on to the next paragraph.

What is it that you would really like to receive by reading this chapter?
- Possibly a confirmation of your current way of working with clients?
- Possibly an expansion, an addition to how you work?
- Possibly permission to try something different with your clients?

What is it you are yearning for in your practice? In your life?
Pause…. Breathe.

My focus for this chapter is to open the possibilities of how and why meditation might be integrated into the therapeutic process. We will look at the application of meditation in counselling therapy through the lens of life force energy. I will also give you a glimpse of Virginia Satir's thoughts about the world and our place in it through examination of her meditations. If you are a therapy supervisor or workshop facilitator, I invite you to use the sessions as a teaching tool.

In the Satir world, the personal and the professional are always linked. Spiritual questions and ideas about consciousness guide both my practice and my life. My beliefs about life energy, the body and connecting to higher consciousness seem to align with those of Satir.

Virginia Satir and Spirituality

Throughout her life's work, Satir's interest in the big picture of humanity shone. In her book, *The New Peoplemaking*, she said:

> My personal ideas and understanding of spirituality began with my own experience as a child, growing up on a dairy farm in Wisconsin [USA]. Everywhere I saw growing things. Very early, I understood that growth was life force revealing itself, a manifestation of spirit… it is the realization that we are spiritual beings in human form. This is the essence of spirituality. The challenge of becoming more fully human is to be open to and to contact that power we call by many names, God being one frequently used. I believe that successful living depends on our making and accepting a relationship to our life force.[1]

Here we see that Satir's early life experiences on the farm nurtured her spiritual growth. I imagine that she witnessed the birth, growth and death cycle repeating over and over. Satir believed, as I do, that we are divine essence in human form. We are powerful! Our thoughts create our reality. Our beliefs lead to our actions and our actions create our context.

MY BACKGROUND

I grew up in Toronto and had a stable life, until I didn't. My parents separated when I was fifteen and got back together a year later "for the sake of the children." What a huge sacrifice it was for my mother and father to give up their happiness for us! I was lucky to have good school friends and a tightly knit summer-time community at our cottage north of Toronto. My grandparents had a cabin next door, our neighbours were our friends, our friends were our neighbours. I have a love for the wilderness and feel at home by the water. At one point, I was a professional athlete, paid to waterski in Europe and Canada in shows at summer resorts and

---

1 Satir, *New Peoplemaking*, 334.

theme parks. Looking back, I think I joined so many activities (sports, music, theatre) to experiment with expressions of life-force energy.

WHY SATIR'S MODEL EXCITES ME

When I first found Satir, I had just finished my PhD in clinical psychology. At this point, I had attended university for sixteen years, although not continuously. I had been seeing clients for a decade and really loved this profession. I had also been exploring various avenues towards altered states of consciousness without the use of substances. As well, I had explored many religions and spiritual practices, curious as to their similarities and open to their differences.

I had my first out-of-body experience when I was seventeen, in a sweat lodge in the Colorado Rockies. I knew then that there is more to this world than this world. In my thirties, I trained in universal shamanic practices. A group of professionals (psychologists, counsellors, physicians and a bookkeeper) came together once every three weeks to explore non-ordinary reality through shamanic journeys. For nine years we experienced many dimensions and morphic fields, being accompanied and guided by non-ordinary beings, healing ourselves and others. These travels had a huge impact on me, and I continue to expand through spiritual teachings and practices. It seems that experiences fall into two categories: ordinary reality and non-ordinary reality.

Because I am particularly interested in living a high vibrational life, I have been exploring higher consciousness concepts and practices for decades and am currently writing a book about choosing to move from suffering to bliss, even while in the midst of difficult circumstances.

When I look back on my life, I know that I am exactly where I am, exactly who I am, because wonderful and devastating events have touched me. I have greater wisdom because I have been faced with difficult choices and made mistakes; I have greater compassion because I have suffered; I have greater courage because I have been terrified and survived; I have greater integrity because I have faced the consequences of lying and being lied to.

We create the world we are living in. If our thoughts are full of suffering, we create a personal world of suffering. If our thoughts are full of fear, we create a world that is scary. If we know that we are powerful co-creators, then we can create a world of love and abundance, no matter where we are or what is happening. I thoroughly enjoy working with clients who are open to the concept of their own divinity and who want to experience a connection with All That Is, the Universal Life Force.

In my three decades in the field of psychology, I have found that most therapeutic models focus on behaviours, emotions and thoughts. Satir's model also connects bodily sensations, existential yearnings and life energy. Satir therapists use the iceberg as a metaphor for the Self [see Leslie's chapter 1], with behaviours partially exposed above the waterline, while all else hides below: emotions, perceptions, expectations and beliefs, with cognitive aspects parsed into separate ideas that require different interventions.

As I continue to explore states of consciousness, meditation and models of therapy, Satir's approach to humans, our relationships to one another and Universal Life Energy continues to fit with my world view and view of life.

To paraphrase Satir, I want you to get excited about who you are, why you are here on the planet, and the possibilities for your life – to know that you can go far beyond where you are right now-- to see the pathway clearly, and to experience receiving love, giving love, and being wholly Love.

INVITATION TO READ MEDITATIONS TWICE

I have chosen lines and passages from specific meditations spoken by Satir that engage the use of bodily sensations and life energy in therapy. I invite you to read a meditation passage once for the experience, and a second time for information. See if you can read the meditation passages more slowly than the elaboration paragraphs, to hear Satir's voice in your mind, to experience and learn on a deeper level. It is my hope that you will come away from this chapter changed, that you will be facing the direction you most long for.

SATIR MEDITATION: *YOU AS ESSENTIAL ENERGY*

In the following guided meditation, Satir reveals some of her spiritual beliefs. Here it is in full so that you may get a sense of the depth of her desire for us to understand that we are in charge of our responses to life's experiences, and that each of us makes a difference to the energetic direction of life on the planet. All depends on what we choose.

Your Choice from Your Spirit

> Now let yourself be in touch with where you are in your chair, on the floor, in this room, at this time, in this building, in this town, in this state, or province, in this country, on the planet. Where you are at this moment in time can be precisely calculated – so many degrees latitude and so many degrees longitude. You are specifically here in the context of the world.
>
> Let yourself become aware that you are one part of the essential energy that moves this planet. You send out energy throughout the world to its furthest places. No one else can take your place. The world is made up of you with five billion others. And to the degree that you allow yourself to be balanced, to be congruent, you contribute to the forward movement of all life on this planet. To the degree that you try to keep yourself in status quo, you stop the movement. To the degree that you send out negative thoughts about yourself, you weaken the fabric of the planet and yourself. The wonderful thing is you can choose. Not your birth, not your money, not your position, nothing can justify not using your choices. Your choice is from the spirit.

With moving forward, we are in touch with life-process. Life moves, we move – not to move is to put up a strong artificial barrier. Life moves through pain and joy, through impediment, and freedom, through disappointment and through accomplishment. That's life, and as we meet life, what we put into the planet depends on how we choose. Perhaps many of us have felt that life defined us, but we choose. So here we are on a wonderful journey that we've all taken in different ways.

Now again, let us become aware of our breathing, and to recognize that our breath comes through effortlessly into the temple we call our body. We are in charge of the receptivity, the relaxation in our body. And to the degree that we allow, encourage, develop, and create our relaxation, our breath can do its work in all parts of ourselves in a better way. Breath fills our body because our body is receptive, and breathing, in our receptivity, in our relaxation, adds up to strength and creative power for us. At any moment in time, we can move from a state of feeling helpless to a state of feeling powerful, because we feel strong. In strength, we can be more creative about whatever crisis or tightness or jam we might be in, because we will be able to see the cracks and act on them. Our choices are from the spirit.

Now again, I'd like you to become aware of the miracle that we own, that is called our body that houses our mind and our spirit and our feelings. These are not separate; they work together, so we are the outcome, at any moment in time, of the interaction between our thoughts, our feelings, and our body and our relationship to the life-force whom we can call God, or whatever other name we want. And it's in the inter-relationship of all of these, freely accepted and freely used, that lays our vitality, our manifestation of life. All the care we give to our thought and feelings and our body and our relationship to life-force will increase our vitality.

Can you now go deep inside and see what it feels like to say, "I love you" to yourself – "I value you. I recognize you as a work of art, as a manifestation of life. Sometimes I feel a sense of awesomeness as I realize I am in charge of helping to make the conditions in which you, my body, my mind, my heart and my relationship to life can manifest."

Now gradually bring yourself back to your room, to this day, this time and when you feel fully back, let your beautiful eyes open, and as they open if any sounds or movements want to come out, just let it happen.[2]

DIVINING SATIR'S BELIEFS FROM "YOUR CHOICE FROM YOUR SPIRIT"

Now let yourself be in touch with where you are in your chair… on the planet. In the first sentence, Satir takes us from the context of sitting in a chair to being on a planet. She broadens our perspective. And seeing ourselves in relation to the planet does not make us small, rather the opposite: in the second paragraph, she emphasizes the significance of each person: *You are one part of the essential energy that moves this planet. You send out energy throughout the world to its furthest places.*

Let's stop and think about that. Satir believed that we send out energy – and not just local energy where we can clear a room if we enter it in a bad mood – *…throughout the world to its furthest places.* That's big. Limitless.

Satir teaches us that we have a responsibility to the Universe to be congruent. *And to the degree that you allow yourself to be balanced, to be congruent, you contribute to the forward movement of all life on this planet.* Our individual choices impact every living thing. She warns us that if we continue to think negatively about ourselves and others, *you weaken the fabric of the planet… nothing can justify not using your choices.*

---

2 Satir, "Your Choice," 46-47.

Now THAT calls forth accountability.

At any moment in time, we can move from a state of feeling helpless to a state of feeling powerful. It is that simple. Not necessarily easy, but simple.

APPLICATION OF GUIDED MEDITATION TO THERAPY

With every workshop I run, every online call, every session with a client, I begin with grounding and centering both myself and the client. When I do a simple grounding and centering guided meditation, the client settles, the workshop participants become quiet and go inwards, and I open to my deeper self. The ongoing list of to-do items, pressure to perform, and responsibilities for others fades away. I ground myself as my clients ground. I settle into my body as I encourage them to settle into their bodies. We focus on breath, bringing us to our centers. I sense a channelling of energy. I connect to my resources. My body opens the channels for my Life Energy to flow. I become less of a busy do-er, more of my Self. I am safe; I am loving; I am fully present. Now, I am holding Sacred Space.

Now, we can begin the session.

Now, half the work is done.

WHAT IS MEDITATION?

Meditation is the act of being present that takes one into a slow synchronous brain-wave state. It may be the act of calming one's thoughts, of blanking out one's thoughts, or peacefully considering new thoughts. Some people consider meditation to be solely the act of having no thoughts. They might describe Satir's style of guided visualization as someone giving directions to focus on a particular image or question. I have always found it easier to come to stillness by focusing on breath, a question or an image, than attempting directly to blank out thoughts.

In essence, meditation is progressive quieting of the mind until it reaches its source: pure consciousness. We get there through active deep listening. Listening to the stillness. Listening for the answers to your questions. Listening, not to the ramblings of the hyper-speed asynchronous brain-waves monkey mind; rather, listening to the stillness of the present moment. If we listen long enough, we tap into the fields where we are connected to All That Is. Then we hear what we most need to hear. And in the act of listening, we become still.

WHY DO I USE MEDITATION?

Meditation is an integral piece of tapping into the less conscious, the subconscious and the unconscious. Meditation accesses an altered state of consciousness. For that reason, I love it! And I love to use it in my therapy practice.

Einstein said that we cannot solve a problem in the same state of consciousness in which we created it. When I go into an altered state of consciousness, answers to life's challenges seem to appear. I usually gain a new perspective. I often see life from an eagle's vantage point, from very high, with a very broad scope. The troublesome issue often shifts into a tiny detail that is minuscule in the grand adventure of life. I also see ahead in time and know that this overwhelming issue will be in the distant past when I am in the far future. Trouble becomes less overwhelming.

I want this for my clients. My belief is that my clients can solve their own problems; I am not there to solve their problems for them. Therefore, one of the best gifts I can give is to help them enter a different state of awareness.

I believe that the goals of meditation are to get in touch with the true Self, to get in touch with the Source of all existence, and to get in touch with the highest emotions of gratitude, bliss, peace, joy, love and compassion. I am smiling as I write these words, as they seem to represent such lofty ideas, impossibly large tasks. Yet they are tasks possible to fulfill. I can never predict which I might get in touch with when I practise, but I do know that something will happen. And that the more often I meditate, the more deeply and more quickly I will drop into peace, joy and compassion.

I use meditation for many different reasons. I meditate to bring my life energy up to a higher vibration. I meditate to contemplate alternative ideas to beliefs that I already hold. I meditate to bring myself to stillness. I meditate for my Self to connect with All That Is. I meditate to expand my consciousness. I meditate to enjoy wild experiences that many people only access through substance use.

HOW DOES MEDITATION CONTRIBUTE TO THE THERAPEUTIC PROCESS?

Meditation takes people inside quickly. If people are in their heads and telling stories, they are talking about what happened *to* them rather than relating to the impact an event has had on them inside. Meditation helps get them away from stories and go inside. They might have told the same story over and over; meditation can bring them into the present moment, aware of what is happening to their body right now. It helps them clear their mind and really focus on the essential elements of what they want to say. Instead of taking fifteen or twenty minutes to verbally process one perspective of an argument that the client has had at home, we can take a few minutes to go inside, connect with the body, connect with the emotions and find the essential core of why the incident is so upsetting to the client.

Using metaphor in meditation taps into the unconscious and subconscious parts of our self. We want to make changes on a deep level, and we want to bring unconscious and subconscious material to the conscious level. Meditation, then, becomes a practical anchoring tool for changes that we can remember in our conscious daily life. We take charge of our life. We bring mindfulness right into the behavioural level of the iceberg, into daily action.

SATIR'S OPENING MEDITATION THAT INCLUDES ENERGIES

Let's examine another of Satir's opening meditations. You will hear her refer to three distinct energies – groundedness, creativity and connection – that I invite you to be aware of when she calls on the listener to connect with the body.

> Now let us again become in touch with the centre of the Earth, which is always there, and remains only for us to become aware that it is there for us.... Energy that moves upward through our feet and legs and into our torso... bringing with it the ability to be grounded, to be realistic, to be practical... and to be in touch with the energy from the heavens, which brings us our ability to be sensitive, intuitive, imaginative, creative.... And these energies of creativity and intuition... meeting the energy of groundedness... creating still a third energy: the energy to be connected to our fellow human beings.[3]

As we experience in this meditation, Satir invites us to use our imagination, without giving explicit direction. Of course, we are not physically touching the center of the Earth, but, with her invitation to *be in touch with the center of the Earth,* we easily imagine that solid, ever-present aspect of life. It is reassuring. And a calming begins. She pulls in the concept that the Earth *is there for us.* The listener experiences that he or she is not alone.

The centre of the Earth is large, larger and older perhaps than we can conceive of. The Earth is solid, ever-present, everywhere we are. Although Satir does not use the word, such language is evocative of the concept behind the word God: larger and older than we can conceive of, ever-present, everywhere. Satir often used the words Universal Life

---

3   Satir, "Our Resources", 51.

Energy. Here, she simply states that the Earth *is there for us*; this is almost "the Universe has your back." I interpret this as not only are we not alone, but there is also an inherent Goodness that cares about us.

Next, she moves on to engaging the body through awareness. It could be that we *imagine* that energy is moving *upward through our feet and legs and into our torso,* or it could be that we become aware that it actually *is* moving in that direction. Either way, it takes us to a clear experience of connecting our bodies with energy from the Earth. This gives us the experience that the inside of our body and the outside of the Earth are not actually inside and outside. The boundary is loosened and permeable.

Then we move to *the energy from the heavens.* For me, this beautiful phrase conjures up stars and galaxies, swirling spots of light in infinite space, and I experience *sensitive, intuitive, imaginative, creative* energies pouring through me, inside my blood, to meet the grounded energies at my heart centre, then together flowing out of my heart as love towards a person of my choosing, or towards the Earth in general. You can see with eyes closed, the Earth, the heavens and the body – that there is a connection between the personal and the cosmic. Eyes closed takes me into a state of consciousness beyond body boundaries. Personal problems diminish in size next to the limitless possibilities of the infinite.

This meditation has been the template for my own opening meditation for clients as we begin each therapy session.

WHY MEDITATION AT THE BEGINNING OF SESSION

Meditation at the beginning of a therapy session helps the client separate from their rush to get to the session, their concern about their children, their to-do lists, etcetera. Meditation lets them leave all of that outside the door.

Meditation between one session and the next helps me disperse any residue from the last client and clear my head for the next. In a clear space, I am able to connect energetically with the new client in front of me. I can attune to her facial expressions, her body energy, and create a sacred holding space for us to do our work together.

When I lead a client through a meditation, I am saying the words for the client, and at the same time, I am following my own instructions. As I ask the client to feel his sit-bones in the chair and feel his feet flat on the floor, I am doing the same thing. When I ask my client to focus on her breath and come to the present moment, I am doing the same thing. And when I ask my client to focus on what they would really like out of this session, I am helping them set a positive direction for where we will go in the next hour. I am opening to the client's agenda.

By connecting myself, the client and the Cosmos, I am also opening to the highest possibilities and opportunities for the client's healing.

When I introduce meditation into a therapeutic session, I give the client the choice to open their eyes and soften their gaze or to close their eyes to feel safe. Closing their eyes can help clients access what is deep inside without visual distractions, without having to pay attention and possibly unconsciously scan my face for signs of acceptance or rejection. Like Satir, I use phrases such as "invite" or "allow yourself" or "if you choose, can you give yourself permission to...." This leaves the client in the driver's seat. Choice increases their sense of safety. Then, with our feet flat on the floor, feeling our bodies fully supported in the chair, our arms supported by the chair arms, we continue, metaphorically aware of being supported in the present moment. My eyes are open. I am sensing my body inside and grounding myself. I am slowing my breathing down. Mirror neurons help regulate the client's emotions, breathing and heart rate. At the same time, I am observing my client very closely. I am watching for shifts in a breathing pattern, relaxation or tightening of facial muscles, tensing of the body and shoulders or letting go and releasing.

Case study: **Michelle**
Accessing Life Energy and the Body in Therapy

Michelle is a thirty-year-old house cleaner who has been through many wounding events in her childhood. She is also a yoga instructor and used to breath work and tuning in to her body. She has come to me for help with changing her relationship to herself and to her partner so that she will not repeat her own or her parents' unfruitful patterns. We have been working together for a while and have an easy way of being together.

"It's so good to see you today!" I say. I feel an outpouring of love for her, and I am sure it is shining through my eyes and smile.

"You too! I was really looking forward to today's session. Lots is going on and I really need this time with you. I am so scattered and upset. I can't think straight."

"Okay then, let's get right into it." I shift and adjust my sitting position, as does she. "Breathing out…" I exhale fully. "Allowing your beautiful eyes to gently close as I close mine…" I continue to breathe in and out, exhaling loudly enough so that she can hear me. "Tuning in to your breath…." I allow my own breath to become quiet. "I invite you to feel your feet flat on the floor, pushing down with your toes and then your heels… feel the connection between your feet and the floor… imagining roots going down into the earth, cool beautiful earth, through the aquifers, the pure water as you cleanse yourself…. Breathe… it washes over you and through you… going down further and further into the warm core of the centre of the Earth and bringing that beautiful clean pure energy back up with you… up through the floor… through your feet into your body…. Bring your awareness up through your calves, your knees, your sit bones…. Feeling yourself held and supported by the chair… and breathe… drawing your attention further up your chest to your lungs, allowing that beautiful clean air to fill your body, dropping your shoulders even further… and breathe… taking your attention down your arms and relaxing your hands, allowing them to really relax, whether they are palms up or whether they are palms down…." I open my eyes, and see that she adjusts her hands, trying it out, settling on a position. "And sending your hands some gratitude. They do so much for you…..

"Bringing your awareness to your shoulders and dropping them even further…." I close my eyes again and drop my shoulders. "Breathe…." I tune in to what still needs to happen in my own body to really relax, and my next words reflect this. "Allowing your eye muscles to relax and your cheeks to melt down.... Allowing your jaw to go slack... and exhale... relaxing your face even more.... Bringing your attention to the top of your head, and out beyond the sky, beyond the sun, out to the cosmos... inviting beautiful light to pour over you and through you and around you, bringing with it creative intelligence, flowing through you and all around you... and the creative intelligence meets the grounded practical energy, mingling in your heart center—" I put my hand on my heart "—where a third energy of love and connectedness beams out to someone who needs it.... Beam that person *love*... and I invite you to add in yourself, at whatever age comes up for you, it could be today, it could be a younger you... so that You are beaming out love to your self....

"In the interest of the highest and best for all concerned, allow to come to mind what it is that you most want to work on today. What is it you most want to work on right now? When you have your answer, open your beautiful eyes and come back to the room to let me know."

Michelle opens her eyes. She takes her time to answer. I wait in silence. She smiles at me. "I feel different than when I sat down." Her eyes are looking up and around. "I feel a bit spacey... and yet really in touch with my body. My body is finally relaxing. It's been a whirlwind week. Now it's as if I see a path cutting through the fog, light all around. The fog is blowing away."

"Anything else?"

"I am ready to tackle this, to face it."

"And by 'it,' you mean...? What's the focus of our work today?"

"Daniel is leaving, and I have to decide what I am going to do. Do I go with him, or do I stay?"

Let's pause here and see what has transpired so far. The meditation was just over four minutes. What has happened?

UNPACKING THE OPENING

Notice that I began the meditation within the first minute. I do that for several reasons. The main reason is that I want to attune with my client as quickly as possible. Also, I want her to come to her centre. We get far more done in a session if my client is in a state where reflection is possible. Clients often come in quite distressed, as they are thinking about their problems and pain, or the traffic to get to my office, or a myriad of other stressful possibilities. Their autonomic nervous systems are possibly on high alert. Breathing in and out at a slow purposeful pace helps people to calm down. They experience a sense of safety in their body and in my office, even though we are shortly going to talk about challenging issues. I also want to make sure that my actual state of being is centered and grounded, flowing with creative, intelligent, loving energy. I do not want to simply be in a state of being where the words come from my left hemisphere, where I am disconnected from my emotions, sensations and spiritual self; rather I want my words to come from knowingness, my whole self, body and energetic field.

Allowing your beautiful eyes to gently close as I close mine.... As Satir did, I use the language of permission, *allowing*. The nurturing words *beautiful* and *gently* may invoke a feeling of warmth, acceptance and honouring. I once worked with a translator who did not approve of my style. In one of my workshops, she translated the above as "Close eyes." A bilingual participant alerted me to the discrepancy, as he had experienced a big difference between my intention and what was being said and felt that the workshop was being sabotaged. The words we choose do make a difference. Of course, the tone of voice, the pacing and the intention behind our words make a tremendous difference as well.

I close my own eyes for a few reasons. At the beginning, I do not want the client to feel that they are being watched with their eyes closed. Closing my eyes creates a sense of safety for them. As well, I go quickly into my own deep inner connection. Because I have a meditation practice where I close my eyes and tune in to my breathing, I immediately drop into a peaceful alert place. It is practised and therefore natural to do so. I might then open my eyes to observe my client, particularly if they are new. If they are not new, I might keep my eyes closed.

Tuning in to your breath.... Many meditation practices across many cultures focus on the breath. The English word "spirit" comes from the Latin word *spiritus,* which means "breath." When we tune into our breath, we become conscious of our body sensations. And we may become conscious of our core Life Energy, or spirit, linked with our breath. A goal with this therapeutic meditation is to have my conscious thoughts (mind), sensations (body), emotions (heart) and Life Energy (soul or spirit) linked with the client's thoughts, sensations, emotions and Life Energy, and both of us conscious of our links with Universal Life Energy. The link is always there. The practice is about becoming conscious of it. That, indeed, is a step further than being linked. We become aware that our Life Energy is part of the whole of Universal Life Energy. And a step further than awareness is the experience of the whole. Even if the client is not aware of *spiritus,* the link between breath and spirit, I am. And I experience us as being part of a greater whole, and that is the holding space, the container that is created, for both of us entering a session of therapeutic change.

Next, I use language that creates awareness of body sensation. *Feel your feet flat on the floor, pushing down with your toes and then your heels....* At this point, the to-do list is being left behind. The mind has other thoughts to occupy it. A step-by-step connection is created with what is occurring in the present moment.

Now I slip into language that creates links between our imaginations and our interior worlds: *...feel the connection between your feet and the floor....* And I expand the imagery: *...imagining roots going down into the Earth.... Breathe... it washes over you and through you.* I think of being clean, no guilt, no shame, no anger, our pure Self, as we came into this world. Anything that does not support this purity is washed away. For me, this is the vantage point from which to view our troubles. When we are washed clean in our imaginations, we are on a higher vibrational plane of existence. If my client can experience herself as clear of guilt, shame and anger, or of whatever else she feels sullied by, we are off to a good start.

My language expands into active imagery. ...*Going down further and further into the warm core of the centre of the Earth and bringing that beautiful clean pure energy back up with you... up through the floor... through your feet into your body.... Bring your awareness up through your calves, your knees, your sit bones...* When I say this, I feel sensations coming up through my own body. I am connecting the energy with body awareness. We are lifting our imaginations to fill with something greater than our body selves.

... drawing your attention further up your chest to your lungs, allowing that beautiful clean air to fill your body, dropping your shoulders even further... and breathe... taking your attention down your arms... relaxing your hands, allowing them to really relax, whether they are palms up or whether they are palms down... I add in choices in my meditations, so that the person feels somewhat in control of their experience. *...And sending your hands some gratitude. They do so much for you....* This is a suggestion to invite in a higher vibratory level of emotional experience, such as gratitude. Because Michelle cleans houses, I believe that my recognition of her hands will help her feel seen. Personalizing each meditation for the individual facilitates their yearnings being met, which allows them to access their resources, and opens the energetic flow necessary to feel confident, competent and congruent.

Bringing your awareness to your shoulders and dropping them even further.... Breathe.... Allowing your eye muscles to relax and your cheeks to melt down... your jaw to go slack... and exhale... relaxing your face even more.... In this section, I am not only connecting her awareness to her relaxing body, I am intentionally relaxing myself, and attuning our relaxation to each other.

Bringing your attention to the top of your head, and out beyond the sky, beyond the sun, out to the Cosmos.... In one sentence, I go from our interior world to our connection with the infinite. I use the top of the head to invoke a sense of a portal, a gateway to connect the interior with All That Is. For those clients who have used the words God or Creator or another powerful term, I will use their language. Otherwise, I find that the term Cosmos flows easily off my tongue and transports me to what is large and powerful.

...inviting beautiful light to pour over you and through you and around you, bringing with it creative intelligence, flowing through you and all around you.... This strong visual image brings awareness of both of our resources of intelligent creativity. I begin to feel that I am filled with light as I connect with my client, and that I have the capacity to work with whatever she brings to the session. When I experience the light, I feel alert, peaceful, grateful, eager and happy. I am vibrant.

...and the creative intelligence meets the grounded practical energy, mingling in your heart center, where a third energy of love and connectedness beams out to someone who needs it.... If practical groundedness is metaphorically the solid body, and creative intelligence is the mind, we want to bring in the energy of love and connection, which is the heart. I put my hand on my heart because it connects me right to it. People who follow HeartMath like to touch their heart to make a physical connection with the heart, experiencing through the lens of love, rather than through an emotionally disconnected thought process. Sometimes I have the client simply experience love streaming out, like a beam of light. Often, I suggest beaming the light to someone who needs it. It seems to give beginners a concrete experience when they direct love towards a particular being; they have more success grasping the concept of love travelling along a light beam.

Beam that person love... and I invite you to add in yourself, at whatever age comes up for you... it could be today, it could be a younger you.... I want Michelle to love herself, to include herself as someone who deserves love. It seems easier for many to direct love first towards someone else, or a cat or dog, and then afterwards direct love to themselves. I am also curious what age comes up in the client's image of herself, as that will likely have some bearing on the issue in the session.

...so that You are beaming out love to your self.... Notice that the first You is capitalized. I am speaking to the Self, the core, the spirit, the essence, the personal life energy. Of course, the client cannot hear my capitalization of the letter Y; however, I know to Whom I am referring.

…In the interest of the highest and best for all concerned.... The highest and best for all concerned includes the highest and best for my client. We are all One. I am not at peace if you are not at peace. At a Life Energy level, we are all in the big soup of Universal Life Energy. I know that what is highest and best for my client is also highest and best for all those whose lives she touches.

...allow to come to mind what it is that you most want to work on today. What is it you most want to work on right now? When you have your answer, open your beautiful eyes and come back to the room to let me know. I end each meditation with a request for the client to commit to a focus for change within our session. Then I wait. I say nothing. If the person does not respond, I ask, "What is it we are working on today?" Or I might say, "How was that for you?" Then I ask her again to tell me what we are focusing on today.

We are not here to chat. We are not here for her to tell me terrible stories of her awful life and the horrible people in it that refuse to change. Neither are we here for my agenda. We are here to do her personal growth work. She is in charge of *what* we work on. I am in charge of *how* we do that. When asked this question, each client soon realizes that they must reflect and pinpoint what needs examining. If they do not answer, I make the request again and sit in silence until they choose a focus.

We are now deep into therapy. I am fully connected to myself, my client and Universal Life Energy. I have thoroughly let go of thoughts of my previous client and their issues. I am connected with my current client. My client is centered and grounded. She feels supported and capable. She is more relaxed than when she arrived. She is in touch with creative, intelligent energy, with gratitude and with love. She is focused on what it is she most wants to change. She is "ready to tackle this, to face it."

All of that happened in four minutes.

HIGHLIGHTING BODY AND ENERGY ASPECTS

Let's continue the session. I encourage you to notice how both energy and body are incorporated into therapy.

"It seems that you both have choices about staying together or not, and choices about where you will live...."

"He is leaving to do what he wants," Michelle says, "regardless of what I decide to do."

"Close your eyes again if you'd like to...." Michelle closes her eyes. I keep my eyes open and watch her minute facial movements. "...And breathe out...." We both exhale. "What's happening in your body now?"

"I feel something in my stomach."

"Let's go there. Put your hand on your stomach, there where you feel it." I also put my hand on my stomach. "What's the emotion that's coming up?"

Pause.

"It's sadness, big sadness."

"Put your other hand on your heart...." I also put my other hand on my heart. We are mirror images of each other. "Hold that for a bit.... Stay with it...."

Tears are leaking out of Michelle's eyes.

"What's happening for you now?" I ask.

"Huge waves of sadness...." Tears are streaming down her face. Her eyes are still shut. "I'm just so sad...."

A pause with silence while Michelle cries. Her face begins to contort, her mouth grimacing, tilting up, eyes still closed. She is trying to swallow.

I say quietly, "Move the hand on your heart up to your throat." Michelle moves her hand, as do I. "What message do the tears bring? Just sit with it and ask... the answer will come.... Now move the hand on your belly to your lower *dantian*, a few inches below your belly-button. Allow the energy to move between your hands, allowing your throat to voice the Truth."

Michelle moves her other hand. I again mirror her. Her eyes are closed and mine open. I wait. Michelle's eyes pop open. "It's not what I thought! I thought I was sad because we were either breaking up or I had to give up the life that I have created here, my friends, my job. It's not that at all." She puts her hands down. I do the same. "The sadness is that he doesn't see me, he doesn't love me the way I love him. He doesn't value me. He is going whether I stay or go, whether we stay together or break up."

"Breathe into that. Big breath in... and exhale." I do the same.

Michelle closes her eyes on her own.

"What's happening for you now?"

"Oh, I feel it in my shoulders... things are changing... it's anger."

"Tell me about that. Describe it."

With eyes still closed, she says, "Oh, it's big. Wow, that's new. Yes, it's really big. I feel it all down my arms and in my hands.... Yep, that's anger."

"Stay with it... what were you expecting with Daniel that didn't happen?"

"I was expecting him to at least talk to me first. He made his decision without taking me into account. As if it wouldn't impact me." She opens her eyes. "He actually didn't *ask* me to go with him to Europe. So we are breaking up, and he expects me to be happy for him, which is ridiculous. I've been feeling guilty because he thinks I should be happy for him, and I am happy that he got the job he wanted, but I'm *not* happy that it means we are splitting. He didn't even ask what was going on for me."

"I'm wondering if there might be a lot of assumptions underlying what you're telling me. They may or may not be true. Let's slow down and look at the meaning you're making right now.... What meanings are you making about him? About you? About your relationship?"

Michelle pauses, eyes closed, and checks in with herself.

"He doesn't care about me. I wasn't significant enough to include in the decision."

"What's the belief about yourself?"

"I'm insignificant. I don't matter."

"Where is that in your body?"

"Here...." She points to her solar plexus.

"Let's go there. Put your hand there." I do the same. "Breathe out.... Focus. What's the emotion that is coming up?"

There is a long pause. I wait as Michelle focuses. She says quietly, "It's moved to my stomach. I feel sick to my stomach."

"Move your hand where you feel it." I do the same. "What's the emotion now?"

"It's shame. I feel so much shame. I feel really little. And scared. Now I feel scared.... They're connected. Shame and fear."

"Focus on that.... When else have you felt this? How old do you feel?"

"Oh, I feel really young. Maybe six? I remember sitting in the back seat of the car, not knowing where we were going, Mom and Dad yelling at each other. I'm trying to hide, but I can't. I'm trying to curl up and be small."

"Can you fold your arms across your chest? And now pat on your arms, right, left, right, left, right, left.... That's it... keep going...." I am patting on my arms too. "Okay, now pause and wipe down your arms from shoulder to wrist. Wipe off anything you no longer need.... Kindly and firmly, not harshly, just kindly...." I wipe my arms off as well. "What's happening now?"

"I'm remembering when Dad moved out. I couldn't stop him. I was totally powerless. I just watched him leave. One day he was there, and then he was gone. I thought it was because.... I thought if I had tried harder to be good, Dad would have stayed. If I had been more interesting, more fun, maybe he would have stayed. I wasn't... I wasn't enough."

UNPACKING MICHELLE'S SESSION

Body awareness

In this short excerpt, I bring attention to the body fifteen times by referencing hands, lower *dantian*, wrists, heart, throat, arms, shoulders, eyes and belly button, as well as tears and breath. While constantly aware of parts of the body and the whole body, I ask questions to bring attention to feelings, emotions, meaning-making, beliefs and assumptions.

Life energy

When Michelle pays attention to her shifting sensations, she is tracking the movement of energy through her body. I observe and track both of us, constantly aware of this changing energy. I know when there is a block and when there is an opening. You might call it intuition.

Surfacing subconscious yearnings

It's not what I thought!... It's not that at all... he doesn't see me, he doesn't love me.... He doesn't value me.

Here, given time and silence, with her eyes closed, connected to her body, Michelle does her own work. She articulates her subconscious yearnings to be seen, to be loved and to be valued. Now we can go to the source of those unfulfilled yearnings.

Surfacing the unconscious

Notice that Michelle, in a very short time, has been able to access her childhood wounds. She is deep enough in her internal experience that with a few directed questions, such as "When else have you felt this?" and "How old do you feel?", an originating incident surfaces. "I'm remembering when Dad moved out. I couldn't stop him. I was totally powerless." And then she speaks her long-held belief: "I'm insignificant. I don't matter." This is the lens through which she has seen all her relationships. We are there.

WHY MIGHT I USE MEDITATION IN THE MIDDLE OF SESSION?

In the middle of the session, I might guide another meditation, just a couple of minutes long. Using meditation in the middle of a session does not mean interrupting the session. If the client is chatting away, and having difficulty focusing on what it is she wants to change, I might take charge and have her close her eyes. Then I might start a very focused, intentional visualization in order to slow down and deepen the session. If she is having trouble identifying what she is feeling, or if she says she is not feeling much of anything, I might ask her to close her eyes and feel what is happening inside her body. Then I would have her focus on that part of the body to see what emotion is associated with that feeling tone, what comes up for her then. Say her belly feels tight, I might have her put a hand on that tight part and ask, "What is this block about? What is coming up for you?" We will follow what is happening for her in her body, moment to moment. The modality Somatic Experiencing uses some of these techniques.

In most sessions, at one point, I have my client touch their heart. I touch my own heart as they do. When clients are really connected to their resources, there is a clear flow of energy between their hand on their belly and their hand on their heart. You will find similar exercises in HeartMath.

A clear flow of energy can expand beyond the belly, can drop lower, and beyond the heart can rise higher, in a linear fashion. As I do my work, the energy meridians that run through the body have fewer and fewer blockages. When someone is acutely tuned into their energy, we are doing therapy at a deep level. The client will more easily be able to incorporate such work into the rest of her life, to see connections without judgement, to make decisions that are aligned with her values. Energy work always involves chakras and energy meridians. During a session I don't need to name the chakra. I don't need to say, "throat chakra" (although as chakra work gets more and more mainstream through the practice of yoga, it's not uncommon for me to name the chakra with clients who are into yoga, such as Michelle who is a yoga instructor); rather, I use my knowledge of chakras and meridians to inform myself about what's happening for my client regarding energy flow and blockages.

When we come to a place, as we have here, where an incident is found to be traumatic, and the memory comes up as an image or sound, I often see micro-shifts in the facial muscles or eyes or hear shifts in breathing. At this point, I often use bilateral hemispheric stimulation, such as EMDR [Eye Movement Desensitization and Reprocessing] or patting kindly and firmly on both biceps. This type of body stimulation engages both right and left hemispheres. It also slows down the pace of therapy. Because my session with Michelle was over the internet, I asked her to use double-arm patting (arms folded in a self-hug). We had used this multiple times in the past, and so I did not have to introduce it. I also use this technique with in-person clients who like to close their eyes when we do inner body work. It seems to have a soothing effect on them. Michelle would often continue hugging herself afterwards.

MID-SESSION MEDITATION TO TARGET AN ISSUE

Later in the session, after working on the current impact of the wounds from Michelle's parents' divorce, I offer a short meditation.

"Are you willing to try something that might help get past that block?"

"Of course!"

"Okay, I invite you to close your beautiful eyes again... and breathe out.... This time, allow your hands to move, one onto your lower *dantian*, just below your belly, and one onto your heart, feeling the energy flow between them... and breathe.... Now move one hand up to your throat, sending your throat some love... sending your throat compassion for all those times you wanted to speak but couldn't... sending your throat gratitude for keeping you safe at those times... and now, sending your throat strength to speak your truth, as much as you choose.... If your throat were to allow the truth to come out, what would you say?"

Michelle, eyes closed, hand on throat, hand on lower *dantian*, says: "I do matter. I always have. I mattered when I was a little girl and I matter now. He can't take that away from me."

Michelle relaxes her muscles through steady, slow breathing, which also helps her heart rate slow. She connects to her body with her hand on her heart and her belly. Not only is this soothing, it also allows energy to flow between the two hands. I believe she is accessing resources of love, compassion, gratitude and strength. Her higher Self directs them towards her egoic self. As she moves her hands higher, up to her throat, the energy flows further, as does her awareness.

I gave her permission to speak in a way that didn't force; rather, it drew on the imagination: *if your throat were to allow the truth to come out, what would you say?* I often use this way of accessing what is real in the moment. Because she was having trouble swallowing, I focused on the throat. In other sessions, or with other clients, I might notice other areas signalling and ask whether other body parts wanted to voice their truth. You might imagine the various responses from various clients: they might ask the head to speak, the heart, the eyes or ears, the genitals. I cannot predict what the person will say.

I do matter. I always have. I mattered when I was a little girl and I matter now. He can't take that away from me. Michelle speaks our essential truth. She has come to her own conclusion of self-worth.

HOW TO USE MEDITATION FOR ANCHORING

Here is a meditation to anchor a positive decision.

> I invite you to close your beautiful eyes once again. Silently inside, repeat the words of your new decision, knowing this is a commitment to yourself. Not to me, not to your spouse, but to your Self… and now try it out loud. Put one hand on your belly to really connect inside. Feel that connection. What is happening in your body right now as you speak this new decision out loud?

Clients often respond with words such as "calm," "connected," or "peaceful."

Place your second hand on your heart and repeat your new decision. What is happening in your body now?

I often hear words such as "expansion," "lighter" or "happy."

I might ask the client to stand up out of their chair and assume a position of congruence: feet hip-width apart, body held with good posture, arms at the side, hands open, palms forward, chin up, and speak their decision out loud. Now I have taken them from an inward, body-centred, meditative position in the chair to a congruent, strong standing stance. At this time, I might ask again what is happening in their body, and often I hear the words "freedom," "strength," "clarity" and "courage."

IS THERE A MEDITATION FOR DEPRESSION?

When I work from my home office, I often do standing meditations outside on my deck with clients. I can also do a standing meditation in a small clinical office. The physical space need not restrict the intention to ground and to activate energy. For those with depression, I have adapted a meditation exercise from Qi-Gong which I call Sun and Moon:

Standing with your feet hip-width apart and facing forward... gripping with your toes, feel your feet pressing into the floor, and down into the earth, and pull the energy up from the Earth... as you bring that practical grounded energy up your legs, feel your calves tighten, then your thighs, your buttocks, your core... keeping it all activated, move the energy down your arms, tightening your biceps and your forearms, tightening every finger, making fists, and now opening your palms, each finger spread and activated... feeling your entire body activated... each muscle.... Now raise your palms, holding the moon in one hand and the sun in the other. Feel that strength! Raise your hands above your head until the two palms are almost touching as you stretch up! up! up! Lift your face to the sun with a smile, feel that warmth, that heat from the sun on your face, and stretch way up, feeling your hands and your whole body vibrating with energy, every single muscle activated! Now, on the count of three, push the energy down with your hands, quickly and forcefully, down and away, and release the energy. One, Two, Three!… Shake it off.

I do the exercise at the same time as the client. We shake our arms and legs vigorously, shake our bodies, shake our jowls, and come to a resting place. We repeat this three times. One's body is usually buzzing. I am always shaking, my muscles all aquiver. Life energy is flowing. We feel very alive. This is particularly useful for clients who are feeling depressed as it rouses them out of their dull lethargic state.

USE OF MEDITATION AT THE END OF A SESSION

I often end my sessions with a short meditation to teach clients that we are in charge of our energy. "Breathing out, let go of what you no longer need. Breathing in, take in exactly what you do need at this moment in time. Everything you need is right here for you right now. You simply need to make room for it and become aware that it is already here." We generate energy. Our life energy is inside us – it is just waiting for us to access it. We can control the flow.

BENEFITS OF MEDITATION IN THERAPY

Safety

After a few sessions with me, clients know what to expect. The regular use of guided meditations at the beginning, during or end of a session helps the client feel safe. Once, a client told me he was holding a humiliating incident that happened a decade ago. He was worried that he would be re-traumatized if we were to work on the event. We did the work, using meditations to calm him each time he became agitated, so that we could stay within his window of tolerance. In total we did six two-minute meditations. As the session drew to a close, he said, "The meditations really help. Now I can visualize the dance at high school and remain calm in my body. I'm fairly relaxed, even though we worked on tough stuff all session. I didn't think I could do it, but I did!"

Energetic Attunement

With guided meditation there is a very quick energetic attunement between therapist and client. We end up working on a deep level almost instantly. I can lead clients swiftly through the levels of the Personal Iceberg Metaphor of the self, deep into their yearnings. Working at the level of yearnings is profoundly different from other therapeutic processes.

Cutting through to the essence of change

Through the use of meditation in a therapy session I can easily and quickly get to what in a person's life needs to change in order for the person to thrive. By engaging in a combination of intervention meditations to tap into the intra-psychic realms, we can facilitate change.

Use of self

Each time I guide my client in a meditation, I am re-calibrating to the highest and best part of myself – my Self – and that leads to magnificent results. I see the client's issues from a cosmic point of view, and I know that he is on a soul journey here on Earth. He is here to learn lessons at a soul level. I have absolute faith that my client is capable of resolving his issues.

NEUROSCIENCE AND MEDITATION

When we go through traumatic events in our life or when we are suffering afterwards, adrenaline courses through our body sending signals to protect ourselves and survive. Many books and papers discuss the benefits of meditation on the autonomic nervous system, so I need not dive into that here. What I do think is important to mention is that meditation can slow down our brain waves and take us into deeper states of consciousness.

When we are in a triggered state, even if the danger is not present, our right brain gets more activated and it is as if our left hemisphere goes offline. There is hyper-activation for the right hemisphere, and hypo-activation for the left hemisphere.

Meditation can help synchronize the two hemispheres, and our brain can slow down to an alpha- or even a theta-state. When our brainwaves are in alpha or theta, we are able to access creativity. This means both client and therapist, during a session, can grasp new perspectives, new thoughts and new solutions which may have been elusive before.

DIFFERING SPIRITUAL BELIEFS

I do not have to share the same religious or spiritual beliefs as a client in order to work with them. I can adapt my spiritual language. If the person refers to God, Creator, Jesus, Buddha, chakras, or Ra and the Law of One, I shift my language to what they are most comfortable with. I make it my business to understand, not assume.

I recently worked with a client who was struggling with grief over the death of his wife, and when I asked about spiritual beliefs, he said, "I am an atheist. This is it. This urn of ashes and bones is all there is." I was stuck for a bit because my own beliefs are so different. In a later session, we talked about energy being neither lost nor created; rather, energy changes forms. And there was possibility in that.

Still, I find it easier to work with clients who believe in something greater than themselves, that there is much more to this world and this universe than we can conceive of.

Case Study: **Claire**
I am lovable, and I am Love.

In the next case study, the client wants to address her self-criticism and shame. Claire is a highly educated, high-achieving professional with a strong tendency to perfectionism and judgement of self and others. She was raised in a multi-generational home. In her culture, men may marry more than one woman, and her maternal Grandfather was married to two women at the same time, living together in the same household with children and grandchildren. She refers to the three elders as Grandfather, Grandfather's First Wife, and Grandmother. We work on the impact of this hierarchical situation over several sessions; First Wife held a position of honour and respect in the family, while Grandmother was more of a subservant, receiving little respect from others. First Wife acted in cruel and dismissive ways, expecting very high standards of Claire, while Grandmother was loving and accepting; but at the beginning of our work together Claire shows no respect or appreciation for Grandmother.

Because English is Claire's second language, you will notice grammatical errors as I have transcribed the session *verbatim*. You may also notice that I sometimes switch direction when I realize we have misunderstood each other.

I have included the times of our pauses, how long I waited without speaking, so that you can get a sense of the pace of this session. There was no pressure from me for her to make an analytical response. Claire went into a deep theta state and the pacing allowed her to stay there.

The following session comes late in our work. Let's begin.

"Closing your beautiful eyes... and coming to the present moment... feeling into your body and allowing your shoulders to drop down, and release with your outward breath... and then when you are breathing in, just allowing everything to expand, knowing everything is here for you... with your feet planted on the planet and your mind open to the universe, and your heart connected to the Source of Love.... Breathing in exactly what you need...." I inhale loudly enough that she can hear me. "...Breathing out what you no longer need...." I exhale, again loudly enough to be heard. "...And allowing to come to mind where it is you most want to go today, and when you are ready, opening your beautiful eyes... and letting me know."

21 seconds of silence while I wait

Claire keeps her eyes closed. "Now, it seems like some feelings is moving inside me. Maybe two words came to my mind. One word is belongings.... Ya... belongings... ya, belongings."

"Mmm... okay... and what's happening in your body as you say that?"

13 seconds

"It seems like I'm here but... do I have... I'm not sure how to say this.... Do I have the right to be here, or, ya, or do I need to have a reason to be here?"

"Let me explain what I'm hearing and then tell me if I've got it, or if it needs more explaining for me. What I'm hearing is that you're wondering if you have the right just to exist? Is it okay just to be here? Or do I have to have a purpose. Do I have to be doing something for other people on the planet? Or for myself on the planet? There has to be a reason. Did I get that?"

"Ya. Yes. Just now when I said, "Do I need a reason to be here?" something comes out, some feelings, and I think this sentence connects with my heart. That's my heart said.... Maybe in subconscious, they need a reason to be here. What kind of reason? Maybe I need to prove my value. I have to, I need to be valuable, so I have a reason to be here, to exist, in this place."

8 seconds

"And what if you did have a reason to exist? What would that mean then?"

21 seconds

"I'm not sure... because in the family of my Mother, the valuable thing is your gender. Boys... boys... boys are valuable, men are valuable."

"So what if you did not have a reason to exist? What does that mean? What do you do with that?"

"Would you please say it again? This sentence?"

"You were talking about a reason to exist, if there is one. And so, what if the answer is yes, there is a reason? And what if the answer is no, there is not a reason? What do both those things mean for you, as you go down either of those paths?"

"Yes, there is a reason!"

"Okay!"

"And the reason may be, you need to prove that you are valuable."

"And how do you prove that when you are born a girl?"

"When I was a girl, I studied very hard. I was obedient. I was somewhat excellent at that age. But I was not happy when I was young."

"And now, as a woman, what do you do to prove that you deserve to exist?"

"My achievements, my professional ability, my love...." Tears come into her eyes. "When I say my love, I was very touched by this part."

"What's happening inside?"

Claire's eyes are still closed. "When I say my achievements, that means I need to work very hard. When I say, my professional ability, I know that comes from my… let me find this English word… as a natural gift. And when I say, *my love*, it seems like I do not need to do a lot of things, I can just be here...." She is crying.

"What are the tears saying? What's their message?"

"When I said, 'I can just be here without doing a lot of things,' it touches me."

"Is it a relief? Or a sadness about the past? A relief of 'I'm Okay'? Or something else?"

"It is reconciliation."

"And what if the only reason you're here is to love?"

Many tears are falling from her closed eyes. Twenty seconds of silence pass. "Maybe this is true, but this overturns my belief in the past. Subconsciously, I work very hard. There is a strength. An invisible strength that always pushes me forward and I can't stop. This has happened a very long time in my life. And when you said, 'The only reason is to feel love for me in my life,' this really overturned my belief." She opens her eyes. "Could you please say it again?"

"Yes. What if the reason you are here is to love, and to be loved, and third, to be Love. My whole being is Love. That's what I Am. My body vibrates with love. I can see this rock," I hold up a pink quartz rock, "as a miracle. I can see this water," I hold up my glass, "as a miracle. I look at flowers and I love them." I gesture outside my window. "And the trees, and I love them. And I love each human being that appears right in front of me." I gesture towards her. "I just love them. Until all that I am is Love."

Claire closes her eyes again, crying. "At this moment, it seems like my body wants to absorb what you said just now."

"Mmmhmmm. Take your time. Ya."

After a silence, Claire opens her eyes. "Would you please say it again?"

"Yes. I'm here to love, as a verb. And I'm here to be loved, as a verb, a receiving. And then, I Am Love. Every fibre of my being, every cell of my Being is Love." I'm now laughing. "And it makes me happy! And Claire, you are right in front of me, and you are amazing. You are an amazing human being. The things that make us stand out as human beings are not about 'perfect.' It's about expressing. And expansion. And love. And that's how I see you, what I wish for you."

Claire cries for 37 seconds.

"So the reason I here is to love and... be Love."

"Yes."

"And I love."

"Yes."

Claire closes her eyes again.

1 minute, 11 seconds

I ask, "What's happening in your body? Breathe that in. Breathe it in. Breathe it in all through your body."

"A kind of vibration. And...." *Silence for 14 seconds.* "...And seems like my body changed something into new, into new things."

13 seconds

"Breathe that in."

54 seconds

"And I feel peaceful now."

10 seconds

"Tell me about belonging," I say.

1 minute, 12 seconds

"It seems that at this moment, I can connect with my Grandfather who died at his young age, and also my two Grandmothers. One is the First Wife of my Grandfather and the other is my real grandmother...."

"I remember you telling me about them."

"Yes."

"And if they have messages for you, what might they be? What would they want you to know?"

31 seconds

"My Grandfather said...." *23 seconds.* "'Thank you....'" Tears are streaming. Silence. "'We are proud of you.'"

"Take that in, Claire. Take that in. Take that in all over."

1 minute

"He said, 'You have done which I could not, I did not. Thank you.'" Claire is crying as she breathes out.

1 minute, 10 seconds

"And the First Wife of my Grandfather say, 'You were born to be fruitful, rich... and you are okay.... You are lovable.'"

"Breathe that in."

"And my Grandmother looked at me, smiling... I can feel from her eyes a lot of love." Claire is smiling, radiant, beaming. Her eyes are still closed. She breathes out a big sigh and her shoulders drop, relaxing, releasing.

"Is there anything that you would like to say to them?" *Silence 10 seconds.* "You don't have to.... You can just receive. Or you can speak, using your voice, your *truth*."

9 seconds

"Let me feel if I have something I would like to say to them...." *Silence for 15 seconds.* "I would like to say to my Grandfather—" her voice changes as she speaks to him "'—This is my first time to hear you say these words... I have waited for such a long time.'" *34 seconds.* "'...At this moment, I can feel I am one of this family.'"

"You belong."

"Yes.... 'And Grandfather, I wish you happy in your world.' And I would like to say to the First Wife of my Grandfather, 'Now I know why I like to be a big tree, not a tiny tree.'" Laughing, Claire opens her eyes, asks me directly: "Do you remember in the first session you asked me about the tree?"

I'm laughing and smiling too. "I totally see the trees. And I see First Wife of Grandfather's tree. And it was what she could do. It was what she could do. And she is so proud of you and happy for you, that you are the big tree."

"Yes. I think this connection with First Wife of my Grandfather... she came from a rich and big family. So I have something connecting with this. So I would like to say to her, 'Thank you.'"

"Yes. Do you want to go back in and do that?"

Claire closes her eyes for several seconds. In tears, she says, "'Thank you.'" Her tears stop. "'Through you, I can feel the wideness, plenty-ness in the life. And also generosity.'" *Half a minute goes by.* "And I would like to say to my Grandmother... she had not expectation on me. What she gave me is love, only love." Claire's voice changes. "'Thank you for giving me so much love. You let me feel I am loved and I am Love, because you are love... ya... you are Love.... You are not a sacrifice... you are Love.'" Her voice changes back. "Yes."

"Maybe put your hand on your heart and feel that in. Feel that all through you. Breathe in the expansion."

We both put our hands on our hearts and breathe deeply.

17 seconds

"And now that you've had that, are there any new decisions you'd like to make?"

"It seems like you are a message from the God," Claire says. "You always have the right pace to lead me forward. Yes, I need to have a new decision. Let me feel about it."

"Yes, feel it."

52 seconds

Claire says, her eyes still closed, "I'm not very clear, but some words came to my mind. Now I know where I came from. So I do not need to hurry up. I can calm down. Ya. I can be active just like before, but I don't have to. The strength for moving forward is not fear, but it is love. Ya."

"And you know how because you've had a great teacher – your grandmother. She is a great teacher! Just Love! So you know the difference."

"Yes, just Love. Yes... just Love."

"Just Love... and is there anyone who comes to mind?"

"Maybe something will change in my relationship. I cannot say very clearly now, but I feel something will change in my relationship."

"Your relationship with...?"

"With my colleague, with my parents."

"Can I add one more? Can I request one more?"

"Ya... ya...."

"Can you change your relationship with yourself?"

20 seconds

Claire, in tears, smiles. "I appreciate your wisdom.... Ya... Yes!"

I'm smiling too. "That's sounding more positive now. 'Ya... Yes!' Yes, I can!"

"I will change. Something will change in my relationship with myself."

"That sounds like very much in the future. I'm wondering if you could just do it right now?" I smile at her kindly, mischievously. "Just—" I snap my fingers "—like that! Is it possible?"

Claire laughs. "Ya.... Yes!"

"Great!"

We are both laughing together.

Claire opens her eyes wide. "Wow!"

"Oh ya!.. Ya.... That almost sounds like commitment."

"Yes, yes, commitment." She breathes out, smiling.

"And so then... I'm going to push it a little further. Is that okay?"

Claire nods, eyes locked onto mine. "Yes. Okay. I like it."

"Yes, okay, good. So—" I get more serious "—when you are not loving towards yourself, because you'll slip, so when you're not loving towards yourself, I'm hoping that you love yourself anyway, even for not loving yourself, that it is okay. That you don't beat yourself up for beating yourself up." Claire laughs, and I join in. "You just say, 'Ohhh, I did it again. I'm so curious. I'm going back to loving myself.' Just like that. Just like that!" I snap my fingers.

"A beautiful adding. I like that. Yes."

I say: "'How would my Grandmother treat me? What would my Grandmother say?' You can just ask."

"Yes," says Claire. "Yes. She would say, 'Everything will be okay.'"

"'Everything will be okay.'"

"'You are okay. Everything will be okay. It doesn't matter.'"

"'It doesn't matter.'"

"'Everything will be okay.'"

17 seconds

"Where are you right now? How are you in this minute?"

"Warm. My body is light."

"And how about your Life Energy?"

"I'm closer to my Life Energy than I ever have been in the past. This is the first time I'm so near to my Life Energy."

"Wow! I'm getting tingles all over my body. Beautiful."

"Ya. Ya. I think 'belongings' is a very big step for me… I would like to thank you for…. You have done so much for me. I can feel a lot of love from you."

"Great! So now you know what it's like to receive it! Good…. Good... ya…. And I think about myself as a channel. If I can tap in and channel Love, then everything is okay. Everything is okay…. Thank you…. Thank you for saying that, Claire. I will receive that. Thank you."

"You… you match me so much. You are really a channel. You guide me. I like your brilliant work."

"Thank you. Thank you, Claire."

Unpacking the case study

I will unpack the session with Claire to illustrate how and why I do breathwork, how to move in a positive direction, set incremental goals, and encourage better decision making.

OPENING MEDITATION: CLOSING EYES

I sometimes encourage clients to work with their eyes closed, especially in internet sessions. When we work in person, the client may be staring at me, my body and my face, but she is not simultaneously looking into a mirror. On the reflecting screen of a computer, there is great likelihood that a client will be staring at me plus staring at her own body and face – judging her hair, her wrinkles or her contorted face when she grimaces or sobs. Such self-consciousness might distract her, stop her from emoting, and hold her back from going as deep as necessary. Claire spent over ninety percent of the session with her eyes closed.

PRESENT MOMENT

And coming to the present moment... Here I bring the client to the thought that nothing exists outside this particular moment. In therapy, we deal with regrets about the past and fears of the future. By teaching clients to come into the present moment, that nothing exists except what is happening right now, we are letting them know they are safe. In this moment, there is no scary monster in the room. They are alive. They have survived whatever traumatic events occurred in the past. And as for worrisome thoughts about the future, I'm reminded of Michel de Montaigne's witty reflection: "My life has been full of terrible misfortunes, most of which never happened."

AWARENESS OF BODY

Feeling into your body and allowing your shoulders to drop down, and release with your outward breath.... I bring clients into awareness of their body, encouraging relaxation. Satir said:

> If you get tight, oxygen does not reach all parts of your body. If you are loose and relaxed, it has a chance to reach those parts so you can be in touch with and get signals from your body. There will almost always be negative signals when your body is tight. So if you can then, in a moment, relax your body by breathing, you can thus restore it to a positive place. This is not a concept this is a piece of reality. As you breathe and relax, the health of your body has a greater chance to develop and you as a decision-making being have a better chance to make more accurate decisions.[4]

Satir wanted people to "...consciously tune in to your body. And maybe for the rest of your life you can become aware that when you are feeling bad, your body will be tight – when you let your body relax, you can move to a new place."[5]

POSITIVELY DIRECTIONAL IMAGES FOR THE CLIENT'S STRENGTH

And then when you are breathing in, just allowing everything to expand, knowing everything is here for you... with your feet planted on the planet and your mind open to the universe, and your heart connected to the Source of Love.... Here, I am connecting the client to the three source energies: groundedness, creativity and connection. They are all from the unifying source of Love. Here, you can see that my own beliefs and knowledge of the universe are present.

---

4 Satir, "Purpose of my Meditations," 2.
5 Ibid., 2.

CHOICE MAKING

Breathing in exactly what you need... breathing out what you no longer need.... The client chooses what she needs and does not need. I am not in charge of the content; I am in charge of teaching her that she always has choices.

GOAL SETTING

And allowing to come to mind, where it is you most want to go today.... The client sets the goals. I have metagoals in mind, but the client sets the goals based on issues she wants to resolve. She is in charge of what; I am in charge of how. When prompted, Claire asserts that her goal for this session has to do with belonging. I choose not to ask for clarification because I want her to stay deep in her process. Within a minute, she expands the idea: belonging has to do with her family of origin.

Later, after a piece of the work is done, when Claire has come to a feeling of peace, I return to the original goal, and say, "Tell me about belonging." Claire connects with the spirits of Grandmother, Grandfather, and Grandfather's First Wife and has conversations with them, and then reflects on her experience:

At this moment, I can feel I am one of this family, she says.

You belong, I say.

Yes, Claire says.

BREATHWORK

Throughout sessions, I encourage clients to inhale deeply or exhale thoroughly for a variety of reasons. Satir said, "For me, breathing and relaxation equals strength. Also, the conscious effort of breathing and relaxation helps pull together various scattered components, again, giving a sense of power."[6]

---

6 Ibid., 2.

In particular, when clients start to feel good, I emphasize inhalation.

"And I love," Claire says.

"Yes," I say. "What's happening in your body? Breathe that in. Breathe it in. Breathe it in all through your body."

"...a kind of vibration. And... and seems like my body changed something into new, into new things..."

"Breathe that in."

"And I feel peaceful now."

Inhalation expands the chest area, and the shoulders go back. The body is in a position of confidence and courage. Bringing awareness to lung expansion brings awareness to the area of the heart. Deep inhalation expands the belly area, the area of the lower *dantian*. Our core and life force are enlivened, awakened and activated.

An emphasis on exhalation is most useful when the client needs to let go of negative feelings and thoughts. The act of exhaling helps us to calm down, as it gets rid of carbon dioxide built up in the lungs, making room for oxygen. Repeated often enough, blowing out and "letting go" become linked, and then, each time we consciously blow out, we are subconsciously letting go of what we no longer need.

LIFE ENERGY

"I'm closer to my Life Energy than I ever have been in the past."

A reason for therapy is to unblock the Life Energy so that it may express itself. When our yearnings are met and we are in touch with our resources, when we clear up pieces of our past and experience well-being in the present, our Life Energy is palpable.

METAPHORS

Images and metaphors tap into our intuition, our knowing of Truth. My experience is that metaphors activate deep-seated cultural archetypes and stories. The use of metaphors by Satir in her meditations, workshops and therapy sessions was both experiential (in the present) and practical for the future. She engaged people's imaginations by conjuring up metaphors to help them in their conscious daily life. Use of metaphor in individual therapy allows the client to leave a session with tools to draw on long after therapy is complete.

During a mid-session meditation in an early session, Claire had accessed the image of a tree. She spoke of herself as an enormous tree, referring to her own personal massive success, and her grandfather's First Wife as a very tiny tree in the shade of the big tree. Claire experienced confusion, bouncing between feelings of pride and guilt, believing that to be valued, she must work hard and accumulate wealth and property, but to be accepted, she must never overshadow her elder, and we worked on those limiting beliefs and unfulfilled yearnings. In the session above, we both referred to that tree and we did not have to restate the work done previously; instead, we used metaphor to anchor Claire's revelation.

FINAL THOUGHTS ABOUT MEDITATIONS IN THERAPY

Satir used guided meditations in groups to open people up to their intra-psychic systems. In this way, they could listen to their self-talk, observe their own beliefs, and reflect on their psychological coping patterns. She also used meditation to deepen experiences, to move people in a positive direction, and do their own inner work. She often used metaphors in her meditations as they speak to the right hemisphere of the brain. Satir used meditations to create an atmosphere of body-centred and heart-centred energy.

Using meditation in individual therapy works in much the same way. It opens people to their intra-psychic systems. They may listen to their self-talk, observe their own beliefs, and reflect on their psychological coping patterns.

At multiple points in a session, I deliberately use meditation. Meditating provides a container. It allows clients to set goals and reflect on their interior process. It pulls people back into intra-psychic experience and sparks imagination regarding the Self. I often ask existential questions; the possibilities for change are limitless.

Because we share collective consciousness, when I am deeply with a client, the energy can be very powerful. Therefore, it is good to help our clients focus on positively directional ideas. That is when magic happens!

When we facilitate the raising of people's consciousness to a level where they are not in victim mode, but rather tapping into their higher selves, we make a synergistic impact on the world. It is our task to nurture personal growth, to raise our consciousness, to be aware of the energy (positive or negative) that we create.

I like to make the teachings experiential. When I ask a question of someone who has his eyes open, the response will often be from the head, a cognitive left-brain response. When I invite someone to put his hands on his heart and go inside, possibly closing his eyes, and then ask the same question, the responses often are deeper and experienced differently.

We know that our mind is not inside our brain. Our mind is beyond the physical boundaries of our skin. When we are with clients, our consciousness can be used to expand ourselves or contract ourselves, as a collective. I choose expansion.

SATIR MEDITATION: *CONNECTION TO ENERGY*

I'd like to finish this chapter with a final excerpt from one of Satir's meditations. It speaks to me of limitless possibility, saying that we are a magnificent part of the cosmos, and that we are all connected. I deliberately access this knowledge in my sessions and it profoundly shapes the therapeutic outcomes of my work with clients.

Sending Energy to Others

As a creature of this universe, I do have a relationship, an access to energy from the center of the Earth, not because I am good, not because I am smart, only because I am human. All humans have that. Connection to the energy of the center of the Earth is there all the time, it is the heart of the Earth. And as that energy moves upward, contacting us through our feet and upward into our legs and thighs and torso, it brings with it the energy of groundedness – the ability to be cognitive, to think, to analyze, to measure – a wonderful and important need we have.

And then an energy from the heavens, which is ours in the same way because we are human, moves down into our head and face and neck, arms and shoulders, into our torso bringing with it the energy of imagination, of inspiration, of intuition... the marvelous part that brings texture, color and sense into our lives and allows us to paint and to dance and to sing and to feel and write poetry... to give texture to that which was alone and barren. This part of our lives, for many of us, has remained dormant out of ignorance, out of fear, out of a sense of unimportance. But to be fully human, that part is essential, as essential as our ability to be cognitive. We must have the feeling sense as well.

Our third energy is a very important one, the power to connect with those others whose receptors are present and open and will receive me. There is also those out there whose receptors are present, but not open. And I will not be able to make contact with them, not because they are bad or I am bad, simply because it isn't yet possible. There are things I can do as I pass by, such as allowing myself to shed light and remembering that the bud is not yet in place to open to me, and the other person may not even know that. Here's my love gift to you, of energy to use as you need, at this moment in time.[7]

---

7   Satir."Sending Energy," 60.

- How did Satir's meditation resonate with you personally?
- When are you playing with all three energies?
- Would you like to channel all three energies in therapy? In your life?
- Is that a commitment to yourself or to your Self?
- Who is making the commitment?

My wish is that this chapter has sparked your curiosity. I hope you received the understanding that the best thing you can do for a client is to love them. Look at them with eyes of love. The best thing we can all do is love one another. See our partners, children, parents and ex-partners, neighbours, everyone, through eyes of love. As Satir said, "It is essential that the person leading the meditation is coming from a position of love and caring and has a total belief in growth."[8]

---

8 Satir, "Purpose of my Meditations," p.2.

REFERENCES

Banmen, John, ed. *Guided Meditations and Inspirations by Virginia Satir*. Langley: Satir Institute of the Pacific, 2020.

Satir, Virginia. *The New Peoplemaking*. Mountain View: Science and Behavior Books, Inc., 1988.

Satir, Virginia. "The Purpose of my Meditations." In *Guided Meditations and Inspirations by Virginia Satir*, edited by John Banmen, 1-3. Langley: Satir Institute of the Pacific, 2020.

Satir, Virginia. "Your Choice from your Spirit." In *Guided Meditations and Inspirations by Virginia Satir*, edited by John Banmen, 45-47. Langley: Satir Institute of the Pacific, 2020.

Satir, Virginia. "Our Resources and our Energy." In *Guided Meditations and Inspirations by Virginia Satir*, edited by John Banmen, 50-51. Langley: Satir Institute of the Pacific, 2020.

Satir, Virginia. "Sending Energy to Others." In *Guided Meditations and Inspirations by Virginia Satir*, edited by John Banmen, 60-61. Langley: Satir Institute of the Pacific, 2020.

Satir, Virginia. In *Guided Meditations and Inspirations by Virginia Satir*, edited by John Banmen, 60-61. Langley: Satir Institute of the Pacific, 2020.

VII

BODYMIND WISDOM IN SATIR'S MODEL

ANASTACIA LUNDHOLM

Anastacia Lundholm's professional journey began with the study of Somato Respiratory Integration (SRI) in 1997. The next year she joined the training staff in the modality, and nine years later she became International Lead Trainer and Director of SRI Technologies. In 2005 she began studying and integrating Satir's model into her trainings. Since then, she has taught body-centred personal growth and professional development programs and Satir's approach internationally to lay and professional students. She also mentors body-centred professionals and teaches online in Canada, Thailand and China. She is currently an active trainer with the Satir Institute of the Pacific, Yinghe Satir in China and the Satir Institute of Thailand, and adjunct faculty of the Banmen Satir China Management Centre. In 2023 she received a Satir Transformational Systemic Therapy (STST) Leadership Award from Satir Institute of the Pacific.

BODYMIND WISDOM IN SATIR'S MODEL

MY JOURNEY OF TRANSFORMATION THROUGH CONNECTION

When I was a child, I really didn't know what to do with my feelings, and I tuned them out. Simultaneously, I tuned out the body sensations connected to those feelings. Later on, in young adulthood, even if my inner wisdom was trying to shout at me, I couldn't hear it very well. A series of physical injuries in my thirties left me in constant, chronic pain for six years. This pain gave me no choice but to pay attention to my body. In my search for help from many different practitioners I learned so much about myself and my body. I could never have dreamed that early childhood experience could shape my physicality and my life to such a degree. Early body-holding patterns connected to experiences of fear, loss and betrayal seemed to filter the way I perceived and reacted to situations in my adult life. I often felt frozen, unable to act in stressful situations. This affected what I would or wouldn't do, how I felt in relationships and how generally stuck I was. As long-suppressed emotions began to bubble up during the healing process, I was shocked how viscerally I was affected by them. It was like snaking out a clogged drain; I was confronted by all the yucky stuff I had had to suppress for so long. There was no road map to this journey, and I had to make sense of it by myself. I had not discovered Satir yet.

As I explored and transformed the body memory of what was inside me, a new world opened up around me. I didn't hold my breath unconsciously anymore. My posture changed. Emotions could surface more easily and move through me. I felt lighter, freer and more adventurous. I was less shy and more comfortable in my own skin. Above all, I was much more aware of my connection to nature, my intuition and inner knowing. As I witnessed others going through their own healing processes, I became enthralled with the depth and sanctity of each person's embodiment of their life, as well as the possibility that they, too, could become intimate with the process of transforming themselves. I wanted to share with everyone my understanding of the sacred ability they each possessed inside themselves to connect and release.

The depth of my own journey prepared me for my training to work with others. Somato Respiratory Integration (SRI) gave me comprehension of the body-mind-energy system. Some unusual opportunities began to find me. I started teaching classes and workshops and facilitating one-on-one. I went on to work with participants in large-scale transformational events, and later trained facilitators around the world. In my work with SRI, I helped people explore body abilities they didn't know they had, using a variety of coordinated patterns of self-touch, movement, focused attention and breath, sometimes incorporating sound or words. I helped them move through feelings in which they felt stuck, and make breakthroughs. In the course of transforming long-held body and energy patterns, a lot of potential was released. My clients gained wisdom and flexibility to respond to their circumstances with more ease and to live more congruently, as I had. My path took me to North and South America, Europe, Asia and Australia, and even into the Amazon jungle.

The more I learned, the more I wanted to know. I began to wonder how I could make my work more accessible. I was seeking greater presence, depth and mastery. I wanted to help as many people as possible to find their best access point to their own unique internal wisdom so they could fulfill their desire for change. That's when I found Satir's work.

I am passionate about incorporating her approach with my relevant bodymind skills because I have realized that we cannot have a life experience without having a body experience. Every body experience is connected to what is happening or has happened to us, to our learning and assumptions, and to our reactions to these. They are all interconnected. There is infinite potential for healing and wholeness when body wisdom, including mental and emotional wisdom, are leveraged by our deep yearnings.

In this chapter I would like to accomplish three goals. First, I'd like therapists, counsellors and coaches to know that, more than three decades after her passing, Virginia Satir's work is alive and thriving around the world, creating transformational, systemic change in clients. Second, I'd like to illustrate how simply yet profoundly transformative it can be to include the body in any kind of self-exploration and personal growth. Third, I'd like bodyworkers and wellness practitioners to learn how they can integrate Satir's model into their professional work with clients as well as into their personal lives.

For me the body has always been full of possibilities. Whether I'm working with myself or with others as a body-centred personal-growth coach and trainer, Satir's model exponentially expands what is possible.

Her systemic and experiential approach adds so much to personal growth work. My perspective results from combining two worlds: body/energy centered Somato Respiratory Integration and the profound gifts within Satir's approach. To my mind these two modalities are a match made in heaven.

MY INTRODUCTION TO SATIR'S MODEL

I believe the most important thing for our growth as practitioners working with others is to do our own personal work; when we grow as people, we inevitably grow as practitioners. I started my journey with the model to develop abilities to help me go deeper into myself and to serve others better.

Even with the best skills and experience, we all find blind corners in our personal growth from time to time – something in ourselves which we encounter, observe, explore, try to change, but don't feel complete with. Before I discovered Satir, I was experiencing a familiar and perplexing life pattern that I could not move beyond. If anyone had a need, I would promise to help or connect them with someone who could help.

I extended help to everyone even when I didn't have time or energy to do all the communications necessary, or when the needed resource was difficult to identify. I felt it was my responsibility to ensure that everyone fulfilled their goals to help others. If anyone needed help, I should give it to them, all of them. It was like being the administrative assistant to the universe. It was a big job, and it was exhausting.

A colleague recommended that I do some personal work with someone saying, "I can't describe what she does but you have to experience this." I was intrigued. Instinctively, I made two appointments, one for an initial visit and a follow-up a week or two later. I didn't know what the method was, but I was ready for anything. At the first visit, I experienced a version of Satir's Parts Party. Satir had developed a group process to facilitate experiential change in the inner world of the client (the "star") which can be adapted for use in a one-on-one setting. That experience gave me an opportunity to tease apart different parts of my inside world and take a look, assess and interact with them. I experienced parts of myself which had, in the past, seemed problematic had resources that I could now appreciate. My critical part, who was like a judge dispensing criticism from on high, could instead use her skills at evaluation to give me pointers about what might work better next time. I learned that each part had unique messages and gifts. As the session went on, I requested my internal parts, one by one, to collaborate and interact with one another in new ways toward a greater cohesiveness. For instance, my critical-part-turned-advisor could collaborate with my adventurous explorer part and help advise her on other options when she was about to go on a wild goose chase. My accountant part who had been ruthlessly tabulating all my failures and shortcomings could instead begin to track other things, like times I used my loving part, and my creative part. I found a mysterious part I called the White Lotus, who had been performing the task of being administrative assistant to the universe. She had no boundaries and was quite hard for me to pin down and describe. I only had the feeling that she worked unendingly and had no idea that all the other parts were there. She was a mystery to me, but I was so excited by the collaboration among my other parts that the process felt full and complete. I left the office clear-headed and lighthearted. I didn't have a concrete idea of what was different, but I felt good. I went on with my normal life without thinking much about the session. During the following weeks I felt better able to respond to situations and not overextend myself. I felt clearer inside, but I couldn't put my finger on anything specific. My big surprise came at the second appointment.

At that visit, the therapist and I took inventory of the parts of my internal world as they seemed to me at that moment. I noticed, one part after another, that each was operating differently than before. It was as if a housekeeper had come into my internal world and tidied up the place, swept the corners and made every surface shine. All the parts we had identified at the previous appointment (except one) were functioning smoothly as a collective, for my common good. My inner world had been reorganized, in a really good way. My inner critic had adopted her new role as advisor, fear had become a sentry who could alert me to danger and consult with my adventurous part to get more information. My loving part could offer caring help, and was not driven by obligation or duty. The changes instigated at the first appointment had neatly sorted themselves out and, without any conscious effort, I was just *different*.

The most fascinating thing for me was that I could not find the White Lotus inside myself at all. She seemed to have vanished. It was as if she had been an adaptation, a coping mechanism in the form of the ultimate placating reflex, wanting everything to be okay with others so I would be okay, and everybody would be okay. I realized that of course she had had no boundaries, because she did not know herself to be an individual. I no longer had the irresistible urge to offer help to everyone. I could evaluate situations before I spoke, and make the best decision for myself and others. I wondered how the parts of my internal world could have shifted so efficiently and effortlessly.

Satir's work intrigued me. I knew that many others had borrowed from or been influenced by her as they built their own growth or therapy models. I wanted to learn more and go as close to the source as possible.

Three weeks later I started my first six-month training with the Satir Institute of the Pacific (SIP). (What I didn't know at the time was that my mother had seen her work in the 1980s. Some of Satir's books were on the shelves in her collection and I have them today. I had been unconsciously influenced through my mother and primed for the experience of meeting Satir's work when I was ready for it.) Although the Parts Party is just one small aspect of the model, I'm grateful it was my entry point into this beautiful world of systemic and experiential work.

In my first Satir training, I learned the five essential elements of the model and realized I had experienced them all in my first exposure to Satir's work. Each of the elements had been woven into those first two sessions, which prepared me to absorb them cognitively now during training. Those essential elements are:

- Systemic
- Experiential
- Congruent use of self of the therapist
- Positively directional
- Change focused.

In retrospect, I could see that the first session I experienced had been deeply systemic. The therapist creatively engaged and activated many different parts of me at the same time, so that transformation could occur globally within me and in my life. The experiential nature of the session meant that I was not limited to cognitive reflections, but also able to include in the moment the felt sense, emotional intelligence and perceptions of each part. She elicited sensory information astonishingly replete with input from all my different internal perspectives. In addition, the supportive therapist and her use of self (she was deeply grounded and playfully inquisitive) helped me be curious about and explore in safety what I couldn't find my way through on my own. The positively directional focus of the session (through her skilled guidance) helped me make new connections inside that ignited each other: the resources embedded within my problematic parts were working co-operatively toward transforming their roles. Before the session I might have imagined a small change, but I could not have anticipated such wholesale transformation. The whole session had been change-focused (through the therapist's perceptive questions), and this was exciting. I'd had no particular goals in mind at the start, but I participated in their creation as we worked together.

INTEGRATING SATIR'S MODEL INTO MY BODY-CENTRED WORK

Before my exposure to Satir, I'd had a lot of experience helping people find a context in which to make contact with their body and its energy. In each SRI class or workshop, I would teach specific bodymind exercises to help each person find their own relationship to the topic at hand. My intention was to help them discover how to explore their connection to their body and access energetic shifts that they could use to find the next steps in their journey.

I had learned to quickly create trust and safety in fast-paced environments, and double down on that safety when assisting someone in distress or uncertainty. I often accomplished this in energetic and nonverbal ways, through facial expression, body language and tone of voice congruent with my intentions of being attentive and caring. I took my cues from how participants held their bodies, from their facial expressions, tone and volume of voice, hesitations and body mannerisms. To create rapport, I could meet or match a bright strong energy, or be soft and gentle to make contact if I sensed vulnerability or an expansive state. I learned how to carefully create safety, to modulate my energy to meet and serve someone without interrupting or distracting them from their inner process.

As a coach and trainer and teacher/facilitator (I am not and never have been a therapist), I begin assessing as soon as I meet someone. Through SRI work I learned to be very observant of physical posture, tone and position of different areas of the body and energetic changes. This perspective allowed me, during assessment and throughout a session, to read systemic body and energy patterns. I was able to observe their words, tone of voice, facial expression and affect to watch for congruity or incongruity and shifts between internal states.

I learned to trust my ability to sense energy within and around a person and assess the state of that energy to look for latent new states emerging. I could use my eyes to find areas in the field around a person that attracted my attention to "stick" there. I could tune into that spot and find the tone or frequency of that sticky place and decide how to match or use that energy. I tracked patterns' progression and resolution, and adjusted my goals as the interactive experience evolved. I often asked myself what needed to happen first in order for the client's goal to be achieved. In this way, I could plan a several-step process to work toward a goal and make the results more sustainable. I loved working with practitioners of different modalities in healing environments and developed collaborative skills to enable the mutual pursuit of congruent goals while each of us used different skill sets.

My work has always included awareness of the innate sacred nature of each human being and their access to the innate capacity to grow. And because I had worked extensively internationally, this informed my ability to find creative ways to touch the humanness within us across cultural boundaries. Since SRI and Satir both work systemically, experientially and towards positive change, they were easy to combine and integrate. I started with a good foundation, and was ready to learn more when I began training in Satir's model with SIP

I could be nimbler now when clients got frustrated at certain points in their process. When they felt that it was difficult to build energy in their body toward a new breakthrough, for instance, I had deepened perspectives that came out of Satir that illuminated more layers of context to explore with them.

Case Study: **Millie**

Millie wants to achieve a kind of personal power that will allow her to feel free and energized in her body, strong and courageous. In a small group class, she begins to breathe quickly in and out through her nose, and I can see she's building energy in a part of her body connected to that yearning. She suddenly starts to cry. She slumps forward.

"What is coming up right now?" I ask.

"I feel like I'll never be brave."

"Tell me about it, if it feels right."

"I had a terrifying experience when I was about five. A group of older boys came where I was playing. I thought they were going to hurt me. And I ran away. It was so scary. I should have been brave and fought them. I should have stood up for myself. But I didn't."

We take a moment to reflect together.

"You were a little girl," I tell her. "Your fear was reasonable. You made the smartest choice you could have made. You kept yourself safe."

Her eyes shine as she begins to breathe through her nose again. "I did the right thing."

Again, I sense energy building in her body. "Where do you feel all those feelings?"

She puts her hand just above her navel and begins to focus her breath there. Her rhythm speeds up as she claims her courage. A few moments later she completes the process. "I deserve more than I thought I did!" she declares. Her eyes are shining, her face is glowing, her posture is proud and strong. "I have never felt powerful before," she says, "but now it's going to be my favourite way to be!"

Focusing on resources helped me see Millie's potential for positive change even when vulnerability and shame came up, seeming to prevent her from accomplishing her goal of embodying personal power in the moment. When we explored the difficulty, we found embedded resources, catalysts toward deeper change. She realized how clever and resourceful she had been at five years old, and now appreciated the instincts that had kept her safe. By taking the cue from Millie's body and her description of her inner experience, we collaborated to guide the unfolding of her new self-confidence.

Satir's approach is all about collaboration. The process of creating goals and assessing outcomes is shared. The end goal is what the client wants to be different in the long run as a result of our work together. We explore how meeting this goal would affect their life in various contexts. Interim goals are created and revised along the way. By frequently assessing where we started together and where we are now, we build bridges from one incremental change to the next, always working together toward our larger goals.

The model emphasizes transforming the present-day impacts of events that happened in the past. My goal as a facilitator is to have the client experience something inside themselves right now, as opposed to telling me about what once happened. I notice their silences, and don't interrupt if they are paying attention inside, as new awarenesses may be surfacing. Conversely, I might interrupt if they are verbally or physically speeding right by something important, slowing them down with a question or bringing their awareness into the body. "What is happening for you right now inside?"

The intra-psychic and systemic emphases of Satir's model allow me to place my awareness on many levels simultaneously. These include observing facial expressions and other cues such as physical and energetic changes. Where are changes being expressed and where are they not – yet? Every small shift indicates that something is happening inside: large and small movements, stillness, spontaneous stretching or breathing changes can show integration happening. I get very curious. I will often circle back to something observed or mentioned earlier and inquire what's happening in the body now. Constant assessment ensures we are staying in touch with what is true right now, and are not stuck in what was true five minutes ago. It's so important to nurture the new connections and not reinforce the familiar, but perhaps outdated, ones. When I am doing a demonstration in a workshop and lead a group debrief, people are often surprised by things I notice. That's because my commentary will unpack many layers of information that transpired in a few moments, many of those layers nonverbal.

The model can provide structures which, when internalized by the therapist, make connections between seemingly unrelated things heard, seen and felt from the client. Many aspects of the client's inner world can be engaged simultaneously to bring about transformational change. It allows the therapist fluidity and creativity to guide the process organically without being limited to rigidly-prescribed steps. One can embrace the complexity of the client's current experience, past experiences and the context of family and culture in which they were raised. This latter becomes particularly helpful when working in different cultures and countries and with multicultural clients.

Anchoring changes personally and interpersonally is very important. We must own our new abilities and integrate them across contexts in life. One change in perception can be leveraged into growth in many areas, such as in relation to self, to others, or in relation to the world, or life itself. I might ask questions like: "Realizing this deep yearning you have discovered, would you like to explore how to meet that yearning for yourself?" or, "With this change that you are experiencing in yourself right now, how might you be different with your partner tonight?" or, "With this new choice you have made, how will you be different in your work environment?" In this way, anchoring across contexts integrates the changes experienced by the client deeply and systemically. Anchoring can also be accomplished by giving homework to practise and celebrate new abilities. Thus, the stand-alone therapeutic experience can be integrated sustainably in daily life over the long term.

The use of self of the practitioner is such an important element of Satir's approach. It has a profound impact on any process. Whether working with individuals or groups, I connect deeply to myself and my resources – caring, intentions, physicality and willingness, mindful that I am in the energetic field of a relationship or group, with its potential to move toward growth, connection and congruence. In the background of my awareness is my purpose – to connect to my life energy (highest Self) and to serve as a compassionate guide with healthy boundaries – I use direct gaze, relaxed body posture, focused attention and steady tone of voice to radiate acceptance and validation. This conveys without words to others in the field that they can safely explore their inner world. Use of self creates an environment where new ways of experiencing and being can be accessed more easily, and transformation is a byproduct of that.

Since that day in 2005, when I took to the work of Satir like a duck to water, I have taught lay courses that help people connect to their own bodies and find new ways of self-regulation. Students discover more about how their emotions are linked to their bodies to create emotional flow and harmony. They engage with their thoughts and beliefs as they have embodied them and have the choice to change painful patterns through engaging differently with the body. They also learn how to embody their relationship with the energy of the universe, the natural world and their higher selves. In professional trainings, I have taught Satir-trained therapists, social workers and psychiatrists how to integrate the body into the therapeutic process through use of the clients' self-touch and body sensation inquiry, as well as pacing, titration and anchoring. I have taught elements of Satir's model, such as the Personal Iceberg Metaphor and the Change Process, to personal-growth facilitators. The model informs my body-centred coaching every day. It empowers me and those around me to transform our lives.

OUR BODY AND OUR LIFE

Our life impacts our body every day, and vice versa. Life experience is stored in the bodymind.

Let's take a moment to connect experientially to the body to provide context for what we are exploring. Coming from a more right-brain place will help us to be receptive. This is something that we can do easily, but sometimes we forget to do it. I invite you to check in with yourself right now. Is there anything you can do to be more comfortable? You may have some body sensations of stiffness, cold, thirst or something else that would like your attention. Take the opportunity to respond to those internal signals. If you need to stretch or move your body in any particular way, go ahead. If you need to take a deep breath, or even yawn, please do. And if you would like to reposition yourself in your chair so you can be more comfortable, and take more care of your body, please, honour that urge.

This action of bringing your attention inward, to feel the sensations that you are aware of, connects you to what is happening now. You may notice parts of your body that you haven't paid attention to for a few minutes or a few hours.

ACCESSING BODY WISDOM

Body sensations are a doorway to the inner world. By directing a client's attention into the body sensations that they are experiencing right now, the therapist helps them to be present-focused and experiential rather than perceiving themselves cognitively. Satir said:

> Our bodies are miracles. Who could have dreamed up such marvels and then made them work? For the most part, we have been taught to ignore our bodies, except when they are dirty, sick, too fat or too lean, or not the right size or shape. The idea of just appreciating, understanding and communicating with our bodies is just beginning.[1]

Since I started to listen to and interact with my body so many years ago, I have found inner resources which have alerted me, inspired me, guided me and surprised me. I remember once, early in my learning process, feeling some sensation in the area of my liver, and with trepidation putting my hands there. I had no idea what I would find but assumed it would be scary or uncontrollable. I guided my touch, awareness and breath into that area, immersing myself in it. To my great surprise, I found it resonated with joy! Within a few seconds the joyful feeling radiated throughout my body. I learned that it is not only pain in life that we might protect ourselves against, we might also suppress pleasurable feelings, for whatever reason.

When we access our body sensations, we can unlock a trove of internal

---

1 Satir, Virginia. "A Partial Portrait of a Family Therapist," 116.

wisdom and resources. A flutter in the belly, tension in the shoulders or chest, or heaviness in the heart area could all be connected to something deeper. Areas of symptom or sensation may be connected to feelings, thoughts or information the body has been holding for us. Sensations might be subtle, strong or even overwhelming at times. Encouraging our clients to be aware of their body sensations throughout our interactions is one way that we can help them be responsive to their inner world.

Case Study: **Cassandra**

I am working with a client for the first time. We begin with her hands scanning the midline of her torso – chest, lower ribs and navel – to assess her ability to engage with her body and decide what we can work on together. She mentions casually that she has had a pain in her left shoulder for years.

"Can you touch the precise area of discomfort?"

As she does, I can see she is connected deeply to that part. She becomes very quiet as she focuses there.

"When was the first time you felt that?"

"I was seven years old, walking to school in the snow. In Germany, where I grew up. The leather strap of my heavy book bag pulled down my shoulder." Her voice has an edge to it. She opens her eyes suddenly and says, "I was really angry at my parents for pushing me so hard. They really pressured me about my schoolwork." In the next breath, she says, "But it was not permitted to be mad at my parents…." She closes her eyes again and a tear gently rolls down her cheek; her breath deepens into the chest area near her left shoulder. As she feels the emotions of that time flowing, the tension held in her upper chest releases under her hands and her ribcage widens and expands.

I touch her hand. The warmth and vibration I feel tell me something is changing.

She says in astonishment, "This is the first time in fifty years I have felt that pain release." The energetic shift in her chest and shoulders spreads into her pelvis and legs, and everything softens in response. Warmth and tiny movements spread throughout her body like ripples in a pond. As we finish the session, I notice her standing posture has changed. She is more erect through the torso, with shoulders more open and relaxed. Her face has softened, and her smile is contagious. She has found freedom to feel what she hid from herself all those years ago. She has experienced compassion for herself as a child under so much pressure, with all the mixed feelings of that time.

I marvelled that her bodymind could have held that physical and emotional tension for so long. I was amazed at how easily and completely she could connect and release the tension simply by being deeply present with the emotional content held in her body. She found access to long-held feelings and perceptions. I was sure her process would continue as new awareness and feelings surfaced regarding childhood and her relationship with her family. Our growth is a continuous process as we integrate new perspectives and make new meanings from them. I did not have the opportunity to work with Cassandra further, but I trust her process took her forward toward self-compassion, understanding of her relationship to anger, and seeing that her parents' motivations came from caring, in their own way. My perception was that we had moved a huge boulder out of the way of that process.

BODY SENSATIONS

We feel body sensations in the present, but they are often connected to past experiences. When we are very young, and some would say when we're in the womb, we perceive and form our implicit view of ourselves, our caregivers and our environment. We create a picture of how the world is and who we are in it before we have words to describe it. As we grow, we have body sensations or ways of moving or holding energy in our body that often have to do with reactions to stimuli and assumptions we made in those early years. These patterns held in our body become very practised. As we become adults, events may trigger perceptions and feelings that we felt when we were very small; certain events will activate the energy state and the body-holding patterns that we once used to survive, deal with, or adapt to challenging experiences in the past.

In his article "The Neuroscience of Body Memory: From the Self through the Space to the Others," Giuseppe Riva writes:

> Our experience of the body is not direct; rather, it is mediated by perceptual information, influenced by internal information, and recalibrated through stored implicit and explicit body representation (body memory)....[Our] bodily experience is constructed from early development through the continuous integration of sensory and cultural data...[2]

According to Riva, as we develop throughout life, we perceive through our senses, integrating spatial and movement information from muscles, joints and nerve endings. Our body experience is complex and constantly updating. Each body experience is enmeshed with an emotional experience and a relational experience. All experience influences the body map as it is being constructed. Our lived body experience is deeply interconnected with our experience of ourselves, of others, and the world around us.

When I ask a client, "This sensation you are noticing, is it new or does it feel familiar?" I often hear, "Yes, this feels familiar, I have felt this before." As we explore together, we begin to connect to the entire iceberg of their experience. (The Personal Iceberg Metaphor consists of behaviours, sensations, coping or survival patterns, emotions and reactions to emotions, expectations, perceptions, beliefs, yearnings and our core connection to our essence at a given moment in time.) Often the impressions from the past come replete with details that lend insight to the current-time reaction.

Body sensations (such as heaviness, tension, fluttering, pulsing or stillness) give us feedback about what's going on right now. They are a doorway into our experiential world where response patterns that we

---

2 Riva, "The Neuroscience of Body Memory," 241-260.

may have carried for a lifetime are held. Those sensations, if we follow them, will lead to the impacts we are holding from the past, and transform them. As we continue to explore, we can get more insight about ourselves and make new interpretations of the past or decisions about what to do now. As sensations of tightness, heaviness or pain lessen, move or disappear, they tell us that something is changing inside. Are we moving forward on the right path? New sensations can give us feedback: a deep breath of relief, for instance, or a muscle release, or a tingle of excitement or curiosity. When our bodies get activated, we have the opportunity to move forward toward deep healing; and we get direct feedback when something shifts. Body sensations illuminate the path toward transformation, and show us when we have arrived.

BODY WISDOM AND TRANSFORMATION

I approach each new client with the awareness that there is information stored within them that they are unaware of. My job is to help the person connect *safely* to whatever resource is available to them that they are ready to explore and use. I want them to be able to integrate the changes and grow as a result of the experience. By connecting to a body area where unprocessed emotions are held, profound shifts – physical, emotional, mental and spiritual – can occur. My intention is not to "fix" something that is wrong, or heal some illness; I want clients to learn how to connect effectively to their bodies and themselves. By exploring what's there, and interacting with the wisdom and potential that is inside each of us, we change. Transformation is a byproduct of connection to oneself. Respecting the client's capacity to be with what they are experiencing may require slowing down or redirecting attention as needed, to help the client stay present. Identifying a part of the body that radiates dependability, strength or peace can be invaluable; these are touchstones for safety for both therapist and client.

Case Study: *Shelley*

I ask Shelley which areas of her body does she feel greatest connection to, and which areas might want more connection. She requests that we explore the lower abdomen. "I've been experiencing a kind of dullness in that area for some time. It feels kind of inaccessible."

I ask her to put her hands on the exact place that calls to her.

She slides her hands slightly apart and positions them in the general area over her ovaries.

"Be present with that part."

She focuses her touch, gently breathing. She says, "They're afraid!" With eyes closed, she tells me about a surgery she had thirty years ago, during which she had been fully sedated. Her surgeon, intending to do a complete hysterectomy, decided during the procedure to leave the ovaries. "The exact feeling in my ovaries is dread," she says. "It is as if they are still frozen... expecting the surgeon's scalpel to come for them next." Shelley is now completely present with her own touch and focus. She is experiencing the emotional energy held in that area. Her lower belly is responding to her touch and I can see her perceptions updating to the fact that it is safe now. The result is a flow of energy and connection through the inguinal crease, where the torso meets the thighs, and downward into her legs and feet.

"What are you feeling?" I ask.

"There's a feeling of relief. There's a warmth in my belly. My belly is always cool. And there's a shiver down my legs."

"Why not try to walk a bit?"

When she stands and walks, she says, "Wow, I feel sensuous!"

It's clear she has found increased flexibility and availability of the muscles and joints of her whole pelvis.

With Cassandra, in the previous study, unfinished business manifested as pain or dysfunction, but information can be held in the body without the experience of pain. In fact, this is often the case. Shelley's case is an example of how an area in the body can get our attention without the signal of pain. When aware of our body's subtle cues, we can explore the energy from past experiences and integrate the new experience. I hypothesized that Shelley might experience more continuity and freedom of movement, energy and sensation in her lower body after our session, and into the future.

HOW SYMPTOM AREAS CAN BE CONNECTED TO UNRESOLVED EMOTIONS

I typically don't focus on eliminating symptoms. Instead, I focus on where the appropriate next step is for the client to meet their current goals. This might, but doesn't always, include exploring a symptom area, and discovering what it is holding. Sometimes symptoms can shed light on a deeper pattern that can be part of the client's process of growth. If the symptom shifts, that is a bonus, but it is not my goal.

There are cases in which a person may experience complex emotions concurrently with physical trauma. It can be difficult or impossible for the bodymind to process many feelings and the physical injury all at once.

Case Study: **Cindy**

Cindy is a new client who is learning to use the basic bodymind skills of touch, movement, breath and focus to explore herself. She has discovered that some parts of her body are easier to move and more accessible than others. She has more range of motion and greater ability to use fine motor skills with precision in these areas. It's a surprise to her that other places are not moving so well, and she can't coordinate all the elements of the given exercise at the same time in those locations. "It's as if my brain can't find these places as well as the other parts." We note that awareness, and continue to work together to connect with the upper chest. "There is restriction in one shoulder," she says. "It has been frozen for years."

"Can you connect to that exact part of your shoulder with precise touch?"

"Yes." She does so with breaths and gentle movement and I see a surge of emotion. She says, "I remember walking my dog on a leash in a farm field. He suddenly bolted for the road, chasing something. The leash was wrapped around my wrist, and it pulled hard on my arm as I tried to hold on. It wrenched my shoulder as he tore free. He ran out into the road and was killed instantly."

So many emotions appropriate to the time are coming up for Cindy: shock, sorrow, anger, grief, surprise, self-blame, and many more. Too many to feel all at once. Her shoulder has bothered her for years, and she has never made the connection before. As she experiences all the emotions buried in her shoulder while mindful of the context of their origin, she tells me her chest is suffused by vibrations and warmth. I see the tone and tension of her muscles change as her breath expands into her upper ribs. She can move her shoulder freely.

"Is there pain?" I ask.

She shakes her head. "I didn't realize I felt guilty for his accident. All these years I have pushed that feeling down. I didn't know."

After that acknowledgement, deep love for her dog rises up, and gratitude for the joy he brought into her life.

I was amazed at the speed with which her memories surfaced and the body and energy shifts happened. She had truly experienced that small point in her shoulder and all of its unresolved and conflicting feelings, all at once. This experience showed me that the nervous system can reorganize quickly, when the conditions are right. However, if we don't have the ability to connect deeply, in an integrated way, the body will wait faithfully until we do. I saw this in Cindy's body as loyalty: her body held onto that experience for years until she had the capacity to receive it fully.

We all have embedded body memory from life experiences. Places in our adult bodies which react under stress with strong sensations can be access points. When we are guided in connecting experientially to those parts, we can get clues to the earlier context of those feelings; to our reactions to those feelings at that time, and the intrinsic meanings we made. When this wisdom is accessed, transformation can occur within the person. When a client brings conscious awareness to embodied memory, and then receives wisdom from this resource, they can modify those perceptions, keep them, or decide they no longer apply. This is integration. Integration can happen when trust exists between the client and facilitator, and between the client and their body.

Case Study: *Veronica*

Veronica is experiencing transcendent, embodied joy at the end of her session with me. Her joy is so big that anyone witnessing it would also become joyful, in the way that joy is sometimes contagious. Then comes a change. In an instant her joy contracts; she shuts it down. Her facial expression, body posture and affect become anything but joyful. I ask her what is happening inside.

"I feel a sense of dread when feeling that joyful, that something bad might happen as a result." She brings her hands to her contracted heart area which is holding that fear, and a memory surfaces. "I remember when I was a little girl of five. I decorated my Easter bonnet with daffodils from the garden and, in my pretty dress and magnificent hat, I won the prize in the Easter Parade. I was ecstatic. I felt so special and beautiful. But when I went home to show my father the award he was just terrifically angry because I had cut all of his daffodils from the garden without permission."

Veronica realizes in this moment, fifty years later, that since that day she has never let herself get too happy, in dread of something awful happening. She realizes that the Easter parade was then, and she is in the here and now, remembering it. She can make a different meaning about it. In an instant, she makes a new decision for herself. Her face shines. She is able to experience her heart area that has held that anticipatory fear, and let all the feelings come into the present moment, where she is safe. She makes the decision that it is okay to be radiantly joyful now, without fear of repercussions. She is safe now, and she can give herself permission to celebrate!

At subsequent appointments, I notice her facial expression is consistently brighter. She appears relaxed, open and at ease, and smiles more often. This change is consistent over time, and it appears as though a significant part of her inner world has transformed.

PROCESSING STORED INFORMATION IN THE BODYMIND

When we experience a life event which we don't have the ability to fully process, our capacity to resolve the impacts of the event may be overwhelmed. To process and integrate embodied information we must engage not only with the conscious mind, but also with parts of the bodymind that are subconscious. In a session, when a client makes contact with their body, they can allow conscious awareness and unconsciously held body wisdom to be experienced simultaneously. Then the whole person has the opportunity to sense what is going on through sensation, tension and tone. As the client's feelings and associations bubble up from subconscious to conscious mind, they can make decisions about what those feelings and thoughts mean to them now. They can sit with, reframe or resolve any conflicted feelings, perceptions or expectations that arise.

When people use the touch of their hands, focused awareness, subtle breath and movement in an area, their frontal cortex is engaged as they guide and observe the process. At the same time, there is sensory processing (conscious and subconscious), as local nerve endings in the muscles and joints are involved. Proprioceptive, motor and respiratory areas of the brain are also activated, all at the same time, as executive function directs and observes the process. As the client observes what is happening, there can be physiological, energetic and emotional changes, along with new realizations about how their body has organized itself. Such systemic participation informs how their body can reorganize, now. As the body unwinds and releases old patterns the client may stretch, yawn, sweat or tremble. Emotions may flow. Insights can occur that shift the client's inner world. Old stories may be over-written with refreshed perspective. New choices can seem obvious. A revised sense of self can be experienced. This internal cascade of shifts can affect the future trajectory of self-perception, life choices and meaning making.

THE BODY IN TRANSFORMATION AND ANCHORING THE CHANGES

By tracking body sensations, we help clients connect to parts of their body that hold personal wisdom and experience. The embodied information may be related to coping patterns, feelings, expectations, perceptions, beliefs and yearnings connected to an unresolved life event. When these elements are accessed and processed, new possibilities become available: new actions, new ways for clients to see themselves or others, new beliefs about life, etcetera. The person will have a new status quo as a result of their exploration. Gut reactions to a provoking experience will often change. This is a sign of healthy integration, increased congruence and wholeness. When the bodymind is included in a process, transformation can occur so subtly and easily that a new status quo may be quickly established. The client might not be aware of how much has changed. To increase awareness of their growth, the therapist can reflect back changes in breath, posture or facial expression witnessed in the moment. ("I notice you took a deep breath just now." "You are sitting so tall. Do you notice your shoulders are more open?" "It is beautiful to see your smile radiating.") Checking in with the client and allowing them time to verbalize their experience can help validate one's hypotheses and increase the client's self-awareness. The act of owning the changes they have made helps them realize what they have accomplished. It is also useful, from time to time, to reflect on the client's status quo of last week, last month, or last year, and note the changes. This can have a very positive impact;

self-affirming reflections help build a client's self-confidence, self-esteem and trust in the growth process.

CONGRUENCE

For Satir, congruence was the foundation upon which the possibilities for transformation are built. How I am using the parts of myself – my thoughts, feelings, intentions, beliefs, perceptions and yearnings – at any given moment has a huge impact on those I serve. My internal reactions to stress impact my ability to be present for my clients. If I am hurried, worried or distracted, my clients will be affected. I must also deal with what comes up for me personally during our interactions. If I get distracted by a thought or memory activated while working, that could have an impact. If I go into judgement, there will be a subtle, felt sense of that judgement in the room. If I am frustrated with myself, a client or the process, that, too, will have an impact. Whether through tone of voice, facial micro-expressions, body tension, posture or even breathing changes, I am unconsciously communicating signals which can be picked up by clients. For these reasons I prepare myself to embody an intentionally congruent state.

When I am adequately prepared, I feel centered and grounded. In that state, I can attune to my highest motivations for the clients I meet and the work I do. I can access Life Energy from my sense of Self connected to the universe. I can access my hopes and yearnings for clients to be connected to their own hopes and yearnings. I can have healthy boundaries. When I am truly present, I can be aware of all the parts and possibilities of my clients, including the resources and possibilities embedded in their presenting problem. How I use my feelings and thoughts is within my control. I can more easily focus on clients' strengths and abilities. I can be flexible and open to new directions and choices in the healing process.

When I first began teaching, I was asked many times to teach a large group class with just a few minutes' notice. I'd have to observe the energy of the group, decide on the content that fit the context of the program, and invent it on the spot. I also worked regularly in the San Francisco Bay Area at six or seven different healing practices as an adjunct facilitator. Often I would have no idea who I would be working with or how they would present themselves to me until the moment I walked in. As a fledgling facilitator, I often had doubts or misgivings about my abilities or my readiness. Knowing that focusing on my fears or worries would affect all my interactions, I had to create a solution for myself that would help me enter each site with confidence. I learned to ask myself two questions. First: "Am I willing to show up at 100% of my ability?" Inside me a resounding *YES* lifted my heart and stretched my spine with excitement. Then I would ask myself: "Am I ready to do whatever is required of me to honour what comes up?" Another *YES* would resound in my heart and soul. My chest would expand, my feet felt firmly planted on the ground, and the crown of my head extended toward the sky. In that state, I could enter any office, any retreat space, and any stage with a bright smile, confidence and humility, ready for whoever and whatever was waiting.

For the first three years, I silently asked myself these questions every time I entered a healing space. By the end of that time, I had integrated them into my being. They are now part of me. Each time I go into a work environment or teaching situation I step naturally into that state of mind, body, emotions and heart. To this day I am grateful I took ownership of my thoughts, my energy and my mood to optimize my limited time with clients.

When working with clients' body wisdom, our own congruence is essential. The way we use ourselves creates safety for our clients. When we are centred and grounded, we can be aware of our own experience, and at the same time be attuned to clients. Our congruence helps clients to be present with themselves in the moment. We can appreciate and trust their Life Energy, and acknowledge their potential for change, self-determination and hope.

INTRODUCING CLIENTS TO THEIR BODY WISDOM

Relating to the body as a source of inner wisdom is new for many people. Sometimes the body is related to as a thing. For example: *My shoulder hurts, and I hate it. I wish I could get rid of it. I want it to go away.* Relating to our body and body sensations in the third person distances us from ourselves, rather than bringing us insight about what is going on. It is better to think *I* hurt *right here*, or *this part of me* is in pain. That's a good first step. Experience with oneself builds trust in the process. We can begin to ask, "What is going on here? What is my next step? What is this place holding for me?" When we build an even deeper relationship with body wisdom, we can consult with the beloved container for our Self. We can treasure the body as a source of wisdom, a divine mystery of cells and tissues encoded with our deepest truths.

If we are accustomed to tuning out body signals, as I was in my early life, it can be uncomfortable to begin directing attention inward. In order to get messages from inside, we must be curious and give permission to our body to express what it has to share. Contacting what's inside the body may be unfamiliar for the beginning client. They may have unpleasant associations with their body, such as painful or traumatic physical experiences, abuse or neglect. Some people learn to disregard body sensations and consider them distractions or weaknesses, not valuable. Perhaps they have been taught to "tough it out," to not "give in" to their body's needs. When I began my personal growth by learning to communicate with my body, I had the fear that inside me was a Pandora's box full of terrible things ready to fly out at once, and the chaos would be unmanageable. The presence and reassurance of a grounded, centred facilitator gave me the confidence to explore myself safely, to find the resources to deal with whatever I found.

SAFELY PROCESSING BODY WISDOM

By employing pacing and safety elements to match the capacity of the bodymind, the conscious therapist can integrate new awareness and information in each moment. By being permission-based, watching for cues and checking in with our clients along the way, we can ensure that we are moving at an appropriate pace to help them grow without being overwhelmed by the experience. Spending at least as much time with body resources as with unpleasant or uncomfortable body sensations will help clients stay grounded in the safety of the present moment, and connected to their resources. This respects the present-moment capacity of the client for integration and transformation, and provides sufficient grounding and anchoring to create a congruent experience of their new inner state.

Case Study: **Mark**

I am called in by another practitioner to assist a client in integration. I visually assess him and notice that two different areas in his body are activated in different ways. His chest is tight, vibrating and pulsing with activity, and his belly is at ease, softly expanding with his breath. I decide to help him connect to both areas in a way that will help him move through the polarity of holding two different body experiences at the same time. I prompt Mark to move his hands back and forth between his highly charged chest and his peaceful and open belly. I begin to feel a vibratory frequency increase in his hands when he touches his chest. When we go back to his belly, the amplitude reduces and becomes calm. I take the cue and move his hands to the calm area as soon as the vibration starts to increase its amplitude. I know from previous experience that if the vibration's amplitude becomes extreme, it will be accompanied by strong emotional expression with some measure of distress. By using Mark's vibrations as a guide, I monitor his internal experience. We don't talk. We just shift his awareness back and forth between the areas. His jaw, which has been tight almost to the point of teeth chattering, begins to release. His chest comes into an easier rhythm as the muscles release. Mark's process is so gentle that the energy resolves as we work without a big catharsis. Instead, he gets warm and begins to relax as the vibrations recede. It is as if the energy under his hands shifted with his new access to the grace available in his belly.

When clients use their own hands to contact the body, what is inside can waken. Self-touch and participation can facilitate self-regulation and integration.

Satir's videotaped sessions[3] show how she tapped into the wisdom of her clients through touch and presence. I was quite moved by "Of Rocks and Flowers: Dealing with the Abuse of Children." Two young boys had learned physically violent behaviour from their birth mother. The children's new stepmother was very afraid that her husband's older son would be violent towards the new baby coming soon to the blended family. Satir taught the boy to use his "beautiful hands"[4] to show love and express caring feelings. This helped him repurpose touch as an act of love rather than an expression of frustration or anger. Watching the video, I realized that I had often seen people kneading, pushing or poking their symptom areas. Using self-touch in a session might be the first time a client has used their hands to connect to their body in a compassionate way, simply to tune in to what is there. I hypothesize that clients' caring self-touch creates healthy attachment bonds to their body as well as gaining them access to the information it possesses. This could begin to change a person's relationship to their body.

A congruent Satir therapist can teach clients to be aware of and engage with their subtle physical cues by being interactive and intuitive and letting the answers from their inner selves inform the process. We can help clients be secure in their experience and open to new ways of thinking, perceiving themselves and their world. They can conceive of change, experience it and get excited about it. Repeated experience of positive results creates self-confidence, building trust in their inner resources.

---

3   "Virginia Satir Series: Of Rocks and Flowers."
4   Ibid.

USING INTUITION

Intuition is available for the practitioner when the five essential elements of Satir's model are in use. When we use self well, and the client is in the moment (experiential) and connected to their inner self, there is magic in the space between. These conditions of engagement set the stage for intuition to be readily available. Wisdom not usually accessible can emerge. People experience intuition in many ways. I remember my first inkling of the variety of possibilities during an experience of my own intuition at work many years ago.

Case Study: **Gilbert**

Gilbert has done a lot of healing work in different modalities after his cancer treatments. With his cancer resolved for the time, he wants to participate with his body in different ways to process the impacts of the treatments on his physical body, and he also wants to manage his energy day to day. He is a long-time meditator and has great skills of awareness and presence with himself. When I instruct him in various self-awareness exercises, words sometimes drop into my head as we work together. I begin to say these words as I coach him, and they always resonate with him and assist in deepening our practice together. These intuitive words have a slightly different character than the voice of my own thoughts.

Over time, I learned to discern the difference between my own thoughts and these inspired prompts. My first gifts of intuition were auditory, to do with language.

Intuition can surprise us. A while later, I learned that I could receive intuitive information through pictures, too.

Case Study: **Betsy**

Betsy is connecting deeply to herself at the end of a session. I pause to let her be in her experience a bit longer. I sit by, reverently witnessing her peaceful integration process. While she is resting in her meditative state, I see, in my mind's eye, two long lines of people in the space above her body, a line of women and a line of men facing each other, all in clothing from many periods in history; they are making an archway with their raised arms. I see my client walking through this archway. The lines arc up and away into the distance. It's as if she is being accepted, blessed and celebrated by passing through this archway of ancestors. When she has finished resting, she sits up and tells me that she was adopted and doesn't know her birth family. During her rest, she felt that she had been accepted by them and was connected to them even though she would never know them.

This experience had a strong impact on me. Since then, in sessions with other clients, I always hold the awareness that healing is possible on many levels, some of which I may be unaware of. By paying attention deeply during the integration phase, I tune into impressions and sensations that tell me that something important is going on inside the client which deserves my patience and respect. This helps me know when clients need more integration time, and guides me to ask brief, specific anchoring questions to tie each client's internal experience into the context of their journey.

One day I learned that the subtle vibratory frequencies I felt through touch could communicate information. That was the day I realized I could use my own body awareness to discover the tone of vibratory sensations and intuit their possible messages.

Case Study: *Melody*

A practitioner asks me to assist Melody with connection to her body. As we begin to work together, she gets curious about a tight zone around her lower ribs. As she explores it, I ask permission to touch her hand with my hands. She agrees. As I touch her hands, I begin to feel a vibratory frequency in my body. The frequency is being communicated from her body through her hands, into my hand and into my body. I ask myself, "If I were to feel this sensation in every cell of my body, what would I be experiencing?" I realize that I would be on the verge of running away from whatever was happening.

"Does it feel like this part wants to run away?" I ask her.

Her eyes open wide. "Yes! I couldn't have said those exact words, but that's precisely what I'm experiencing."

I feel a rush of acknowledgement from her, and the area lessens its tightness. She breathes more easily into her lower ribs and belly as the tone and its emotional content is received and integrated. The frequency communicated through her hands shifts from anxiety into calmness. She smiles.

To this day, something happens inside me when a client touches a valuable point on their body that is connected to something deeper. Intuition is hard to describe. My body sensations and energetic awareness help me identify where to follow up or what to get curious about. This is a sense of potential, a knowing. As a pure body experience, I would describe it as a subtle, alert feeling running up my spine to the eyes and the crown of my head. Body awareness is key to use of self. It helps me be present-focused and experiential while I am working. Every person will have their own experience of intuition. Perhaps you could take a moment to reflect on your experiences of knowing something intuitively.

In Satir trainings, there are many chances to develop and validate your sense of intuition. At the outset of a practice session, trainees learn to prepare themselves, to focus awareness on their inner experience and set the intention for growth and transformation. They learn to create a safe, receptive space for their clients to co-create goals. The trainee will also take on the role of client and, through experiential exploration, get involved deeply in their own process of exploring some relevant issue in their life. The experience of authentic emotion, thoughts, sensations and yearnings begins to awaken their Life Energy to move and grow. In this dual process, enrolling as both practitioner and client, the trainee co-creates an environment that makes intuition more easily available. After practice sessions, there are opportunities to process the experience for all concerned – client, practitioner and witnesses. In this way, students can validate their intuition and explore different options and pose questions

– such as what worked well and what might have been different – in a rich and non-judgemental learning environment.

In *The New Peoplemaking*, Satir said:
> We are all unique manifestations of life. We are divine in our origins. We are also recipients of what has gone before us, which gives us vast resources from which to draw. I believe we also have a pipeline to universal intelligence through our intuition, which can be tapped through meditation, prayer, relaxation, awareness, the development of higher self-esteem, and a reverence for life. This is how I reach my spirituality.[5]

How you use your intuition is up to you. The Satir approach creates the conditions for deeper exploration of the power of intuition and the resources of a peaceful, creative and focused mind.

ENRICHING YOUR PRACTICE WITH THE SATIR APPROACH

Body-oriented practitioners often begin a relationship with a client around a problem or goal they have. We get to know clients by gathering a complete history and present-day picture of their health and how it affects them day-to-day, as well as getting a sense of their resources and coping strategies. Then we assess what we have learned about them and recommend a way forward, using whatever modality is our area of expertise.

In the initial interview with clients, we listen for certain types of stress, such as injuries, accidents, loss of a loved one, loss of job, moving to a new city, or exposure to toxic chemicals. We may be attuned to discovering "the problem" and finding "the solution," but Satir said: "[t]he problem, the symptom, is not the problem. Coping or not coping is the problem. The symptom is the subconscious solution to the problem."[6]

---

5 Satir, *The New Peoplemaking*, 338.
6 Banmen, "If Depression is the Solution," 245.

Within Satir's model, the problem is not the problem; the way we have coped with stress is the problem, and transformation of what is driving the coping is the solution. This approach invites us to look deeper and more systemically into the client's presenting issues, instead of staying on the surface. By getting curious, we can learn more about what is going on, contextually and at various levels.

Satir began assessing her clients as soon as they entered the room, often before they started to speak. She observed physical tone and tension in their bodies, body position and movements, breathing patterns and dynamics between family members; she even noticed the way they shook hands with her, or didn't. According to Jesse Carlock, she relied on "images, thoughts, feelings and sensations in the moment, and her sense about the energy field between and among all concerned."[7] In these ways, she used her powers of observation and curiosity to direct her exploration of what was going on under the surface of the presenting issue.

When we add the Satir approach, we take note of what clients want to change, and what role they are willing to play in that change. We notice how they see themselves and what beliefs they hold about health. Do they think that this will ever change? Can they envision a healthier life for themselves? What lights our clients up? What gives joy? These are important motivators and anchors for progress. What are their coping styles when they are under stress? We can be aware when those patterns play out in the office. When symptoms flare, we can be curious about the emotions and experiences connected to that symptom and that part of the body. We can engage with our clients as companions on the healing journey. We can awaken in the client self-responsibility and ownership of their process. We can use awareness of family of origin to hypothesize the ways early life experiences might have impacted a client's body and sense of self. We evaluate our clients systemically. As we collect more

---

7 Carlock, Introduction to "When I Meet a Person," 179.

information, we make connections between seemingly disparate parts of their life experience and body experience and see connecting patterns.

It is tremendously exciting to be able to offer a word, an image or a question that can catalyze the change process, to see our words touch emotions and spark energetic changes. Words can stimulate deep thought processes, sometimes outside of a client's awareness. Physical touch directs a spotlight of self-awareness. Simply by being present, we can touch the unseen and unspoken within a client and provide a sense of safety. Acceptance and validation of their steps toward growth gently encourage more of the same. We can help them meet their yearnings: to be seen, validated and accepted, so they can learn to meet other yearnings in other ways in their life. It can be normal for our clients to:

- experience positive changes emotionally as they make positive changes physically
- find new options as they gain new abilities and awareness
- shift their perceptions of themselves, others and the world as they gain a greater sense of wellbeing.

When Satir's approach has been integrated into your practice, you may start to notice that changes in your clients extend well beyond the area of their initial concern. Changes can extend into every corner of their life experience.

WHO CAN BENEFIT?

All body-oriented practitioners can benefit from the model. I'd also like to stress that the model can expand possibilities for all helping professionals. Not only therapists attend Satir Trainings, but also clergy, social workers, nurses, medical doctors, coaches and physical therapists. Any type of practice in which there is interaction with others for their growth and health – physical, emotional or spiritual – can benefit from incorporating the Satir approach, with its goals of growing empowered, embodied and more congruent choice makers. Satir training can teach any helping professional how to effectively use process questions in a transformative interaction and support systemic change.

Throughout my life, I have consulted with practitioners in many different modalities for my own growth and wellness, and all the best of them had a depth of experience beyond what was mentioned on their business card or website. As each of us matures in our profession, we collect a variety of approaches, techniques and modalities that contribute to what we can offer our clients. Adding Satir into my practice has brought joy into creative partnership with my clients. I see my job as holding space for unlimited healing, guiding the process and helping clients witness their transformational changes.

The experiential nature of learning the Satir approach has added value to my personal relationships and professional life. As I went through the trainings, I cleared up unfinished business from my complex family of origin and past relationships. It is amazing how much we can carry around with us! As I acknowledged, processed and transformed what got activated within me, I became more clear in myself. This was integral to my development as a facilitator. Every day I rely on the Personal Iceberg Metaphor to discern quickly what areas of my inner world are activated and to acknowledge my coping patterns and emotions, my underlying expectations, perceptions and beliefs, and find what yearnings are not being met. Then I can connect with myself at the level of Self. I can be more compassionate to myself or change my expectations. I can explore myself systemically to gain a greater sense of congruence.

Satir's model has provided me a nuanced framework in which to organize and evaluate information I hear from clients. I can listen with highly attuned ears, very curious about what's going on. I can hypothesize systemically about what meanings were made in their family of origin, what skills they used to survive and what yearnings might be unmet. I can help them find their aptitudes and internal resources, all potential places for tapping into life energy.

SUMMARY

Satir's model offers an approach that empowers both practitioner and client. It intends to access wisdom encoded in all our bodies from a lifetime of experience – not only impacts of old injuries and hurts, but also impressions and echoes of joys, fears and surprises, as well as unmet expectations, meanings made, deep yearnings and the contexts they connect to.

As practitioners, we use our body wisdom to inform and guide us in our personal growth as well as in our work. We use body sensation to be more aware of our own unfinished business and increase our personal congruence. We gain greater access to our intuition. When we guide our clients to discover what their body holds for them, we are helping them to discover themselves at a deeper level. When the client feels safe, seen and supported, they can have the curiosity and courage to look deeper inside. When they are present within themselves, the bodymind can integrate new information, update itself and reach a new status quo, consciously and unconsciously. Going forward, clients may observe new emotions or reactions to life events or others' actions as a result of their inner changes. Energy is no longer tied up in maintaining the old patterns. Liberated energy affects the body structure, and the emotions and thinking of the client. Long-held perceptions may change, and new beliefs can be formed.

It's quite simple really. We help our clients become aware of their internal shifts when we notice them and reflect that change back to them, so they can see it. I cannot count how many times I have said: "If I think back six months, what you just described to me would not have been possible." And I cannot count the times each client has responded with astonished agreement. When we, as helpers, hold up the mirror, clients can see themselves more clearly. We may start with the body, but we work with the whole person. The Satir approach can help anyone in a helping profession to grow their mastery, and help clients achieve goals beyond their expectations, enhancing their self-empowerment and all of their relationships.

REFERENCES

Banmen, John, ed. *Satir Transformational Systemic Therapy*. Palo Alto: Science and Behavior Books, Inc., 2008.

Banmen, John, ed. *In Her Own Words...Virginia Satir: Collected Papers (1963-1983)*. Phoenix: Zeig, Tucker & Theisen, Inc., 2008.

Carlock, Jesse, "Introduction" to "When I Meet a Person." *In Her Own Words... Virginia Satir Collected Papers 1963-1983,* edited by John Banmen, 179-196. Phoenix: Zeig, Tucker & Theisen, Inc., 2008.

Riva, Giuseppe. "The Neuroscience of Body Memory: From the Self through the Space to the Others." *Cortex* 104, (July 2018): 241-260. https://doi.org/10.1016/j.cortex.2017.07.013.

Satir, Virginia. *The New Peoplemaking*. Mountain View: Science and Behavior Books, Inc., 1988.

"Virginia Satir Series: Of Rocks and Flowers: Dealing with the Abuse of Children." n.d. Psychotherapy.net: Training Videos for Mental Health Professionals. Accessed April 17, 2023. https://www.psychotherapy.net/video/virginia-satir-series-videos.

ACKNOWLEDGEMENTS

As authors we have had the input of a wide-reaching number of gifted teachers and mentors over the years in both therapy and related body and energy fields, who are still with us in person or in spirit. There are too many to thank and mention individually. We trust those still here will appreciate their gifts to us and feel our appreciation for them as they read our chapters. Special mention goes to John Banmen who taught, supervised, and mentored most of us, and was a guiding presence at so many of our many Zoom sessions in creating this book. He is not only a dear friend to each of us, but also an esteemed cheerleader. We owe special mention to Spencer Wade and Sandy Novak, who carefully read every one of our chapters, and to many other readers who provided excellent advice and support.

We have been gifted with exceptional editing and publishing professionals, who have offered their time, expertise, and deep listening presence to enable our writing to be not only true to our own voices, but also more accessible to those we were hoping to reach. We offer thanks to Barbara Kmiec, an editor, who joined with us in our early days of writing with supportive resources and a belief in our goal. She saw, in time, that we would benefit from shifting to Michael Kenyon, an experienced editor and counsellor. Michael has been a gift in so many ways through his patience with each of us, his keen eye and ability to find just the right tone and words to convey our messages. Barb also connected us to Bruce and Marsha Batchelor of Agio Publishing House, after noting our struggle to find the right fit for us in the publishing world. Not every editor and publisher would tackle a book with seven individual writers and content that was far from mainstream; having such experienced and gracious professionals who could embrace each of our styles of writing and guide us through this process so smoothly has been an immeasurable gift.

We want to express our thanks to the Satir Institute of the Pacific where most of us have taken extensive training over the last 25 years for their excellent training programs. Special mention goes to their amazing administrator, Cindi Mueller, who fully embraced and supported our passion to write together. The administrator, several board members and members of The Virginia Satir Global Network, likewise have been very supportive with their interest in our project, reading our drafts, encouraging us, and providing resources and advice re the logistics of publishing.

Last of all, but not least, is our collective gratitude to our families and friends who stepped in to provide the time, space, and support to keep us going through many ups and downs during our years of writing together. We could not have accomplished this feat without your involvement, support and patience. *We offer our deep gratitude to each and everyone of you.*